Heads-Up
No-Limit Hold 'em

Expert Advice for
Winning Heads-Up Poker Matches

By
Collin Moshman

A product of Two Plus Two Publishing LLC
www.twoplustwo.com

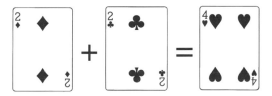

FIRST EDITION
FIRST PRINTING: SEPTEMBER 2008

Printing and Binding
Creel Printing Co.
Las Vegas, Nevada

Printed in the United States of America

Heads-Up
No-Limit Hold 'em
Expert Advice for
Winning Heads-Up Poker Matches

Copyright © 2008 by
Two Plus Two Publishing LLC

For information contact: **Two Plus Two Publishing LLC**
32 Commerce Center Drive
Suite H-89
Henderson, NV 89014
www.twoplustwo.com

ISBN: 1-880685-44-2
ISBN13: 978-1-880685-44-0

Dedication

To my fiancée, Katie

Table of Contents

i

About Collin Moshman

Collin Moshman has always held a deep interest for mathematics and games. He received an honors degree in theoretical math from the California Institute of Technology in 2003. He then abandoned his graduate studies in economics after discovering that he could make a better living gambling.

Although Collin started by playing 10¢-25¢ cash no-limit hold 'em, he quickly began specializing in 1-table sit 'n go tournaments. These games require a specific math-based approach which Collin mastered through his own online games and detailed in *Sit 'n Go Strategy: Expert Advice for Beating One-Table Poker Tournaments*. Also published by Two Plus Two.

Collin started off playing heads-up poker for the challenge; he quickly discovered that the tight strategy required for normal sit 'n go's was inadequate for these matches. A loose-aggressive style with strong elements of unpredictability was required, and he set to work mastering the math and logic of this new game. He consulted with experts in cash and tournament play to verify his theories and put them to paper. The result is this book.

Collin earns the majority of his income playing online poker, both full sit 'n go's and heads-up matches. He has written articles for publications such as *Poker Pro* and the *Two Plus Two Internet Magazine*. He also produces videos of his own games for the instructional site www.Stoxpoker.com. Collin lives in Washington, DC with his fiancée Katie.

Acknowledgements

I would like to thank Mason Malmuth, David Sklansky, and everyone at Two Plus Two Publishing LLC for their invaluable strategic and editorial advice. I have greatly appreciated the knowledge and support of Two Plus Two during the process of writing and publishing both my poker books.

I would also like to acknowledge the entire "Heads-Up No Limit Forum" at www.twoplustwo.com, whose posters have helped me extensively to develop and refine my heads-up game. A sincere thanks to ChicagoRy, CWar, TNixon, Jay_Shark, CreedOfHubris, and the many other posters who have made so many valuable contributions to heads-up theory.

Thanks also to Gary Alstatt of Creel Printing for his artwork through this book and to graphic designer Jason "Gonso" Hughes for his terrific cover design. Lastly, I would like to thank photographer Bryan Ranharter for my back cover photo and Jeff Neuman for his unflagging support and poker knowledge.

Introduction

The characteristic that defines a hand as "heads-up" is that only two players can act during the hand. Throughout this text, we will use standard conventions for describing a heads-up hand.

The button is the player who posts the small blind. He acts first before the flop, and second on every subsequent betting round. The big blind is the player who posts the big blind. He acts second before the flop, and first on every subsequent betting round. The player whose perspective we are considering is named "Hero," or sometimes "You" or "We" since the reader and I will be playing along. His opponent is "Villain."

Becoming a good heads-up player is to your benefit because it will help to develop important poker skills since one-on-one play is the format requiring the most aggressive and read-dependent approach. The tools to be examined in this book will be useful in many contexts.

We begin Part One by discussing the fundamentals of heads-up gameplay, including such universal concepts as expected value, pot odds, and value betting. In Part Two, we focus on the different playing styles — both for playing them yourself, and for exploiting opponents who fall into the most common categories. Part Three is an in-depth look at pot size manipulation and the process of making an optimal "Bet-Number" decision based on hand strength and opponent type.

Part Four covers a variety of important topics from preflop three-betting to calling all-ins and the split pot rule. While much of the book focuses on examples and concepts applicable to any heads-up match, Part Five examines the differences between cash and tournament situations. Metagame, the continually evolving strategies and perceptions of two players involved in many consecutive hands, is the focus of Part Six. And the concluding

Part Seven discusses the many details of heads-up career play, such as bankroll requirements and the poker business.

There are also many hand examples throughout this book. The ones featuring famous players, if not specified, come from the inaugural *NBC National Heads-Up Poker Championships* in 2005. And if you enjoy heads-up play, this is a can't miss show.

And finally, in various spots in the text, hand percentages appear. These come from the freeware program *PokerStove* which I highly recommend for those of you who are interested in doing similar calculations.

A note of caution: This book is not designed to beat expert heads-up players. Following any set of pre-given strategies will not be sufficient against top-notch opponents. However, you will be given the tools to beat intermediate competition. After enough playing experience and thought away from the table, you may be able to do even better.

Part One

The Fundamentals

The Fundamentals

Introduction

Many of the crucial concepts presented in this first section are universal to all poker variations. We discuss them now in a heads-up specific context, including:

- Pot Odds and Percentages
- Expected Value
- Showdown Equity and Fold Equity
- Continuation Betting
- Value Betting
- Solving Heads-Up Problems Mathematically.

You may go through the opening sections of "Part One: The Fundamentals" at a quicker pace if you are an experienced player, although reviewing fundamentals never hurts no matter how well you may play. Advanced topics such as metagame and Nash Equilibria are important for the expert player, but understanding pot odds and value betting are concepts at the heart of winning play.

The chapter, "Solving Heads-up Hands Mathematically," is especially important since it will be used in many of the hand examples. Knowing how to translate assumptions about your opponent into an optimal decision is a skill we will use throughout this text. One important application is a quantitative analysis of the all-in decision: We will calculate the profitability of raising all-in based on how we believe our opponent is likely to behave.

Pot Odds and Percentages

Pot odds are a mathematical expression giving your risk-to-reward ratio for calling a bet. They are a number designed to help your decision-making in such situations as whether to call an all-in bet with a particular draw, and how often your opponent must be bluffing for you to profit from calling an unexpected river bet.

Pot odds are calculated by taking the ratio of the pot relative to what it costs to call. For example, if you are the small blind, you are getting 3-to-1 on a preflop call because the current pot is your opponent's big blind (BB) plus your small blind (SB), and it costs you one SB to call. Since one big blind is equivalent to two small blinds, your pot odds are 3 SB-to-1 SB, or 3-to-1. This means that the current pot size is three times the cost of staying in the hand.

Now suppose a pot heading into the river is $1,000. You check your low pair and your opponent bets $200. Should you call?

The pot is $1,000 + $200, and it costs you $200 to call. So you are getting $1,200-to-$200, or 6-to-1, on your call. You should call if these odds are good enough. Often it will be easier to think in terms of percentages.

> If you are getting odds of X-to-Y, then you should call if you think you will win more often than Y times in (X+Y).

So, the question now is: Will your opponent be betting an inferior hand more often than 1 time in (1+6), or 14 percent? Call if that's the case, otherwise fold.

One common example of pot odds pertains to draws. Your opponent puts you all-in on the flop, and you have a flush draw. You believe your hand will be best if and only if you make the flush. You are a 1.9-to-1 underdog to hit your flush with two cards to come — see "Appendix B: Drawing Odds" on page 377, so call if the pot odds are better. For instance, if the pot was $50 on the flop (after his bet) and it cost you $25 to call your opponent's all-in bet, then these 2-to-1 odds would be good enough for a profitable call (unless you are playing a freezeout against a bad player who is likely to give you much bigger edges on future hands).

> Always evaluate your pot odds when deciding whether to call a bet.

Pot odds, while an excellent framework for call/fold decisions, typically only compare the decisions of calling and folding. The third option, raising, may be more profitable than either a call or a fold. Note also that unless your call closes the action at the river, or you are deciding whether to call an all-in bet, pot odds do not account for future betting that may occur later in the hand.

Here's an example. You hold

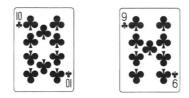

and both you and your opponent have $1,500. The flop is

giving you a straight draw. The pot contains $50. Your opponent bets $50. Do the pot odds say to call with your straight draw?

Neither. First, since you have many more chips, you could raise as well. If you think your opponent is unlikely to have the king, raising now as a semi-bluff is a strong play. You could win immediately, getting him to fold a low pair or better high card. This play may prevent him from winning with two lower cards when he would otherwise have spiked a pair later in the hand.

Also, your pot odds alone do not tell what opportunities/ hazards future betting will bring. The odds are 2-to-1, so you would fold if your opponent's bet were an all-in since straight draws on the flop are worse than 2-to-1 to hit by the river. But now suppose your opponent is very loose. If you hit your straight and he has even a low pair, it is likely you can win all his chips.

From a strictly call/fold perspective, you should certainly at least call this reckless opponent's bet. You are risking $50 to win a probable $1,550. This ratio of expected betting on all betting rounds to current bet size is called *implied odds*, and in this extreme example, your implied odds of over 30-to-1 ($1,550-to-$50) make this an easy call.

Conversely, future betting may also work to your disadvantage. For example, suppose you flop top pair on a flop of 9♠8♠7♠. You hold 9♣2♣. The pot is $100 and it costs you $100 to call. Even if you believe your hand is best now more than 1 time in 3 (since you are getting 2-to-1 pot odds), you should consider folding. This is because future betting will often occur when your hand is much weaker, such as when a fourth card to a straight or flush falls on the turn or river.

> Always consider whether future betting works for or against you when calling a bet early in the hand.

While pot odds can often tell you whether calling a bet is profitable, they do not say by how much. That is one reason why we also need the concept of expected value.

Expected Value

Your expected value (EV) tells you how many chips you expect to gain or lose, on average, from a particular play. It is calculated by taking all possible scenarios that may arise from your decision and adding up how much you win or lose from each, weighted by their probability of occurrence.

The classic examples for calculating EV are flipping coins and rolling dice. For instance, you are offered a bet where a standard die is rolled and you win $12 if it lands on 3, otherwise, you lose $6. What is the EV of this bet?

There are two outcomes: either the die lands 3 or it lands on another number. The first outcome happens 1 time in 6, and it results in a $12 reward. The second outcome happens 5 times in 6, and it costs $6. Therefore this bet, on average, loses $3.

$$-\$3 = \left(\frac{1}{6}\right)(\$12) + \left(\frac{5}{6}\right)(-\$6)$$

Let's now look at some poker expected value calculations.

EV of Calling an All-In

You hold the

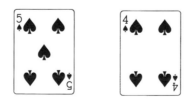

The flop is the

Your opponent goes all-in for $100 in a $400 pot. You believe he has a pair of aces. So what is your expected value if you call?

You will win this hand if and only if you complete your straight.[1] From "Appendix B: Drawing Odds Chart" on page 377, you will complete the straight 32 percent of the time, resulting in a $500 win. When you lose, you forfeit the $100 it costs to call this bet. Therefore, your expected value for calling is $92.

$$\$92 = (.32)(\$500) + (.68)(-\$100)$$

So even though any individual time you call this all-in bet with your straight draw, you will either lose $100 or win $500, your long run expectation will be approximately $92.

EV of Folding

The expected value when you fold is always precisely zero. It does not matter how you have gotten in the situation or how many chips you have already invested. Expected value only pertains to future decision-making, and when you fold, you necessarily win or lose no more chips in the hand.

---

[1] We are ignoring the chance that your read is wrong, as well as the remote possibility of either one of you hitting other backdoor hands.

EV of Calling, Folding, and Raising

You hold the 3♣2♣ at the river. The final board is the A♠J♠9♠6♠4♥. The pot is $1,000 and your opponent bets $500. What is your expected value of folding, calling, and raising to $1,500?

The expected value of folding is always zero. The expected value of calling is around -$500. You are ahead of no hand he could hold, and there is only the slight chance you could split the pot if he is holding another trey-deuce, also with no spade. So calling essentially guarantees a loss of $500.

But what if you raise to $1,500? One of two things will happen:

1. Your opponent will call or reraise, in which case you lose the hand. When this occurs, you lose $1,500.

2. Your opponent folds. Then you will win the $1,000 pot plus Villain's $500 bet.

Let us label the probability of a call or reraise as "X" and the probability of a fold as "Y." Since your opponent must either fold or call/raise, we know that X + Y = 1, and therefore X = 1 - Y. So your EV of raising to $1,500 is:

$$(\$1,500)(Y) + (-\$1,500)(1 - Y)$$
$$= (\$3,000)(Y) - \$1,500$$

Therefore, you win money on your raise if:

$$(\$3,000)(Y) - (\$1,500) > 0 \Rightarrow$$
$$(\$3,000)(Y) > \$1,500 \Rightarrow$$
$$Y > \frac{1}{2}$$

So if you believe your opponent will fold more than half the time, then making a bluff-raise to $1,500 will show a profit.[2]

Lastly, note that in many cases, you will not be able to calculate an exact EV for a particular play. For instance, suppose you hold 2♠2♦ with $10,000 effective stacks.

The flop is K♠Q♦8♥. Your opponent bets $200 into a pot of $1,000. You do not know your EV for calling here because when you call so many future alternatives are possible. For instance, after you call:

- You could lose the pot after the turn and river get checked.

- You could win the pot after two more checks.

- Your opponent could bluff you off the better hand with a big bet on the turn.

- You could bet and win with an inferior hand at the river. Or,

- You could make a set against your opponent's top two pair and win his entire $10,000.

The possibilities are many. Nonetheless, while expected value often cannot produce an exact answer for the profitability of every conceivable action, it is nonetheless an excellent tool for quantitatively comparing possible decisions.

---

[2] Of course, in this particular case, this is easy to see as you are risking $1,500 to win $1,500.

Showdown
Equity and Fold Equity

Equity is your "rightful share" of the pot. Your expectation if the hand went to the showdown without further betting.

Here is an example, the board is the

You hold the

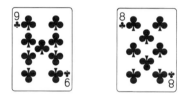

The pot is $600. What is your showdown equity?

Assuming you need to hit your straight to win, you have 17 percent pot equity or $102.

$$\$102 = (.17)(\$600)$$

Suppose you go all-in for another $600. If you knew your opponent would call, then the total pot would be $1,800, and so our 17 percent winning chances give us an equity of $306. Since we bet $600 for $306 in equity, our expectation on this bet is to lose $294.

$$-\$294 = \$306 - \$600$$

But our opponent could also fold. Let us suppose your opponent will only call with an ace or a king, and you estimate he has such a hand 40 percent of the time. Then we know he will fold the remaining 60 percent of time. When he folds, we win $600. Therefore our EV on this semi-bluff all-in raise is $242.40.

$$\$242.40 = (.60)(\$600) + (.40)(-\$294)$$

This is simpler than the calculation we would make using the method from last section. Using this method, we still win $600 the 60 percent of the time he folds. The remaining 40 percent, we are 17 percent to win the $600 pot plus the $600 bet he has called, and 83 percent to lose the $600 bet. Therefore the expectation is the same as before or $242.40

$$\$242.40 = (.60)(\$600) + (.40)\big[(.17)(\$1{,}200) + (.83)(-\$600)\big]$$

The first component, common to both equations, is called the fold equity — the expected gain from the chance your opponent will fold. Not only will fold equity sometimes ease expected value calculations, but we will often discuss it in a more qualitative sense. For instance, "I knew my queen-high gutshot draw had little showdown value after he raised the turn. But the pot was large, and I thought he might be bluffing, so I reraised because there was so much fold equity."

Aggression
and Hyper-Aggression

With rare exceptions, whenever you play poker, in the early rounds you need a stronger hand to call than you would to bet or raise. This is because betting and raising allow the possibility of winning the pot immediately since your opponent might fold. But you can never win immediately by calling.

This principle was formulated as the Gap Concept by David Sklansky. (See *Tournament Poker for Advanced Players: Expanded Edition.*) For now, simply observe that you should make a habit of being the aggressor. This brings us to "The Aggression Principle:"

> Being the bettor/raiser is almost always better than being the caller. This is because betting and raising allow for the possibility of winning the pot immediately since everyone may fold.

The Aggression Principle, or Gap Concept applies to all forms of poker from cash draw poker to no-limit multi-table tournaments. However, "The *Hyper*-Aggression Principle" is unique to heads-up play.

> In heads-up play, the majority of the time neither player has a "good" hand. So the person who bets and raises most aggressively will frequently have an edge when other aspects are equal.

This strategic guideline is based on probability. For instance, the chance that you are against a pocket pair rises with number of opponents; against only one person, that probability is 6 percent.

Similarly, the likelihood that you are against someone who has made at least one pair on the flop decreases with fewer opponents. Against one person, it is 65 percent likely that your opponent has not paired, provided he started with cards of different ranks.

So against only one opponent, you are much less likely to be up against a stronger hand preflop or post-flop relative to fuller table play. It is similarly less probable that your opponent has hit a possible draw or connected with a scare card.

For instance, suppose there was a preflop raise and the flop comes with a low pair and a mid card, such as the

A hand like the

is a marginal hand playing a full game with 3 or 4 players seeing this flop. But heads-up, it will often be best.

One way to understand the Hyper-Aggression Principle is through the "Difficult to Play Against Criterion."

> Strategies that are difficult to play against are more effective than those which are easily countered.

This may be an obvious idea, but it is a useful framework for evaluating strategic effectiveness. This principle explains, for instance, why aggression is so important heads-up. It is difficult to play against an opponent who bets and raises aggressively in a format where you generally have a "weak" hand.

Meanwhile, consider a tight-passive style where you rarely raise your button, fail to defend your blind against small raises, and tend to check/fold the flop unless you connect. There are theoretical arguments against such a style, but one easy way to see its weakness is to consider playing such an opponent.

You would gain a significant edge simply by frequently betting and raising — winning many small pots, while folding those times you have a weak hand and your opponent shows strength. This person is much easier to play against than his aggressive counterpart, which leads to our next topic ...

Continuation Betting

A continuation bet (C-Bet) is a bet made after the flop by the preflop aggressor. It is common for the player who raises before the flop to bet after it, and correctly so. This is because:

1. You will often be raising before the flop with your better hands, and so you are more likely to have a stronger hand post-flop.

2. If your opponent misses, he will often fold after you show strength in the first two betting rounds.

The C-bet is very common in all no-limit variations, particularly after its discussion in the *Harrington on Hold 'em* books. A common C-bet size is one-half to two-thirds of the pot. Here's an example.

Stacks: $2,800
Blinds: $40-$80

Your hand: T♥9♥
Villain's hand: A♣7♠

Action: You raise to $210 on the button. Villain calls. The pot is $420.

Flop: K♠J♠6♦

Action: Villain checks. You bet $250. Villain folds.

Analysis: Villain has the better hand, yet you force him to lay it down with your C-bet since you raised preflop representing strength. The flop comes and it misses your opponent. You bet again. Unless Villain wants to call or raise with only a high card, his only alternative is to fold.

When in doubt, bet the flop after raising preflop. The best flops for this play are ones that are consistent with your preflop raise, and also unlikely to have hit your opponent.

For instance, a flop of

is unlikely to have helped your opponent. Only five possible hole cards connect with this hand (K♣, K♥, K♠, 2♦, 2♣), and there are no possible straight or flush draws. Meanwhile, your preflop raise is quite consistent with hands containing a king, such as king-jack offsuit or king-eight suited.

Now consider a flop such as

Your opponent could have paired with any of nine possible hole cards, rather than five. There are also a myriad of straight draws and a possible flush draw. So this flop is more likely to have hit him in some way. In addition, the most common hand to raise with preflop, two unpaired high cards, has not connected in any way. Since your opponent is more likely to have made something with this second flop, and less likely to believe you have hit it, you should be less inclined to C-bet than with the first example.

Value Betting

A value bet is designed to win chips by being frequently called with a weaker hand. While there is not a clear line as to how strong a hand must be to value bet, the most basic guideline is to simply bet those hands strong enough that weaker hands might reasonably call.

The reason value betting is important is that it is the simplest way to win chips. Bluffs, semi-bluff check-raises, and other plays are often solid chip-winners, but the most common way to accumulate chips is betting because you believe your hand is best. In addition, your value bets will sometimes serve the dual purpose of being defensive bets when the turn or river card could give your opponent a better hand. Here's an example.

Effective stacks: $1,500
Blinds: $10-$20

Your hand: J♥J♣

Action: You raise to $60 on the button and Villain calls. The pot is $120.

Flop: T♠6♣4♠

Action: Villain checks. You bet $100. He folds.

Question: *Why bet?*
> **Answer:** The preflop raise was a value raise. We most likely have the best hand, and gain when called by a worse hand. The flop bet is also for value since again our hand looks best. We could certainly be called by worse hands — a pair of tens, sixes, or fours in particular. The flop bet also serves as

a defensive bet since a turn of a queen or higher, and possibly a card such as the 5♠, could give our opponent a better hand. So not only do we want to win chips by being called with a worse hand, we do not want to give a free card that may beat us.

We now turn to our first *NBC National Heads-up Poker Championship* hand. But first, some preliminary remarks. When these hands were actually played, the participants had more information at their disposal than we will have in these hand examples. In particular:

1. Players might pick up physical tells on their opponents.

2. The participants often have extensive previous experience playing each other, and modify their play in these hands based on observations of prior play. And,

3. Lastly, the analysis in this book is done from an "armchair" perspective; the actual hands take place with limited time, cameras, and a substantial amount of money on the line.

So when we state a given player has made a mistake, he may actually be playing much better than it appears. In other words, our analysis is for the purposes of preparing you to handle similar situations. It's not to make someone like Doyle Brunson or Gus Hansen play better. They already play quite well.

Value Betting the Nuts

Here's a hand between former World Series of Poker (WSOP) Champion Jamie Gold and actress turned poker player Jennifer Tilly. It occurred in the first round of the *2007 National Heads-Up Poker Championship.*

Tilly: $22,400
Gold: $17,600

Blinds: $200-$400

Gold's hand: 4♠3♣
Tilly's hand: K♠Q♠

Action: Tilly raises to $1,200 on the button and Gold calls. The pot is $2,400.

Analysis: Tilly has a strong hand and makes a standard three big blind raise. Gold is out of position holding a junk hand. This combination of unfavorable factors makes Gold's call a mistake even if he believes he can outplay the non-professional Tilly post-flop.

Flop: A♠7♠5♠

Action: Both players check.

Analysis: Tilly should bet. She has the strongest possible hand which gives her an excellent way to accumulate chips — value betting each street. When you flop a strong hand, particularly against a loose opponent, your first thought should be: "How can I win the most chips possible?"

So there is no reason to slowplay. Indeed, Gold would expect her to C-bet with almost any cards she initially raised with, and he might therefore call or raise widely. Hands he might play back with include a straight draw, an inferior flush draw, any ace, most sevens, or possibly a stone bluff. In addition, Tilly's checking behind keeps the pot small and might make her opponent suspicious.

Turn: 2♣

Action: Gold bets $2,000 and Tilly calls. The pot is $6,400.

Analysis: This is a solid bet by Gold. He has hit a strong hand on a board with many draws, and he leads out with a full pot-sized bet.

The commentator suggests that Tilly is correct to only call. But her failure to raise will only limit her ability to win many chips, ideally an all-in, by the river. Raising this turn bet is not only for value. If Gold is on a draw or weaker made hand, he will probably call a small raise now, but be hesitant to bluff if Tilly calls and the river card does not improve him.

River: 2♠

Action: Gold checks. Tilly bets $4,000. Gold folds.

Analysis: Gold's check-fold is reasonable as his 4♠ can only beat a bluff on this four-spade board. Meanwhile, Tilly makes the value bet she has been reluctant to do throughout the hand. Unfortunately, it is too late, and she must settle for winning fewer chips than she might have if she had bet throughout the hand.

Value Betting the River

This hand is between former WSOP champion Phil Hellmuth and Paul Phillips.

Blinds: $1,000-$2,000

Hellmuth's hand: A♥8♥
Phillips' hand: 7♦3♣

Action: Hellmuth calls on the button and Phillips checks. The pot is $4,000.

Analysis: While Hellmuth likes to play a "small-ball" style, a mid-high suited ace is too strong not to raise unless your opponent frequently attacks button limps.

Flop: 7♥6♦5♠

Action: Phillips bets $4,000 and Hellmuth calls. The pot is $12,000.

Analysis: Phillips's bet with top pair (and a weak straight draw) is clear. Hellmuth knows that even if his ace-high is not best, he has as many as 12 outs — 8 straight outs, three for a pair of aces, and approximately one for his backdoor nut flush. (The times that a pair of aces improves him to a second-best hand are roughly counter-balanced by those times a pair of eights does make him the best hand.) So he is nearly 50-50 to improve by the river, and he must therefore at least call getting 2-to-1 odds. Raising is a solid alternative as well.

Turn: 4♥

Action: Phillips checks. Hellmuth bets $4,000 and Phillips calls. The pot is $20,000.

Analysis: With the ignorant end of the straight, Phillips is either way ahead or way behind. This is one time where check-calling is actually good strategy since a worse hand will probably not call a raise with four to a straight on board, and a better straight is certainly not folding.

Hellmuth makes a small value bet. He has what figures to be the best hand, as well as a redraw to the nut flush if any heart lands on the river. Also, Hellmuth routinely makes small bets, often as inexpensive jabs to take the pot. By making a small bet with a quality hand as well, he prevents Phillips from being able to narrow down his hand range since he could have many hands here.

River: 9♣

Action: Philips checks. Hellmuth bets $10,000 and Philips calls.

Analysis: For similar reasons as the turn, Phillip's check-call is still his best option. Hellmuth most likely puts Philips on two-pair, a set, or a smaller straight. With anything weaker, he will probably fold. With a worse straight, two-pair, etc., Hellmuth believes that the 3-to-1 pot odds will be too compelling for Phillips to fold, and he is right. So this is a solid river value bet.

Failing to extract value from strong hands is a significant mistake. So keep in mind that you will have the opportunity to make this error often, and it costs a lot when you do make it.

Effective Stack Sizes

The effective stack size is the smaller of the two stacks. For example:

Player A has $1,000

Player B has $2,000

Then the effective stack size is $1,000 because Player B cannot bet anything beyond A's $1,000 stack without automatically winning this amount in an uncontested sidepot. So in this example, both players have $1,000.

The effective stacks, relative to the blinds, will be a paramount consideration in all of our decisions. For instance, suppose you have the button and are dealt the

If the effective stack sizes are under 10 BB — ten multiples of the big blind — you should generally raise all-in. Other plays may work well too, but raising all-in is always a solid default move with a good starting hand and shallow stacks. If the blinds are $50-$100, this would mean that at least one player has fewer than $1,000. Perhaps you have $9,200 and your opponent has $700.

But if the effective stacks are over 100 BB, raising all-in would be your worst possible option since you are risking your entire stack to win a tiny pot (because we can assume your opponent won't call unless his hand is favored over you). So calling, making a smaller raise, or even folding are better options.

So in this case, over 100 BB means that both you and your opponent have over $10,000, such as stacks of $11,000 and $13,000.

You always want at least an estimation of the effective stacks as one criterion in deciding how best to play your hand. It will not only impact strategy before the flop, but can influence your decisions on the other rounds as well.

Solving Heads-Up Problems Mathematically

Is there a best way you can play a hand? In fact, it is often possible to determine your exact best option. The catch is that you might need to make many assumptions about your opponent's behavior. For instance...

Effective stacks: $800
Blinds: $15-$30

Your hand: 6♠4♠

Action: Villain, a loose and over-aggressive player, raises to $90 on the button, and you make a loose call. (Folding is a good alternative.) The pot is $180.

Flop: 8♠5♥2♣

Question: You have flopped a strong draw. *Is it better to bet out or go for a check-raise?* (I assume you have rejected the third alternative of check-calling.)
    Answer: Theoretically we can solve this problem exactly, but it requires many assumptions. Here is a sample list:

1. If we bet $120, Villian will fold any time he has flopped no pair, no draw, and raise all-in otherwise.

2. If we check, Villian will bet $120 regardless of his hand. If we raise, he will shove all-in or fold based on whether or not he has connected with the flop.

3. He will make this preflop raise with any two cards.

4. Villain will miss the flop at least 50 percent of the time, even if we account for the many overcard hands and draws.

Notice we have assumed that he will never call our flop bet. If we bet out $120, 50 percent of the time he will fold. The remainder of the time, he will raise all-in, we fold. So half the time we win $180, and half we lose $120. This makes our expectation (EV) $30.

$$\$30 = (.50)(\$180) + (.50)(-\$120)$$

If we check-raise, then 50 percent of the time we win $300 (the $180 pot plus his $120 bet), and the remaining 50 percent we gamble for the remaining stacks. Lose this gamble and we lose the remaining $710 in the $800 effective stacks. Win the gamble, and we win the remaining $710 stacks plus the $180 pot, for $890 total.

Besides the double straight draw, we have a backdoor flush draw, and catching a pair might win it for us. So let's assume we have around 10 outs if called, from "Appendix B: Drawing Odds Chart" on page 377 we see that our showdown equity is 38 percent. Thus our expectation is $99.

$$\$99 = (.50)(\$300) + (.50)\big[(.62)(-\$710) + (.38)(\$890)\big]$$

So we win an extra $69 by check-raising rather than betting.

When playing, we can often use more reasonable and inclusive assumptions to get solid answers. These situations where more exact answers are possible often involve the decision to commit all our chips with an all-in raise. There will be many examples to follow in this book. Otherwise, we will need to use other skills that will be addressed.

The All-In Decision:
A Quantitative Analysis

In a widely anticipated match-up, Daniel Negreanu makes an all-in semi-bluff reraise at a crucial point against experienced amateur Jerry Buss. Was this a play with positive expectation?

Negreanu: $22,100
Buss: $17,900

Buss's hand: 4♠4♦
Negreanu's hand: 9♦8♦

Blinds: $200-$400

Action: Buss limps from the button. Negreanu raises to $1,200. Buss calls. The pot is $2,400

Analysis: Buss should be inclined to raise with a pocket pair in position, particularly when facing an expert opponent.

Flop: T♥7♠3♣

Action: Negreanu bets $1,200. Buss raises to $2,500. Negreanu reraises all-in, and Buss ...?

Analysis: Negreanu makes a normal leadout bet after his preflop raise. Buss's decision to raise is good since this is an excellent flop for a small pair. Negreanu only has him beat if he is holding a ten, seven, or pocket pair above deuces. However, any turn card besides a deuce or a four reduces the chances of Buss's hand remaining best, and Buss should be looking to force Negreanu to play a large pot or abandon the hand. This will be the strategy that will most effectively neutralize Negreanu's skill advantage.

However, this raise is too small. He is offering Negreanu nearly 5-to-1 odds, and it will be difficult to elicit an immediate fold.

Negreanu now has a decision. He is certainly getting the odds with his open-ended straight draw to at least call. But what if he raises?

Out of position, even the most skilled player will have little advantage against a solid amateur, and so Negreanu elects to end the hand early with a reraise. The problem is that he must risk the effective remaining stacks of $15,500 to win the $6,100 on the table, not an ideal risk/reward ratio, and if the nines and eights are not outs, Negreanu will only win the 32 percent of the time he makes a straight.

All this data can be combined into one equation to determine the EV of the all-in raise so long as we make one additional assumption: We must know what hands Buss will call with, and how often he holds these hands. Also, note that even if we determine that the all-in has positive expectation, we will still not be able to state that this play is Negreanu's best option since calling may have higher expectation as well as a smaller raise. Therefore, the final answer for deciding on the best strategy would have to compare the EVs of each possible move. And even then the right answer is not necessarily the play with the higher EV because Daniel is the better player. If it is close, Daniel would rather make the play that extends the match.

Nonetheless, calculating the EV of an all-in is a crucial skill, so let us suppose that Buss requires at least top pair (regardless of kicker) to make this call. Then most of the time, Buss folds and Negreanu wins the $6,100 without a fight. But when Buss makes the call, 32 percent of the time Negreanu wins the $6,100 pot plus Buss's remaining $14,200, and 68 percent of the time Negreanu misses his straight and loses the remaining $15,500 to double Buss up. So letting p equal the probability of a call. The expectation of the all-in reraise is:

$$(1 - p)(\$6,100) + (p)[(.32)(\$20,300) + (.68)((-\$15,500)]$$

Therefore, Negreanu is making a resteal with positive expectation when

$$\$6,100 - \$6,100p - \$4,044p > 0 \Rightarrow$$
$$p < 60.13\%$$

So this all-in wins chips if Buss's hand is top pair or stronger no more than 60 percent of the time. (However, again as just stated above, no matter how often Buss holds a weak hand, Negreanu may still win more chips by calling or making a smaller raise.) In the actual hand, Buss folds to Negreanu's all-in raise.

Restealing All-In Preflop vs Post-flop

Here's a hand between former WSOP champion Chris Fergusen and Gus Hansen.

Ferguson: $35,500
Hansen: $24,500

Blinds: $1,500-$3,000

Ferguson's hand: Q♠Q♣
Hansen's hand: A♣3♦

Action: Ferguson raises to $6,000 on the button and Hansen calls. The pot is $12,000.

Flop: K♦K♥4♥

Action: Hansen checks. Ferguson bets $8,000. Hansen check-raises all-in for $18,500, and Ferguson calls.

Final board: K♦K♥4♥9♠8♦ and Ferguson wins the hand and match.

Analysis: When Hansen check-raises all-in, he is offering Ferguson odds of nearly 4-to-1. There are very few hands Ferguson will fold here. He will certainly call with a king, four, or any pocket pair. It is also likely he will call with any ace, in which case Hansen will be drawing to a split pot (or a trey). So Ferguson would have to hold, and then fold, two cards queen or lower to get an immediate fold.

Question: *Is there any other way Hansen could have played this hand?*

Answer: With an ace-high and under 10 blinds in chips, he could reraise all-in after Ferguson min-raises. When successful, he wins a $9,000 pot without seeing a flop. When called, he will often be a 70-to-30 dog against a better ace or pocket pair, but he might also be up against two broadway cards making him the slight favorite.

More quantitatively, we can ask: How often must Ferguson fold after min-raising for this proposed preflop resteal to show a profit? If we suppose that when called, Hansen's ace-high will have 40 percent showdown equity — which it will facing the top 15 percent or so of starting hands, then his EV on this resteal is:

$$\$9,000p + (1 - p)\left[(.40)(\$27,500) + (.60)(-\$21,500)\right]$$

where

    p is the probability that Ferguson folds.

When Hansen is called and loses, he forfeits his remaining $21,500. And when Hansen calls and wins, he wins $24,500 from Ferguson's stack, plus his original $3,000 blind.

This EV will be positive when:

$$\$9,000p - \$1,900 + \$1,900p > 0 \Rightarrow$$
$$p > 0.17$$

So if Ferguson is discarding any non-negligible portion of his range, Hansen will profit by reraising all-in. This move has the further advantage of simplfying future decision-making as a preflop all-in entirely negates the small blind's positional disadvantage.

However, with an ace, it should also be profitable for Hansen to call. So to make this play he must feel that Ferguson's folding percentage is well above 17 percent.

This next hand features Antonio Esfandiari and Ted Forrest. It shows that reraising all-in is not necessarily a cure-all solution.

Esfandiari: $57,800
Forrest: $102,200

Blinds: $1,000-$2,000

Esfandiari's hand: A♥Q♠
Forrest's hand: A♠4♣

Action: Esfandiari raises to $6,100 on the button. Forrest reraises all-in and Esfandiari calls for $51,700 more.

Analysis: It is tough to fault aggression in heads-up play, yet Forrest's reraise here has a poor risk/reward ratio. If Esfandiari folds, he wins $8,100. If Esfandiari calls, then Forrest figures to be roughly a 70-to-30 underdog against a mid-high pocket pair or better ace.

Question: *How often must Esfandiari fold for Forrest to show a positive expectation?*

    Answer: Letting p equal the probability that Esfandiari calls, then Forrest shows a profit if:

$$(1 - p)(\$8,100) + (p)[(0.7)(-\$55,800) + (0.3)(\$59,800)] > 0 \Rightarrow$$
$$\$8,100 - \$8,100p - \$21,120p > 0 \Rightarrow$$
$$p < 0.277$$

Therefore Forrest profits, relative to a fold, only if Esfandiari folds over 72 percent of the time.

Unless your opponent is raising with a very wide range and then only calling with top hands, this reraise will lose chips. It will also greatly increase swings which will hurt the restealer when he believes he has an advantage in future hands.

Later in this same match, Forrest elects to call with a stronger hand and shallower effective stacks.

Esfandiari: $76,500
Forrest: $83,500

Blinds: $1,500-$3,000

Esfandiari's hand: Q♣Q♦
Forrest's hand:8♣8♠

Action: Esfandiari raises to $9,000 on the button and Forrest calls. The pot is $18,000.

Analysis: Earlier in this match, Forrest three-bets all-in preflop with A♠4♣. In that hand, there was a higher fraction of the effective stacks on the table after Esfandiari's preflop raise, and Forrest's 8♣8♠ play better against hands that Esfandiari might call with. So if Forrest was willing to resteal earlier, it is surprising he declines to do so here.

Flop: 9♠9♣4♥

Action: Forrest checks. Esfandiari bets $12,500. Forrest raises all-in and Esfandiari calls for an extra $55,000.

Analysis: Forrest knows he cannot get away from this flop with a large pot and a hand that is best unless his opponent holds a nine, two fours, or a higher pair. Since Esfandiari is very likely to C-bet if Forrest checks, he lets Esfandiari make this extra bet before committing his chips.

Sample Match No. 1: Introduction to Heads-Up Gameplay

Many of the hands given in this book will be from matches with a common online format. The starting stacks are $1,500 and the levels are as follows:

Level I: $10-$20	**Level IV:** $50-$100
Level II: $15-$30	**Level V:** $75-$150
Level III: $25-$50	**Level VI:** $100-$200

This particular sample match consists of the most important hands from an online $16 heads-up match. Some of the topics will be addressed later in this book, so consider this an introduction.

Playing a Weak Face Card in Position

Blinds: $10-$20

Hand: Q♠4♦

Action: We limp on the button and Villain checks.

Analysis: Weak face cards are strong enough to play, but they fare better in small pots. Tend to make a small raise against a tight opponent, particularly those who might fold. And limping is also fine, especially against a calling station.

36

Flop: J♥T♥4♠

Action: Villain checks. We bet $30 and he folds.

Analysis: Our strategy in limped pots with position will be to make standard value bets with any pair, which will generally be best. If we missed entirely, a check might be better, but bottom pair is good enough to bet and charge him for a possible draw, or sticking around with a high card. If he called, we would probably try to check it down rather than play a large pot. If he plays back, it's usually best to fold.

Evaluating Outs and Pot Odds

Effective stacks: $1,480

Blinds: $10-$20

Hand: A♣8♦

Action: Villain raises to $60 on the button and we call. The pot is $120.

Analysis: A mid ace is strong enough to play, and you could also reraise. The plan when only calling is to play our hand when we connect, and otherwise try for a cheap showdown with ace-high.

Flop: 9♣7♦6♣

Action: We check. Villain bets $60. We raise to $200. He reraises all-in and we fold.

Analysis: We have connected solidly with the flop. We have 8 outs with our open-ended straight draw, 3 possible outs to top pair, and 1.5 outs for the backdoor nut flush draw. We may weigh this strong draw similarly to 10 full outs discounting the value of the top pair outs to be conservative. In addition, ace-high could be the better hand right now.

So this hand is strong enough to play aggressively, and the only question is whether to lead or check-raise. With draws, as opposed to made hands, it is often better to check-raise. That's because if your opponent checks behind, you still benefit from getting a free card which might complete your draw. But with a made hand, such as a pair, you want value immediately, and future cards are more likely to help your opponent than you.

So we check, happy to get a free chance to hit a straight or overpair if he checks, and intending to check-raise otherwise. But when he then three-bets all-in after our check-raise, representing a monster hand, we cannot call. The pot is $1,740 — his $1,480 stack, plus our $260 contribution. It costs us $1,280 to call. Therefore our pot odds are $1,740-to-$1,280, or about 1.4-to-1. Since our ten outs make us a 1.6-to-1 underdog to improve by the river, we elect to fold. Plus the action indicates that we may now have less than ten outs.

Several hands later, we are dealt Q♦8♥ on the button.

Action: We raise to $50 and Villain folds.

Analysis: He is capable of folding to small preflop raises, useful information.

Bluffing an Unraised Pot

Effective stacks: $1,300
Blinds: $10-$20

Hand: 7♠4♣

Action: We limp on the button and Villain checks. The pot is $40.

Flop: Q♣9♦6♥

Action: Villain checks. We bet $25 and he calls. The pot is $90.

Analysis: Our 7-high has very little showdown equity. But we do have fold equity. Since we have seen him fold to small bets, we take a stab at the pot. If he plays back, we lose little, and when he folds, we win a pot we would probably lose. And we expect him to fold often enough for this to be a profitable play. But since our opponent calls and shows strength, we now decide to check/fold on future streets.

Turn: 4♦

Action: We both check.

Analysis: We have bottom pair with a weak kicker. We want the cheapest showdown possible with our marginal hand since it may be best.

River: A♣

Action: We both check. Villain shows A♠4♥ and his two-pair takes the pot.

Analysis: After he checks the river, we have no reason to bet. With a hand like bottom pair, you want to play a small pot, so we gladly take the free showdown. But our opponent's river play was a mistake. We showed weakness checking the turn, and his best chance to win chips on the end is to bet unless he thinks we are prone to bluff. Since many weaker hands will call, he should make a normal value bet.

We now win a couple of small pots in succession, bringing the effective stacks close to the starting $1,500. The blinds rise to $15-$30.

Calling with Ace-High

Hand: A♠T♥

Action: We raise to $90 on the button and Villain calls. The pot is $180.

Flop: K♦J♣3♠

Action: Villain checks. We bet $100 and he calls. The pot is $380.

Analysis: We C-bet this flop, a bet that Villain will have difficulty calling without a king or a jack. Furthermore, our ace-high will often be best, plus we have a gutshot straight draw if called by a better hand.

Turn: 7♥

Action: Villain bets $40 and we call. The pot is $460.

Analysis: After Villain calls our flop bet and we do not improve, our normal play would be to give up on the hand. But this unusual bet of $40 might indicate any hand, and the pot odds of over 10-to-1 are almost good enough to call for the gutshot straight draw alone since we are a 10.6-to-1 underdog to hit a queen. If we win even a small bet on the river when this happens, calling will show a profit.

River: 3♥

Action: Villain bets $40 and we call. He shows Q♦3♥, and his trip treys take the pot.

Analysis: We can only beat a bluff, and it is unlikely that Villain is bluffing. But we are getting over 12-to-1. If our ace-high is best more than one time in thirteen, then this call is a chip-winner. This strange river bet will probably be a bluff at least this often, so calling is correct.

Reraising a Strong Hand Preflop

The next hand we are dealt is Q♠Q♥ in the big blind.

Action: Villain raises to $120. We reraise to $380. He folds.

Analysis: We reraise our queens not only for value, but because this hand is difficult to play after the flop when an ace or king hits and we are out of position. Also, facing a reraise, Villain could go all-in with a much weaker hand than ours such as a pair of eights or ace-jack. And when he folds immediately, as he does here, we still win a healthy amount.

Value Betting
After a Loose Preflop Raise

We now trail $1,400 to $1,600 with blinds still at $15-$30.

Hand: 9♠6♣

Action: We raise to $90 on the button and Villain calls. The pot is $180.

Flop: Q♦6♥5♣

Action: Villain checks. We bet $120 and he calls. The pot is $420.

Analysis: Mid pair is strong enough to bet heads-up. We might be called by a pair of fives or a straight draw possibly a high card, and we do not want two higher cards than our six to get a free chance at pairing. Note also that we would still C-bet if we had missed.

Turn: 8♣

Action: We both check.

Analysis: After his call and another card higher than a six falling, our hand is not as strong. It is unlikely our opponent will call two more bets with fives or worse. Furthermore, we have picked up a 4-out gutshot draw, making for 9 cards that improve us to a better hand. (The other 5 are the remaining nines and sixes.) So we are happy to check and take a free card.

River: T♦

Action: We both check. Villain shows the 7♦6♦ and our nine kicker wins the pot.

Analysis: At the river, we are again looking for another check/check sequence since our pair of sixes could be best. If we bet, stronger hands than our weak second pair should call, and weaker hands will normally fold. His actual hand of 7♦6♦ is a likely exception as he probably would have called a small bet.

Effective stacks: $1,390

Hand: A♥J♣

Action: Villain limps on the button. We raise to $150, both for value and because we do not mind ending a hand early when playing out of position. He folds.

Putting an Opponent on a Hand

Effective stacks: $1,100
Blinds: $15-$30

Hand: Q♦T♣

Action: Villain limps on the button and we check. The pot is $60.

Analysis: This is a passive check. You should tend to raise a button limp when you have a stronger hand such as queen-ten.

Flop: T♠8♥5♥

Action: We bet $60. Villain raises to $270. We…? The pot is $390 and it is our turn to act.

Analysis: On the flop, we have a vulnerable top pair. So we decide to bet for value and to defend our hand against overcards and other possible draws.

Question: *When Villain raises, do we still like our hand?*
    Answer: Let's consider the hands that have us beat right now, as well as how consistent they are with the information we currently have.

Hand	Does He Hold?
King-ten	Possible. But two tens are already accounted for, and most likely he would have raised preflop with this hand, particularly suited.
Ace-ten	It is likely he would raise preflop.
Overpair	It is likely he would raise preflop.
Tens	This could only be one specific hand, T♥T♦, since two tens are already out. Also, we would have expected a preflop raise with tens.
Eights or Fives	Possible. But there are only six of these hands total, and, as above, he would probably have raised a pocket pair preflop — particularly eights.
Ten-eight or ten-five	Two tens and an eight are already accounted for, but these hands are definitely possible.
Eight-five	Consistent with all of Villain's actions.

Notice that the two primary ways that we can label a hand as "unlikely" are examining hand combinations and previous actions. Pocket tens, for instance, is the least likely hand on all fronts. Most players will raise this hand preflop, whereas Villain limped preflop. And since a ten flopped and we hold one as well, that means there are only two tens left. Unless he holds both of them, he does not have pocket tens.

So while Villain could hold a set or an overpair, we are most worried about five hands: KT, AT, T8, T5, or 85. But now let us consider all the hands consistent with his actions that have us ahead at the moment. These include: JT, J8+ (or possibly a lower eight, and less likely a five with an overcard kicker), T9 - T6, T4 - T2, or a solid draw such as 7♥4♥. Each of these hands could quite reasonably be limped on the button, and then aggressively raised on the flop.

Since the pot is already $390, we have a lot of fold equity if we reraise, and based on his hand range, we also like our showdown equity. Since calling leaves us out of position in a large pot, we simply reraise all-in.

Resolution: We reraise all-in and he calls. He shows T♥4♣, and we win the pot and match with a final board of T♠8♥5♥8♥4♦. (Notice that his pair of fours is counterfeited; we each have two-pair tens and eights, while his kicker is only the board's 5♥.)

Part Two

Playing Styles
and Exploiting Styles

Playing Styles and Exploiting Styles

Introduction

There are many winning heads-up styles, all sharing one common element: aggression. In this section of the book, we will outline several ways to approach winning, aggressive play. This will include tight-aggressive and loose-aggressive strategies.

We will then discuss how to take advantage of those playing passive styles, as well as the best ways to counter opponents also playing aggressively. We will then conclude with a full discussion on the "hit-to-win style," and a series of sample matches tying it all together.

We'll begin with a deceptively simple style, the Basic-Aggressive Style, that shows the power of aggressive play even when used in a very basic manner. From there, we'll move on to other strategies and finally to tactics designed to counter how your opponent might be playing.

The Basic-Aggressive Style

The Basic-Aggressive Style has the player following a simple strategy throughout the match.[3] Playing this way, you will min-raise before the flop regardless of position. You will then bet the minimum each subsequent betting round. If your opponent folds, or he calls until the river, your play is entirely independent of your cards. But if he raises or bets at any point, you then make subsequent decisions based on your cards. Here's an example.

It is the first hand of an online heads-up sit 'n go. You are playing the basic aggressive strategy.

Effective stacks: $1,500
Blinds: $10-$20

Action: You min-raise to $40 on the button, independent of your cards, and your opponent calls. The pot is $80.

Flop: K♦J♥2♦

Action: You opponent checks. You min-bet $20 and he calls. The pot is $120

Turn: 4♠

Action: Your opponent checks. You min-bet $20. He raises to $140.

---

[3] This style was originally discussed in Daniel Negreanu's poker blog of April 13, 2006.

Up until this point, your cards have been irrelevant to the decision-making process. But facing this turn check-raise, you consider your cards. For instance, you might fold a ten-high, reraise a straight flush draw, or call with second pair. Regardless of your holding, you now transition from following a formula to making a hand-dependent play.

This deceptively simple strategy has two distinct benefits:

1. It is supremely aggressive because your default play is to raise preflop and then bet every street of every hand.

2. It gives your opponent no information about your hand since you play in a manner that is not dependent on your cards. So unless he makes an aggressive play himself, your opponent cannot learn any information about your hand based on your betting patterns.

The downside to the Basic-Aggressive Style is a near-complete lack of flexibility. For instance, if you are playing with short stacks and want to go all-in before the flop, the min-raise would be contrary to this goal. Or perhaps you are out of position and flop a weak top pair. The Basic-Aggressive Style prevents you from making the large bet you might normally make to get value and make it incorrect for your opponent to call with many hands.[4] Furthermore, you still must make normal poker decisions when your opponent does not cooperate with your min-betting.

We are not discussing the Basic-Aggressive Style as a suggested way to play, although it can be quite effective. Rather, you should realize that even without fancy plays, or even following conventional strategy, you can do better than you might think by playing a simple, aggressive style.

---

[4] One modification to the Basic-Aggressive Style that works to address the problem of offering favorable odds is to make the post-flop bets proportional to the pot size, such as a constant 20 percent of the pot.

The Loose-
Aggressive Style

Like the Basic-Aggressive Style, you are playing many hands with the Loose-Aggressive Style (LAG), and playing them aggressively. But min-raises and min-bets are now the exception rather than the rule.

One very powerful play in heads-up poker is raising your button preflop, and then betting the flop if checked to you. This is the continuation bet we saw earlier in "Part One: The Fundamentals."

One shortcoming of the Basic-Aggressive Style is the nearly irresistible pot odds you are offering your opponent to call your C-bet. So while your raise amounts are no longer set in stone with the Loose-Aggressive Style, you will be offering your opponents a much less attractive call after you bet.

Playing the Loose-Aggressive Style, when it is your button, you raise the majority of your preflop starting hands, limping or folding the rest. Your default raise size is between 2 to 4 BB, most often 2, 2.5, or 3 BB. When checked to you on the flop, tend to make a continuation bet of around two-thirds the pot.

In the big blind, raise to 4 BB with strong hands when your opponent limps, then if called fire a C-bet on the flop. When your opponent raises his button, reraise with your strong hands. These reraises should generally be 3 or 4 multiples of your opponent's raise, and should usually be followed up with a flop bet if called.

Often your opponent will interrupt these plans by raising or reraising preflop, leading out or check-raising post-flop, and so forth. If he does indeed play back in this manner, or if he usually calls your flop bet, it is time to evaluate your options just as you would with the Basic-Aggressive Style. If you have connected with the board in any way, you will generally continue to bet and raise.

We will consider many examples of loose-aggressive play in the many hand and match examples in this text. These will include the details on preflop and post-flop raise-sizing, when not to C-bet, the later streets, and so forth. For now, it's important to understand the basic mechanics behind the Loose-Aggressive Style. Namely, you are betting and raising relentlessly, knowing that in the majority of heads-up hands, your opponent will not have anything of value.

This makes you difficult to play against, especially since if your opponent does play back, it is still possible that you have a strong hand. Here are two examples of loose-aggressive play.

Effective stacks: $1,500
Blinds: $10-$20

Hand: 9♣6♣

Action: You raise to $60 on the button and your opponent calls. The pot is $120.

Flop: K♣7♦2♦

Action: Your opponent checks. You bet $80 and he calls. The pot is $280.

Turn: 4♣

Action: Your opponent checks. You bet $200. He folds.

Analysis: Preflop you raise with a seemingly weak hand, and then bet the flop even after missing it entirely. This is a common betting pattern for the Loose-Aggressive Style. You raise widely preflop, and then C-bet most flops.

On the turn, you would often not fire again after your flop bet is called, but here you pick up a flush draw. This allows you to bet again as a semi-bluff, hoping to win immediately, but having 9 outs to a strong hand in case of a call.

Effective stacks: $1,200
Blinds: $10-$20

Hand: A♦2♦

Action: Villain calls from the button. You raise to $80 and he calls. The pot is $160.

Flop: J♥J♦5♦

Action: You lead with a pot-sized bet of $160. Villain raises to $400. You reraise all-in.

Analysis: If Villain does not have a jack, five, or pocket pair, he will likely fold to your reraise — you win $710. And when he does call, you have 12 outs to improve, unless he holds a jack, making you nearly even money to win by the river. (See " Appendix B: Drawing Odds Chart" on page 377. Your 12 outs here are the 3 aces and the 9 remaining diamonds.)

Since your reraise will sometimes win a large pot immediately, and you will often be close to even money when called, this is a reraise that the loose-aggressive player is very comfortable making. Note also that some opponents would not raise your flop bet, thus deciding to slowplay. Since there is also an extra five that Villain could hold, relative to only two jacks remaining, his raise will often indicate a hand weaker than trip jacks.

One consequence of playing the loose-aggressive style is that you cannot be afraid to commit all your chips when you have a good hand and the pot is large. By always having an all-in threat looming over your opponents, they will be much less likely to play back against your aggression. You will therefore win most pots when neither of you has a good hand.

> The loose-aggressive style is a very powerful playing style in heads-up poker.

However, the most common playing style in other forms of poker can also sometimes be quite effective in heads-up.

The Tight-
Aggressive Style

The Tight-Aggressive Style is the most common winning strategy in full games. You simply fold your weak hands and only get involved in a pot when you have the advantage. This usually means starting with a quality hand. So when you raise before the flop your hand is usually best. When called, you C-bet often, and your quality starting hand will flop a strong hand more often than a random hand.

The problem with playing any "tight" style when heads-up is since you are posting a blind every hand, you may get blinded out waiting for premium starting hands. There is, however, a middle ground. With the tight-aggressive style, you still play non-premium starting hands, like the loose-aggressive style, but more selectively. Now, from the button, you raise perhaps the top one-third to one-half of your starting hands, limping or folding the rest. From the big blind, the tight-aggressive style will require a strong hand to raise or reraise since you will be playing without position after the flop.

(We'll discuss the issue of button-limping versus button-folding later. For now, when we refer to "playing" a hand, it means opening with a raise before the flop.)

Flop tight-aggressive play more closely resembles the loose-aggressive style. You still C-bet as your default play when your opponent calls your preflop raise. If this C-bet is called or raised, you then continue based on hand strength, what you know about your opponent, and so forth. However, since you start with better hands, you will have stronger hands post-flop with greater frequency.

The primary post-flop difference is that your standards for continuing on with a hand are higher. Marginal draws or weak pairs that a loose-aggressive player might raise or reraise are often folded by the tight player, consistent with his strategy of having higher standards to get involved, or stay involved, in a hand.

Playing tight-aggressive ensures you generally have good cards when playing a big pot. However, you also miss out on the many smaller pots that a loose-aggressive player naturally picks up through his constant betting and raising.

The primary criterion for deciding whether to play a tight-aggressive or loose-aggressive style is your opponent. As we discuss below, the tighter your opponent plays, the more you should be inclined to be loose-aggressive since a tight player is more likely to concede to your bets and raises when he does not have a hand. Some loose players will simply call bet after bet, in which case you should stick to value betting stronger hands.

Another factor determining your strategy is your post-flop ability. You get involved in many marginal hands playing loose and aggressive, and these often require keen post-flop skills to navigate. The more comfortable you are playing after the flop, the looser you can play.

Let's look at two examples. In each case, you are playing an online match without knowing much about your opponent. The blinds are $15-$30 with stacks of $1,500, and we contrast the tight-aggressive (TAG) and loose-aggressive (LAG) approaches.

Example No. 1

You have

on the button. *What is your play?*

The tight-aggressive player will tend to limp or fold this weak hand. J♠2♥ is in the bottom 25 percent of hands (See "Appendix C: Top N Percent Starting Hands" on page 381.) It plays poorly after the flop. So you might limp or raise facing a weak or passive opponent, but this is not a hand the TAG is happy to "play" by coming in with a raise.

By contrast, the LAG will be inclined to raise. He too might sometimes limp, but a loose-aggressive player is certainly willing to play any hand with a face card. One advantage to this approach is that your opponent could fold to one of your early bets, as he could when you raise with any cards. And one disadvantage is that you will often have a tough post-flop decision, such as when you flop top pair, bottom kicker and your opponent begins betting big. Are you willing to commit all your chips to see a showdown with this hand?

Example No. 2

Your hand: T♠9♠

Action: You raise to $90 on the button and Villain calls. The pot is $180.

Flop: 8♥4♥2♠

Action: Villain checks. You bet $120. He calls. The pot is $420.

Turn: 7♦

Action: Villain bets $350.

Question: *What is your play?*
  Answer: First, note that the preflop and flop plays are standard for both styles. Your mid-high suited connectors are

certainly strong enough to raise preflop, and at the flop you C-bet, which is again the common play, regardless of style. The two styles diverge, however, at the turn. Villain's bet is unexpected since you have aggressively bet at each opportunity. Is he bluffing, betting a draw, or suddenly attacking with a strong hand?

The loose-aggressive player will raise much more often than his tight-aggressive counterpart in this situation. (An aggressive style makes flat-calling this large bet unattractive, particularly without deep stacks.[5])

The LAG will reason that the pot is large, his opponent could have many hands not strong enough to call an all-in bet, and even when he is called he still has 8 outs to complete his open-ended straight draw — as well as another 6 outs to an often-best top pair. So lacking a read, he will often raise this bet.

But the TAG will be much less inclined to make an all-in semi-bluff. His hand is likely behind at the moment, his opponent is representing a strong hand, and he has only invested two bets in this pot. So the TAG will more often fold and wait for a more favorable spot to get his chips in.

This distinction is perhaps artificial. A loose winning player will often fold instead, such as when he knows his opponent is tight, and is unlikely to make this $350 bet as a bluff. And a winning tight player could raise, particularly if he knew his opponent was capable of bluffing or semi-bluffing. However, the bottom line is that the loose-aggressive player is simply more willing to put chips in the pot as a bluff or semi-bluff. The tight-aggressive player,

---

[5] With starting stacks of $5,000, for instance, we might call and potentially win a very large pot when we complete our straight. We could also miss the straight, and bluff if checked to. But these river possibilities are much more limited having started with only 50 BB stacks and facing a bet which would commit nearly half this stack.

meanwhile, places a bigger emphasis on present hand strength.

The main point you should pull from this chapter and the two preceding is:

You should play an aggressive style in heads-up no-limit poker.

In addition, labeling your style does not lock you into playing only this way. You can certainly play a mixed strategy, switching up your bet sizes and starting hand standards during the match. Indeed, doing so is often advantageous. Your opponent will have difficulty getting a solid read on your play, and most importantly, switching up your style allows for exploiting your opponent's style.

Exploiting Your Opponent's Style

You will encounter all types of opponents in heads-up poker. For instance, while you should not play a passive style yourself, many players do just that. Other opponents will play recklessly, unpredictably, or in such a fashion that you're never really sure.

Heads-up is a game of information. Your goal when playing a match is to figure out your opponent's style as soon as possible. You must then know how to exploit it. In this chapter, we outline a method to play against the four most categorizable styles:

1. Tight-aggressive
2. Tight-passive
3. Loose-aggressive
4. Loose-passive

While each style requires its own modifications to exploit, there is one common theme. Always ask yourself:

> If this was my approach, what would I not want my opponent to do?

The Tight-Passive Opponent

The passive styles are the easiest to play against. This is the fundamental reason to play aggressively.

The tight-passive (TP) player will require an above-average hand to call bets, and a strong hand to bet himself. Against a tight-passive opponent, simply play a loose-aggressive style, which will allow you to win many small pots, but never get involved in a large pot unless you have a strong hand.

The TP style is arguably the weakest one heads-up. You can bet and raise to take your opponent off hand after hand, chipping away at his stack and winning the most chips in the long run.

Effective stacks: $1,000
Blinds: $10-$20
Note: Your opponent is playing a tight-passive style.

Your hand: 7♣4♥

Action: Your opponent limps and you check in the big blind. The pot is $40.

Flop: 3♠2♦2♣

Action: You bet $30 and your opponent folds.

Analysis: Preflop you should raise button limps with many hands against a tight-passive opponent since he will often fold immediately. And when he does call, your C-bet will frequently win uncontested since these opponents need a good hand to call. With a trash hand, however, checking is best.

The reason you should often bet the flop is that unless your opponent has a rare pocket pair, only five cards connect with this flop — the three treys, and the two remaining deuces. So your tight-passive opponent is likely to have missed and not be willing to call a bet. Meanwhile, your 7-high has no showdown equity, so bet now. If called, simply shut down and stop betting as you are certainly facing a better hand.

Effective stacks: $1,500
Blinds: $25-$50

Your hand: J♥2♠ on the button.

Question: What is your play?
    Answer: Raise. The loose-aggressive play of raising preflop any hand with a face card is your best approach against a tight opponent since he will fold immediately much more often than loose or "normal" opponents.

The Loose-Passive Opponent

The loose-passive player is exploitable as well, but requires a little more caution. This player will only bet with strong hands, but he will call with many holdings.

You should play a tight-aggressive style against this opponent. They will call bet after bet, so wait until you have an above-average hand, and then bet for value. Preflop, avoid raising with your weaker hands, raising only your strong ones for value. Since passive opponents require a strong hand to raise, tend to limp, rather than fold, with your weak hands. If your opponent plays back, be inclined to fold as he will generally need a solid hand to attack preflop.

After the flop, continue playing a tight-aggressive style. Tight because there is little point betting with the idea of moving your opponent off a hand when he will call widely, often with an overcard, backdoor draw, or similarly weak hands. Aggressively, because when you do connect, you must exploit your opponent's weakness by extracting as much value as possible.

Loose-passive opponents are often referred to derogatorily as "calling stations." Players often get frustrated against someone who cannot be bluffed. Aggressive players facing loose-passive opponents will complain, "He's playing so badly I don't know what to do. I semi-bluffed the turn and made a follow-up bluff on the river because I knew he didn't have anything, but he called me down with queen-high!"

These players are missing the point. If your opponent will never fold, bet relentlessly for value any time you have a hand that figures to be best. Forget about fancy plays, recognize when your hand figures to be best, and when it does, bet. It's that simple.

Effective stacks: $1,000
Blinds: $5-$10

Your hand: J♠T♠

Action: You raise to $30 on the button and Villain calls. The pot is $60.

Flop: A♥Q♥7♦

Action: You both check.

Turn: A♦

Action: You both check.

River: 2♣

Action: You both check. Villain shows 4♣4♦ and his low pair takes the pot.

Analysis: Preflop you have an above-average hand, so you raise for value based on hand strength. You do not connect with the board in any way, so you simply check the hand down. If Villain has a better hand with a pair or king-high, he will probably call. So just check and hope you hit your gutshot straight draw, or your jack-high holds up. If your opponent is only moderately loose-passive, you can still C-bet and only check/fold if this does not win the pot.

When you lose this pot, do not fault yourself for failing to bet. Your loose-passive opponent would most likely call one or two significant bets with his low pair, so trying to move him off this marginal hand would have only cost chips.

Now let us modify your starting hand.

Effective stacks: $1,000
Blinds: $5-$10
Note: Your opponent plays a loose-passive style.

Your hand: Q♠2♣

Action: You call on the button and Villain checks. The pot is $20.

Analysis: Many tight-aggressive players habitually fold weak face card hands before the flop. This is a mistake against a passive player since he will require a strong hand to attack your preflop limp, and when you are raised, you can make an easy laydown. So call with your weak hands. Your strategy post-flop will be to bet any flop against a tight-passive opponent, usually winning immediately, and otherwise losing only a few chips. Meanwhile, against the loose-passive opponent, bet for value if you catch any piece, and otherwise check the hand down. Here, your low offsuit queen is too weak to raise preflop, but calling getting 3-to-1 pot odds is a must.

Flop: Q♣T♥4♦

Action: Villain checks. You bet $15 and he calls. The pot is $50.

Analysis: After the flop, you make a standard value bet. Since your loose-passive opponent cannot be bluffed out of pots, you are exploiting this tendency by betting with a made hand. Heads-up, top pair is strong. You would also value bet with middle or bottom pair.

Turn: A♠

Action: You both check.

Analyis: Betting is the stronger play. It's true that this ace is not the best card, but your second pair is still strong enough to bet for value. You might get called not only by any lower pair, but also by a king or jack. If your opponent had king-eight, for instance, he might call the flop bet with an overcard, and call the turn bet with a gutshot straight draw.

River: 7♦

Action: Villain checks. You bet $35. He calls and shows 6♠4♠. Your queens take the pot.

Analysis: A much bigger mistake than checking the turn would be to check behind on the river. We have second pair against a weak opponent who has checked consecutive streets, a situation requiring a value bet. The actual bet of two-thirds the pot is a good default number, and indeed, we win a healthy $120 pot through simple value betting.

> Against loose-passive opponents, bet for value when you have a hand you believe is best, and tend to check/fold otherwise.

The Loose-Aggressive Opponent

The aggressive styles are much harder to play against, none more so than the Loose-Aggressive Style. Before we discuss the general approach to countering loose-aggressive play, it will help to discuss maniacs who plays an exaggerated version of this style — betting, raising, and reraising with very little regard to hand strength. Your opponent might be a maniac if …

- He raises almost any two cards preflop.

- He bets and raises unusually high amounts. And,

- If he is the preflop raiser, he will frequently make at least two large bets after the flop, bluffing if necessary.

You will often know you are playing against a maniac within the first several hands. For instance, suppose you are playing a cash game with blinds of $1-$2 and effective stacks of $200.

Hand No. 1: Villain raises his button to $10 and you fold A♠4♥.

Hand No. 2: You raise to $6 and he reraises to $20. You call with 7♠7♦. The flop comes Q♣T♥8♥ and he leads out for $45. You fold.

Hand No. 3: He raises his button to $9 and you fold K♠2♥.

Only three hands have passed, but you should have strong suspicions you are playing against a maniac. On the surface, this style is difficult to play against. In our three sample hands, Villain could well have gotten us to lay down the best hand each time. And he did so simply by playing hyper-aggressively and overbetting. You rarely have a strong hand in heads-up play, and against these opponents, you are constantly being forced to call large bets or make pot-committing reraises if you refuse to surrender a pot.

What do you do? Let's go back to the question we posed earlier. What prevents you from playing such a "raise any two cards, overbet all pots" strategy? Think about this for a moment.

Okay, most likely you're thinking along the lines: "These plays are risking too much for too small a reward. Sure I'll take the blinds a lot preflop and win a lot of small pots after the flop, but when my opponent actually has a hand, he can simply call me down and take all my chips."

And indeed, when you have a hand you believe is best, simply call your opponent down. You will lose many small pots by folding to large bets early, but when you get involved, you will have the opportunity to win much larger pots with marginal hands.

You must have courage when playing against the maniac. When you have a hand that figures to be best, you will often play a larger pot than you feel comfortable playing. In fact, one reason the maniac style can be so tough to counter is that even players who understand how to beat it are often reluctant to follow through with proper strategy since it may require you to put many chips at risk with a much weaker hand than you normally would.

When you have the button, raise less often because your opponent will often reraise, and unless you have a strong hand, you would rather see a flop before committing many chips. This way, you can connect with a flop and then let the maniac do the betting for you.

Effective stacks: $7,500
Blinds: $50-$100
Note: Your opponent is recklessly aggressive.

Your hand: K♠T♣

Action: You limp on the button.

Normally this would be a weak limp, but it's acceptable against someone who will raise almost any two cards when facing a button limp.

Action: Villain does indeed raise another $500. You call, expecting to have a better hand going into the flop. The pot is $1,000.

Flop: X Y Z

Question: *What is your game plan if Villain comes out with a large bet, as we expect?*
    Answer: Raise or call with almost any piece of the flop, and fold otherwise.

Flop No. 1: A♥9♦2♣. He bets $1,200. You should fold. Your king-high might well be best, but you did not connect with the flop, and Villain will usually fire at least one more sizeable bet if you call. So fold now.

Flop No. 2: K♥9♦2♣. He bets $1,200. You should call. Now Villain's wildly loose playing standards and the likelihood of future bets work in your favor. You strongly figure to have the best hand against an opponent who bets incessantly. Take full advantage by calling him down and often win a large pot by showdown.

Flop No. 3: T♥9♦2♣. He bets $1,200. While folding is the only real mistake you can make, be inclined to raise. Again, your hand figures to be best, but many fourth street cards devalue it (particularly any of the 18 remaining aces, queens, jacks, nines, or deuces).

Flop No. 4: A♦T♥2♣. He bets $1,200. You should at least call. And against a player who will literally bet/raise each betting round regardless of hand strength, you must be willing to call three large bets.

Maniacs will often force you to commit all your chips when you would rather not, such as when you flop top pair, weak kicker, with relatively deep stacks. Accept that your fluctuations will be larger, and assume bigger risks against these opponents. If you fail to take a stand with your better hands, then he will simply chip you away. Now let's consider playing against the maniac from the big blind.

When facing any style, particularly a loose style, you should tend to base your preflop actions mostly on hand strength when playing from the big blind. Against the maniac, however, you should look to call raises slightly more often than you would against a "normal" opponent. The bigger the stacks, the wider your calling range since you are calling his preflop raise in an attempt to win a large pot after the flop when you do connect, taking advantage of the maniac's constant betting.

When you like the flop, check/call more often since the maniac is so likely to bet. If you have a draw, semi-bluffing is less valuable since the chance of the maniac folding is diminished, but realize that your implied odds are better than usual.

Effective stacks: $1,000
Blinds: $5-$10

Your hand: T♠9♠

Action: Villain, a maniac, raises to $35 from the button and you call. The pot is $70.

Question: *What is your game plan after each of the following flops?*

Flop No. 1: K♣8♥2♣
Answer: Check/fold. A bluff is unlikely to succeed, and even if your 10-high is best (against hands such as seven-six offsuit or five-trey suited), you cannot call three large bets to find out.

Flop No. 2: Q♥9♣2♣
Answer: Tend to check/call each street with what figures to be the best hand. Do not fold. Be prepared to play a large pot with your second pair.

Flop No. 3: 9♣5♦4♣
Answer: Check-raise or bet out. Your top pair is very strong, but many turn cards devalue it that you should charge the maniac for any draws. An alternative approach is to lead out, and if you are raised, reraise all-in.

Flop No. 4: Q♠8♥7♦
Answer: Tend to check/call. You should normally play your draws aggressively, either leading out or check/raising as a semi-bluff, but if Villain is the type who will not fold, check/calling is usually best. You have a disguised draw to the nuts, and pairing either card will give you a probable best hand.

Against a reckless opponent, your implied odds make a call quite profitable in Flop No.4. Suppose Villain's normal play is to make pot-sized bets each street. Then you show a large profit calling here. In this case, you would call $70 now, expecting to win a pot of $1,035.

$1,035 = The current pot ($70) + Villain's flop bet ($70), turn bet ($210), and river bet ($685 all - in)

So your implied odds for calling the flop bet are over 14-to-1, and you are only a 4.8-to-1 underdog to hit your straight on the turn.

Indeed, we can make conservative assumptions and still make a tidy profit. For instance, suppose Villain only makes one more pot-sized bet, and we will never win extra chips beyond that when we make our straight. Then we must call the same $70 to win a pot of $350, and these 5-to-1 pot odds are still better than we need to show a chip profit. So the passive play of check/calling is often a good option against the maniac.

We discuss this style at such length because if you can play against a maniac, and you can play against a tighter player, then you can also play against a loose-aggressive player. That's because a LAG is just a tighter version of a maniac. You still must be willing to commit chips when you believe you have the best hand, or you will lose to these opponents.

Raise more often preflop playing a LAG than a maniac, but not as often as you would against a tight player. Assuming your LAG opponent will sometimes fold to your aggression, it is then occasionally profitable to bluff and semi-bluff. But you should still stick primarily to extracting value from your stronger hands. Plays like reraising a straight draw work better on tight opponents who are much more likely to fold without a hand.

A LAG is like a smart maniac. He understands the benefits of the maniac's incessant aggression, but he is capable of folding when clearly beat. This style is generally the most difficult to counter heads-up, and is precisely why you should tend to play this way.

The Tight-Aggressive Style

Your strategy against the tight-aggressive player (TAG) is to play loose-aggressive. The tight-aggressive player is a tougher adversary than his tight-passive counterpart, but you can still exploit his tighter standards for playing a hand (through loose and aggressive play) to win many small pots.

Bet and raise often, with a default strategy of raising your button with many hands and making frequent C-bets, then giving up if played back at or your early bets in the hand are called and you have missed. This playing sequence is highly effective against tight players regardless of their aggression. However, you should still usually fold to button raises when out of position since you are playing at a positional disadvantage against an aggressive opponent. Here are two examples.

Effective stacks: $1,500
Blinds: $15-$30
Note: Your opponent is playing a tight-aggressive style.

Your hand: J♣6♣

Action: You raise to $90 on the button and your opponent calls. The pot is $180.

Flop: 9♣4♦2♠

Action: Your opponent checks. You bet $120. He folds.

Analysis: When the TAG calls preflop, his most likely holding is an ace or two decent high cards: A7, KT, QTs, etc. These players tend to fold weaker hands, and reraise with most pocket pairs or premium high card holdings. So it is unlikely this flop helped your opponent; he would have to be holding a random nine (K♠9♠), low suited ace or face card (e.g. A♣2♣ or K♦4♦), or a pocket pair. So despite having missed entirely, you should go ahead and C-bet.

Now suppose instead the flop were...

Flop: A♣J♥T♦

Action: Your opponent checks. You bet $120. He raises to $260.

Question: *What is your play?*

Answer: You should fold. Against a loose-aggressive opponent, you would need greater evidence you were beat before laying down second pair, particularly getting pots odds well over 2-to-1. But the tight-aggressive player is telling you, with his raise, that he has at least a jack with a better kicker, if not a pair of aces or better. Such a statement is also quite consistent with his preflop call. He might be bluffing, or semi-bluffing with a draw, but realize if you do call that you cannot beat any hand he is representing. So your hand is a bluff-catcher, and even if ahead, you may still be outdrawn. Fold and find a better spot.

The Hit-to-Win Style

Hit-to-win refers to a playing style where you plan to commit more chips after the flop if and only if you connect. This can be a winning idea in certain ring game situations, such as when you call behind a series of limpers with mid-suited connectors. But you should usually avoid such a passive style when facing a single opponent.

It is much easier to fall into this trap playing out-of-position. On the button, you always have the potential to steal the pot if your opponent shows weakness. The one situation to avoid from the button is calling a significant raise or three-bet with the idea of only continuing if you connect on the flop. Most flops miss most hands, and those times when you "hit" a second-best hand can significantly offset your gains when you do connect well. Here's an example of falling prey to hit-to-win on the button.

Effective stacks: $1,400
Blinds: $15-$30

Your hand: K♥T♣

Action: You raise to $75 on the button. The big blind reraises to $275. You call.

Analysis: Calling is a mistake. This hand will usually end when your opponent C-bets a flop that does not pair you, and you are forced to either fold or play a very large pot with king-high. When you do pair, your hand will frequently be good, but your opponent's three-bet is consistent with the higher kings and overpairs that still have you beat. So you should cut your losses rather than continuing with a hit-to-win strategy.

Now suppose you are the big blind. When the button raises, you should tend to fold as a default. If your hand is strong enough to play, then often reraise. By reraising and being the one to show the most preflop strength, your bet will normally take the pot when both you and your opponent miss.

The primary times to call from the big blind and play hit-to-win are when your opponent is loose enough that you figure to win a large pot when you do connect with the flop. But lacking this read, you should not follow this strategy facing a button raise. It is simply too passive to be profitable against most opponents.

> When in doubt facing a preflop button raise, fold.

Here are two examples:

Effective stacks: $1,500
Blinds: $10-$20

Action: It is the first hand of an online sit 'n go. Your opponent raises to $60 on the button and you are not an experienced heads-up player.

Question: *What are good default plays with the following hands:*

1. K♠9♥
2. K♠J♠
3. A♥2♣
4. 8♠6♠

   Answers:

1. Fold. King-nine offsuit is a weak hand. You have little straight and no flush possibility, and you may even be outkicked when you do connect. Do not play it out of

position, facing a preflop raise, unless you have a read on your opponent.

2.   Reraise. King-jack suited is much stronger. You now have straight and flush possibilities, as well as two cards that could make top pair with a higher kicker. Even when your preflop three-bet is called and you miss, your C-bet will often be a semi-bluff with overcard(s) and a draw to either a straight or a flush.

3.   Fold. An experienced player can make profitable calls with weak aces facing a button raise since any ace is a relatively strong hand in heads-up. However, weak aces can be difficult to play out of position on the flop and the later streets, and thus an inexperienced player is usually better off folding.

4.   Be inclined to call but occasionally three-bet. Mid suited semi-connectors play well after the flop since your cards tend to be live and can make many different hands. The rationale for sometimes reraising is discussed in the chapter "Three-Betting Preflop" in "Part Four: Crucial Heads-Up Concepts and Situations" starting on page 175. If you call, you are not playing strictly hit-to-win since flopped draws can be bet.

Approach heads-up matches with the strategy of value-betting all your good hands when you have the button, and attacking tight players who might fold. Simply do not get involved out of position unless you have a strong hand, and/or you feel that you have a significant advantage after the flop.

I say "significant" because your opponent gets to see you act first on every betting round. This is an enormous built-in advantage, and you can always fold and wait until you have the button. Most opponents will be willing to give you more action than you should give them when it is their turn to be the big blind. This is exactly what you want. Let most of the larger pots occur when you have the button, and you get to see your opponent's actions first each betting round. Without the button or a strong hand, tend to fold early.

As your heads-up skills develop along with more post-flop experience, you can expand your hand range for calling button raises. The topic of playing flops out of position is discussed in the chapter, "Calling Button Raises" in "Part Four: Crucial Heads-Up Concepts and Situations" starting on page 157.

As we discussed, the most common situation to call an out-of-position raise is against a very loose and aggressive opponent.

Effective stacks: $10,000
Blinds: $50-$100

Your hand: 2♠2♣

Action: Your opponent, who is recklessly aggressive, raises to $300 on the button.

Question: *What is your play?*
    Answer: You call. You will flop a set more often than 1 time in 9. So if your opponent will put more than $1,200[6] into the pot after the flop, your implied odds justify calling. This is because for each 8 times you call and lose $200, one time you will flop a set and win $1,600 ($400 preflop pot plus $1,200 more post-flop). So against this reckless opponent, calling with a hit-to-win strategy is profitable.

---

[6] Actually, a bit more than $1,200 since you will occasionally flop a set and still lose while almost never winning without flopping a set.

If you failed to recognize situations where you were correct to call button raises playing from the big blind, you would not maximize your long-run profits. But lightly calling raises out of position with regularity is a bigger mistake since there are many more opportunities to do this. So if you call this raise, make sure you have a good reason to do so.

Exploiting Hit-To-Win

When your opponent is playing hit-to-win, you can exploit this tendency just as you would exploit the style of any tight-passive opponent. The loose-passive style is not an example of hit-to-win because this player will put chips in the pot regardless of whether he connects or not. But the tight-passive opponent is a classic example of this mindset, as are certain tight-aggressive players.

Since your opponent will miss the flop much more often than he hits, simply take a stab at any pot where this player was not the preflop aggressor. If he plays back, fold. This will allow you to steadily chip away at such foes.

The most effective strategy against a hit-to-win player is to raise many hands preflop when on the button, and then C-betting. This normally effective betting sequence is even more effective against these opponents since they will fold preflop with a weak hand, or on the flop after they miss. And when they do play back, you can fold when you have not connected.

Playing Hit-to-Win on the Button

Here's a hand between Antonio Esfandiari and Phil Hellmuth.

Blinds: $800-$1,600

Esfandiari's hand: 8♠3♥
Hellmuth's hand: K♠Q♦

Action: Hellmuth calls on the button. Esfandiari raises to $8,200 and Hellmuth calls. The pot is $16,400.

Analysis: Esfandiari has the right idea attacking a button limp, but making a large raise is a better play with cards that have some post-flop potential. That's because if Esfandiari is called, he could win not only from a standard C-bet, but also due to hand strength. For instance, five-four suited is not a premium holding, but you can still win a large pot when your opponent connects and you make a strong, disguised hand. But note, if Esfandiari's opponent is someone who will almost always fold or reraise, then it actually is better to make these large raises only with your very good and very bad hands. See *No-Limit Hold 'em: Theory and Practice* by David Sklansky and Ed Miller for more discussion.

Flop: A♠J♦9♠

Action: Esfandiari bets $10,600 and Hellmuth folds face-up.

Analysis: Both players miss this flop, and so the pot naturally goes to the aggressor. Hellmuth's passive line preflop will often flop him a disguised pair or strong draw, but he ends up playing hit-to-win. Calling an over-sized raise, only to fold upon missing the flop, is a surefire way to lose chips.

Hellmuth may have had a more elaborate game plan than hit-to-win depending on the flop — when he flops two overcards in particular. But in general, you should not call raises preflop with the idea of folding to a missed flop. The primary exception is when your opponent is reckless and figures to bluff away many chips when you do connect.

Sample Match No. 2: Defeating Tight-Aggressive Opponents

Villain is a well-known high-stakes online sit 'n go player, known for playing in full 9-handed games. Based on a player search, he is playing 3 other heads-up sit 'n go's concurrently, as well as one multi-table tournament.

Going into this match, we therefore have an idea of his style. 9-handed sit 'n go strategy requires a tight-aggressive style, and it is tough to play a loose-aggressive style while playing multiple heads-up tables. So our first guess going into this match is that he will be a tight-aggressive opponent.

So our strategy will be to play loose-aggressive, which is always a fine way to start a match. If he plays different than expected, we can modify our style. Another reason we choose this match is to discuss how and when you can categorize your opponent's style based on what you have seen so far. Starting blinds are $10-$20 with $1,500 chip stacks.

Hand No. 1: We raise our button to $45 with the 4♥3♦, and he folds.

Hand No. 2: He folds his button.

Hand No. 3: We limp with 7♣3♥ on the button. Villain checks. The pot is $40. The flop comes K♣Q♦9♦. He checks. We bet $25. He folds.

Analysis: From the big blind it appears Villain is playing hit-to-win, and since this is heads-up and he did not raise our button limp, our chances of winning immediately with a small bet is large. Furthermore, our hand has no showdown value, so we can only win by betting.

Hand No. 4: Villain raises to $60. We fold J♥3♣.

Hand No. 5: We raise to $60 with Q♦7♠. Villain folds.

Hand No. 6: Villain raises to $60. We fold 7♦3♦.

Hand No. 7: We raise to $45 with K♥2♣ and Villain calls. The pot is $90. The flop comes A♠7♦6♦. He checks. We bet $60 and Villain folds.

Hand No. 8: Villain raises to $60 and we fold T♥5♥.

Hand No. 9: We min-raise with T♥6♦ and Villain folds.

Hand No.10: Villain folds his button.

Analysis: The first 10 hands strongly confirm our impression of his style. He has folded his button two times, while raising his other hands three times to 3 BB. From the big blind, he has been playing tight. He has folded to 3 small button raises, ranging from 2 BB to 3 BB. The other two hands he has folded to small bets on the flop. So we will be very aggressive from the button, coming in with constant small raises to win immediately or take it away on the flop.

Let us continue, looking now at only those hands where there is post-flop action or this pattern changes.

Hand No. 12: Villain raises to $60 on the button. We reraise to $200 with A♣Q♦. He folds. Note that a premium hand coupled with being out of position post-flop is a good reason to reraise before the flop.

By hand No.15, we have a chip lead of $1,665 to $1,335 since we have won all pots where we were the button, whereas he has forfeited several of his buttons (legitimately against our ace-queen three-bet, and weakly the several times he's open-folded with position).

Hand No. 15: We limp with 5♠3♣ and Villain checks in the big blind. The flop comes J♦7♠2♠. He leads out with a pot-sized bet of $40. With no piece, facing a tight player's bet, we quickly fold.

Hand No. 28: The blinds are $15-$30 and our chip position has increased to $1,900. We have won literally every button but one, usually preflop with 2BB to 3BB raises, and the remainder with small post-flop bets. This hand, Villain raises his button to $90, and we elect to call with J♦9♦. These mid-high suited semi-connectors play well post-flop, and will usually be live when they hit. The pot is $180. The flop is the 4♣3♣2♣. We both check. Notice that leading on this flop is reasonable since it is unlikely to have helped our opponent, and meanwhile, a jack-high is unlikely (although possible) to be best at the showdown. But if we do check and he checks behind, we will bet almost any turn.

The turn is the 7♥. We bet $120 and he folds. If he had an overpair or high club, he would probably have bet the flop. It's most likely he has two overcards with no club. Therefore, expect him to fold.

Hand No. 45: The pattern continues. From our button, we have limped two hands (winning one with a post-flop min-bet and losing the other when he leads out), and raised the rest. Our raises are 2 to 2.5 BB, and he folds to each. As Villain is still folding a full quarter of his buttons, our chip lead rises.

We now have a 2-to-1 chip lead with blinds rising to $25-$50. He folds his first button at this new level, and we raise ours to $110 with Q♦7♥. He reraises all-in and we fold. Whether he is planning to switch to a looser style with the rising blinds, or simply picked up a hand, we do not know.

Hand No. 48: Villain raises to $125. Getting better than 2-to-1 odds, we call with T♠8♠. The pot is $250. The flop is A♣7♠6♠. We bet $150 and he folds. With a straight flush draw and 6 possible outs to second pair, we are betting our draw for value.

Hand No. 52: With a stack of $875, Villain makes a now-standard raise to $125. We have 4♠4♦ in the big blind. We reraise to $450, effectively putting him all-in if he plays. Our pair figures to be best, but does not play well post-flop from the big blind. There is already $175 on the table, nearly one-fourth of the effective stacks. So we raise big to win immediately. He folds.

Hand No. 55: We have a $2,300-to-$700 chip lead. We limp 7♣4♠. Villain raises all-in. We fold. Since he has not been playing aggressively after his Hand No. 45 shove, we assume he has a legitimate hand, perhaps 22+, A2s+, A5o+, QJ+, or JTs+.

Blinds are now $50-$100 with his stack down to $575.

Hand No. 60: Villain raises all-in, and we call with K♠Q♣. He shows J♦8♣, a reasonable hand to have shoved with a 5 BB stack. The final board is: Q♥8♥7♠6♣3♥.

We win the hand and the match. Villain's error was not this all-in, but rather allowing himself to get short stacked through tight play. In summary, we believed our opponent would play a tight-aggressive style. He confirmed this impression through his routine button-folding and hyper-tight play facing our preflop raises. We then continued to play a loose-aggresive style, and won by chipping away at Villain's stack by winning many small pots.

Sample Match No. 3:
Playing Without Cards
— the Value of Aggression

As we have seen, a common element to winning styles is aggression. So much so, in fact, that simply playing aggressively can do great things for your game, even if you bet and raise "blindly."

I have produced a number of videos for the poker training site www.Stoxpoker.com, and one that received much attention involved me playing a match where software blocked out the cards. Weak cards can distract from clearly favorable situations, such as the preflop raise, post-flop C-bet sequence when facing a tight player. Let us now look at an actual $11 blind heads-up match that was played on www.PokerStars.com where our cards will not be given (as they were not known). Not all the plays are perfect, but the basic idea holds.

Effective stacks: $1,500
Blinds: $10-$20

Hand No. 1: The button raises to $60. We fold.
   Analysis: Unless the button raises widely, we will simply fold when he raises and do not have position. Our strategy will be to aggress in position, but less often from the big blind.

Hand No. 2: We raise our button to $60. Villain folds.

Hand No. 3: Villain raises his button to $60. We fold.

Hand No. 4: We raise our button to $50. Villain folds.

Hand No. 5: Villain raises his button to $60. We reraise to $200. He calls. (Pot:$400.) The flop is the J♦5♦4♥. We bet $245 and Villain folds.

Analysis: Simply folding this hand preflop would be fine. But three-betting preflop, and then betting the flop if called, is an aggressive playing sequence with the potential to win early regardless of cards. This is particularly true against an opponent who appears to be frequently raising hands from the button.

We now have a $1,700-to-$1,300 chip lead.

Hand No. 6: We raise our button to $60. Villain calls. (Pot:$120.) The flop is the 8♠7♠3♣. He checks. We bet $80. He raises to $240 and we fold.

Analysis: We raise preflop and make a two-thirds pot C-bet. When he reraises, we leave the hand without a significant chip loss.

Hand No. 7: Villain folds his button and we take the pot.

Hand No. 8: We min-raise to $40. Villain calls. (Pot: $80.) The flop is the J♦6♦4♥. Villain checks. We bet $60 and he folds.

Hand No. 9: Villain raises his button to $60. We three-bet to $200. He calls. (Pot: $400.) The flop is the T♦9♠2♠. We bet $250, and Villain calls. (Pot: $900.) The turn is the A♦. We bet $600 and Villain folds.

Analysis: We have been very aggressive preflop, but without the benefit of cards, our strategy must incorporate some later-street aggression. So again, you could certainly fold at any earlier point in this hand. Here, after Villain calls our C-bet at the flop, we would generally give up, but the ace is an excellent card to follow-up bluff because our actions so far are consistent with holding an ace, and our opponent would have often raised our flop bet with middle or top pair. Since the pot is already large, and there is a lot of fold equity, we make a turn bet which takes the pot. This play will show a profit if Villain folds more than 40 percent of the time.

We jump to a better than 2-to-1 chip lead. (We will now switch to omitting hands that end with a preflop raise and fold.)

Hand No. 10: We raise our button to $60. Villain reraises all-in. We fold.

Hand No. 12: We limp from the button. Villain checks. Pot: $40. The flop is the Q♣4♣2♥. Villain checks. We bet $30. He raises to $80 and we call. (Pot: $200.) The turn is the T♥. Villain checks. We bet $100. He raises all-in and we fold.
  Analysis: We throw in a limp to mix things up. After Villain checks we bet the flop, and could easily fold to his raise. But we call getting 3-to-1 with position. Our plan is to attack if he checks again, but his turn check-raise indicates he probably has a strong hand.

Hand No. 16: We raise to $45 and Villain calls. (Pot: $90.) The flop is the A♥K♣2♠. He checks. We bet $30 and he folds.
  Analysis: This bet is slightly small, but we are representing a hand that beats even what he is drawing to if he has not connected — a lower pair. So betting a smaller-than-normal amount is reasonable.

Hand No. 18: We raise to $60 and Villain calls. (Pot: $120.) The flop is the J♣8♥3♣. Villain checks. We bet $90 and he folds.

Hand No. 20: We raise to $50 and Villain calls. (Pot: $100.) The flop is the J♥9♠8♣. Villain checks. We bet $80. He raises to $160 and we call. (Pot: $420.) The turn is the 7♣. We both check. The river is the A♠. He bets $120 and we call. Villain shows Q♥T♥ to win the $540 pot with a queen-high straight.

Analysis: We again want to take away the pot on a later street after calling his flop min-raise. When the 7♣ hits we check wanting to show down cheaply, as we could have a piece of this highly connected board. We could also fold on the river, but elect to make a borderline call for three reasons:

1.   The pot odds are 5-to-1 and there is some chance our (unknown) hand is best.

2.   Calling with a potentially weak hand may help our image if Villain believes that we cannot be bluffed. And,

3.   We also want information: *What do his small bets mean?*

Since he shows a flopped nut straight, it appears his smaller bets may indicate strength. This is something we will be looking to confirm in subsequent hands.

We still have a slight chip lead with blinds rising to $15-$30.

Hand No. 23: Villain limps his button. We check. (Pot: $60.) The flop is the J♠7♥4♣. We bet $45. He raises to $145 and we fold.

Hand No. 26: We min-raise to $60. Villain reraises to $120 and we call. (Pot: $240.) The flop is the A♣K♦2♣. He bets $150 and we fold.

Hand No. 29: Villain raises to $90. We reraise to $260 and he calls. (Pot: $520.) The flop is the K♦9♦5♥. We bet $320. Villain raises to $640, and we fold.

Villain now takes a 2-to-1 chip lead.

Hand No. 32: We raise to $70. Villain reraises all-in. We fold.

Hand No. 36: We raise to $90 and Villain calls. (Pot: $180.) The flop is the Q♠9♥7♣. Villain checks. We bet $100 and he calls. (Pot: $380.) The turn is the 5♠. Villain bets $150. We raise all-in to $665 and he folds.

Analysis: There is a lot of fold equity here since the pot is a near stack-sized $530, and furthermore, his unexpected turn leadout is more consistent with a draw or weak hand. If he held the nine or queen, he most likely would have check-raised on the draw-heavy flop. A straight or flush is unlikely from a hand combination perspective. These hands are also less consistent with Villain's unexpected bet because we have taken the lead on each prior betting round, so most players would check the turn in anticipation of collecting another bet.

We now pull to $1,200 in chips.

Hand No. 37: Villain min-raises his button and we call. (Pot: $120.) The flop is the J♥9♠2♦. We both check. The turn is the 6♣. We bet $80 and Villain calls. (Pot: $280.) The river is the 4♣. We bet $30 and he folds.

Analysis: We bet the river as a small price-setting bet since our random hand might be best. Villain most likely folds a busted straight draw. A good lesson is that getting over 10-to-1 (as our opponent was), you must be very convinced you are beat before folding.

The blinds now rise to $25-$50, and Villain has a slight chip lead.

Hand No. 40: We raise our button to $125. Villain reraises all-in. We fold.

Hand No. 41: Villain limps and we check. (Pot: $100.) The flop is the 9♦2♣2♦. We bet $60 and he folds.

Hand No. 42: We raise to $150 on the button and Villain calls. (Pot: $300.) The flop is the 8♦7♠3♦. Villain bets $250. We raise to $750. Villain folds.
> **Analysis:** Again, the combination of a large pot and an unexpected leadout from our opponent give us a good raising opportunity.

We now have a 3-to-2 chip lead.

Hand No. 43: We raise our button to $100. Villain reraises to $300 and we fold.

Hand No. 44: Villain limps his button. We raise to $200. He calls. (Pot: $400.) The flop is the A♣K♥7♠. We bet $140 and Villain calls. (Pot: $680.) The turn is the 5♦. We both check. The river is the Q♥. We bet $90 and he calls. He mucks his hand and we take the pot. The chat window announces that we had a pair of kings.
> **Analysis:** A small flop bet will generally win when our opponent holds neither an ace or a king. Our river bet is again designed to price-set low with our random hand in this large pot. We do indeed take it, showing the power of even two random cards in hand-sparse heads-up play.

We now have a better than 2-to-1 chip lead.

Hand No. 45: We raise to $110 on the button. Villain calls. (Pot: $220.) The flop is the Q♠5♣4♣. Villain checks. We bet $150. He reraises all-in. We fold.

Hand No. 47: We limp our button and Villain checks. (Pot: $100.) The flop is the Q♥9♣6♦. Villain checks. We bet $60 and he folds.

Hand No. 48: Villain raises to $150. We reraise to $600. He shoves all-in for another $378. We call. Villain shows the K♥K♣. The board comes the Q♦5♦3♣2♥6♦. The chips come our way, and the chat window announces we have an ace-high flush.

   Analysis: We were risking his stack size of around $1,000 to win the $200 on the table. This is a reasonable risk/reward ratio for high-blind heads-up play.

   Luck certainly played a role in this victory, but even before the last hand where he happened to hold a high pocket pair and get outdrawn, we managed to hold our own in a competitive 48-hand battle. We accomplished this primarily by making high-percentage aggressive plays that often win without a showdown. In particular, besides a few hands where we made big plays after the flop, our strategy was to show strength before the flop, and then follow-up with aggressive play post-flop. When Villain called or raised our C-bets or post-flop stabs, we generally check/folded, as is most common even when looking at the cards.

Sample Match No. 4: Discerning and Handling a Hyper-Loose Opponent

In our last sample match of this session, we further consider how to classify opponents, and then what to do with this information. We also encounter a different opponent type.

Effective stacks: $1,500
Blinds: $10-$20

Your hand: Q♦2♥

Action: We limp on the button. Villain raises to $80 from the big blind and we fold.

Analysis: We want to avoid playing a weak queen for a big pot. He could easily have a real hand, or be a loose-aggressive player who will frequently attack our button limps.

Your hand: T♣8♦

Action: Villain limps on the button and we check. The pot is $40.

Flop: J♣J♥2♦

Action: We bet $25 and he folds.

Analysis: The paired flop is very unlikely to have hit our opponent. We have yet to figure out his playing style, so we make a standard aggressive play and bet out.

Your hand: 8♠6♥

Action: We raise to $50 on the button and Villain calls. The pot is $100.

Flop: Q♣8♣6♠

Action: Villain bets $120. We raise to $285. He folds.

Analysis: Two mid semi-connectors are worth opening for a raise. If our two-pair were not so vulnerable on the flop, slowplaying would be a reasonable option. But any queen, seven, club and potentially many other cards significantly devalue our bottom two pair. So we make a healthy raise, both for value and to make it incorrect for our opponent to call with many hands. After Villain folds, we make a player note mentioning what we observed in this hand: "Unexpected leadout => weakness?"

   Anytime you raise preflop and your opponent calls and leads out on the flop, you want to figure out what this means. He should expect you to bet since you were the preflop raiser. Is he now betting as a bluff, or is he playing literally with a strong hand? When you find out, make a player note, and you will have a better idea what his future lead-outs are likely to indicate. This note is not set in stone; if future hands paint a different picture, we are fully prepared to change or delete the note. But now, we are on the lookout for this type of behavior since we have an active hypothesis.

Your hand: 9♠4♣

Action: Villain raises to $180 on the button and we fold.

Analysis: His 9 BB raise makes us wonder if he is reckless. After all, what hands make sense for this raise? With a premium hand he would naturally want action, rather than attack with an overbet. With a weaker hand, there is no reason for such a large raise. So we venture another tentative hypothesis that our opponent might be loose-aggressive.

Your hand: T♠5♣

Action: We limp on the button. Villain min-raises to $40 and we call. The pot is $80.

Flop: A♦4♣4♥

Action: Villain min-bets $20 and we fold.

Analysis: This hand Villain wins using the simple aggressive style: He hits the "Raise" button preflop, then the "Bet" button post-flop.

Your hand: 5♦3♦

Action: Villain limps and we check in the big blind. The pot is $40.

Flop: 8♥2♠2♥

Action: We both check.

Turn: 6♦

Action: We bet $30 and Villain calls. The pot is $100.

River: 6♠

Action: We both check. Villain shows K♠T♣ and his king kicker takes the pot.

Analysis: This is a flop we would normally lead into since our 5-high has no showdown value and the board is unlikely to have helped our opponent. Furthermore, he laid down his hand to a flop bet on a paired board in a previous hand.

But checking the flop to mix up your play is fine; you then bet the turn many of those times your opponent also checks. He has now shown weakness, and, in addition, we have picked up a gutshot straight draw in case of a call.

The river puts two pair on board. Since we are now playing the board (our best hand is two pair with an 8 kicker), we can only win by betting. And yet, Villain has called the turn bet, showing strength, and so we decline to follow-up bluff. If he liked a board of 8♥2♠2♥6♦, he will probably like a board of 8♥2♠2♥6♦6♠.

Your hand: Q♠9♣

Action: We raise to $50 on the button and Villain calls. The pot is $100.

Flop: J♠6♣4♥

Action: Villain checks. We bet $70 and he calls. The pot is $240.

Turn: 5♣

Action: We both check.

River: Q♠

Action: Villain checks. We bet $150 and he calls. He shows 4♣2♠ and our top pair wins a $540 pot.

Analysis: After making a small preflop raise and standard post-flop C-bet, we prepare to give up on the hand, hoping to check it down and possibly win with queen-high. When the river gives us top pair, we must bet for value. His call preflop with a weak 4-high, and then continuing to call two bets with the weakest bottom pair, cements our idea that this is a loose opponent — aggression is less sure.

Your hand: 7♠7♥

Action: Villain limps on the button. We raise to $80 and Villain folds.

Analysis: We would check weaker hands here against a loose opponent, but a mid pocket pair is strong enough to raise for value, even if you believe it unlikely your opponent will fold. In this case, however, he does fold. Categorizing an opponent only helps you determine his *likely* actions.

The blinds now rise to $15-$30.

Your hand: 9♣3♣

Action: We limp on the button. Villain raises to $90 and we call. The pot is $180.

Analysis: We are getting over 2-to-1 with position, and we are willing to play many hands when second to act against an opponent likely to pay off when we hit. Folding here is also fine.

Flop: J♣9♦6♣

Action: Villain checks. We bet $60. He raises to $200. We reraise all-in, Villain folds.

Analysis: With a pair and a flush draw, even if behind, we will improve to a better hand over half the time by the river. So this is a good spot to play fast. We will either win a $440 pot now, or gamble for stacks with over 50 percent showdown equity against currently stronger hands.

Your hand: K♥J♥

Action: Villain raises to $90 on the button. We call. The pot is $180.

Analysis: Two high suited cards is a strong hand, but against an opponent who does not often fold, we prefer calling over three-betting. If we catch any piece of the flop, we figure to win a nice pot, and many flops will still give us a strong enough hand to continue, such as when we hit two overcards and a straight draw or flush draw.

Flop: A♦9♦7♦

Action: We check. Villain bets $150 and we fold.

Analysis: This would be a bad situation to force a play. We have missed the flop entirely, and our loose opponent figures to call not only with an ace or lower pair, but many draws as well. So we give up on the hand, electing to check/fold.

Notice that our opponent is making a solid bet almost regardless of his holding. If he holds a pair of aces, for instance, he is correct to bet to give us incorrect odds with many hands that we might hold. And if he has missed entirely, a bluff will be difficult for us to call since we might be afraid of drawing dead against a made hand.

Your hand: J♠8♦

Action: We limp on the button. Villain raises to $100 and we call. The pot is $200.

Analysis: Jack-eight is strong enough to raise, but limping is reasonable against an opponent liable to raise or reraise widely.

Flop: 8♥5♣3♣

Action: Villain bets $740. We reraise all-in. He calls.

Analysis: Villain's bet is essentially an all-in since he would have only $460 left if we called, and so our question is effectively whether we want to call an $1,100 all-in here. The pot is $1,300, so getting 13-to-11, we make this decision based almost entirely on whether we think our hand is best.

Against many opponents, this would be a difficult choice. We do have top pair with an overcard kicker, a strong hand in heads-up play. However, his overbet is a little alarming.

Question: *What does it indicate?*
   Answer: This is where our notes come in handy. We have already observed that our opponent is loose and prone to over-betting, and we also observed that his unexpected

leadouts correlated with weakness. These two notes combine to make his range wide enough that we expect to have the best hand. He may have an overpair or stronger jack, but more often we will see hands such as A♥5♥, Q♣T♣, or 6♠6♣. On balance, our top pair figures to be ahead of this loose opponent's range, and so we commit all our chips.

Action: He calls, showing K♥3♥ for bottom pair, an overcard, and a backdoor flush draw. This is certainly on the weaker side of his possible holdings. The final board is the 9♥9♦8♥5♣3♣, and our pair of eights holds up to win the pot and the match.

In the last hand of this match, we are willing to play a large pot. But this will not always be the case, a topic that is the focus of "Part III: Pot Size Manipulation."

Part Three
Pot Size Manipulation

Pot Size Manipulation

Introduction

Manipulating the pot size is the skill of choosing your bet-sizing (and other actions) so that the pot is large when you want it large, and small when you want it small. The canonical discussion centers around winning a large pot when you have a monster hand.

Suppose you flop a set. With blinds of $10-$20 and $2,500 effective stacks, you raise to $60 on the button with the

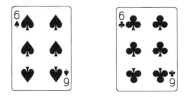

and your opponent calls. The pot is $120.

The flop is

Villain bets $120. With mid set, this is a hand where your goal is to have your entire stack wagered by the river. But how do you accomplish creating a large pot? For instance:

1. You can call the flop bet and then bet or raise the turn.

2. You can reraise all-in on the flop.

3. You can min-raise to $240. Or,

4. You can raise to $300, $500, or some other amount.

And assuming the chips do not all go in on the flop, and your opponent doesn't fold, you will have a similar array of choices on the turn. (In this particular example, a good solution is to raise to $300 or so because it is building the pot in a way that encourages your opponent to stay in.)

Making the checks, bets, and raises most likely to get you all-in by the river is an important component of pot size manipulation. But this skill comes into play in many forms, and consistently forces you to consider such questions as:

● What is the best possible pot size with top pair?

● How do I go about creating this pot size?

● How do I keep the pot small with a probable best hand playing out of position against an aggressive opponent?

> Always consider what size pot you want to be playing, and how best to accomplish this goal.

Pot Control and
the Bets-Per-Hand Number

Manipulating the pot size is much easier when you are the button and act second on each post-flop betting round. This is one of the reasons we suggest playing many hands from the button, and mostly playing relatively premium hands from the big blind. So let's begin by looking at situations where you are in position, and connect with the flop. (If you miss, while you may bluff or semi-bluff, you will want the pot to be as small as possible most of the time.)

Okay, you have position on your opponent, and you connect with the flop in some manner. Now ask yourself: "What size pot do I want to play?" Or the more quantifiable version, "How many bets do I want to go into the middle during the course of this hand?"

You have two competing concerns:

1   Getting maximum value from your holding, and

2.   Not playing a pot so large that your opponent would only stay in if he has you beat.

Thinking in terms of number of bets will help you to balance these concerns.

Here are sample answers to the "How many bets?" question:

At Most One: You have a weak hand with some showdown value. You either make one bet early or check every street, and fold if your opponent raises a bet, or bets himself on multiple streets. While your hand might be best, it is unlikely you will win

102

the pot if multiple bets occur and your opponent is not recklessly aggressive.

Effective stacks: $1,500
Blinds: $10-$20

Your hand: K♠2♣

Action: You limp from the button and your opponent checks. The pot is $40.

Flop: 9♥4♣4♠

Analysis: King-high will often be best in an unraised pot on a paired board, but if more than one bet enters this pot, you are usually behind. So suppose your opponent checks. You bet since your hand will often be best, and do not want your opponent to pair or pick up a draw. But if he raises, then a second bet enters the pot. You will not play this hand for more than one bet, so you fold.

If he calls, you will not commit anymore without improving. So you might bet once, but you need to improve for another bet to go in.

Hands where you answer, "At most one bet," on the flop are ones where your hand is often best, and you are happy to check down or play for one bet. But you know that your holding will rarely be best if more money goes in, so you resolve to leave the hand if your opponent does not allow you to show it down for zero or one bet.

As Many as Possible: You flop a premium hand and want only to get as many bets in during the hand as possible.

Your hand: K♠2♣

Action: You again limp from the button and your opponent calls. The pot is $40.

Flop: K♣K♦2♠

Analysis: Flopping the nuts, your concern is to maximize the number of bets that enter this hand. If your opponent leads out, then three or four bets is realistic — two calls and one raise. For instance, you might call the flop bet, raise a follow-up turn bet, and then bet the river after he checks.

If your opponent checks you might set a more reasonable goal of two bets. It is unlikely he has any piece of this flop, but there is always a chance your opponent will bluff or "keep you honest" with a loose call, and he could also "catch up" by pairing the turn. So here you should tend to check, hoping he pairs the turn or decides to bluff. If he checks again, you must bet to have any chance of reaching your 2-bet goal.

To recap, suppose you have a hand with some potential on the flop. Your first step is determine a good bet-number target. This amount should be designed to maximize your value without being so high that you will only hit this goal when you are beaten. Before looking at another example, here are a few questions that you may have.

Question No. 1: *Isn't the size of the bets important too?*
Answer: Yes. A good default bet size is around two-thirds of the pot.[7] If you or your opponent are betting much more than the pot, or much less than half the pot, than the size of the bet must be accounted for. (For example, obviously a single "all-in" bet means more than 3 normal-sized bets.)

---

[7] See *Professional No-Limit Hold 'em: Volume I* by Matt Flynn, Sunny Mehta, and Ed Miller for more discussion.

Suppose your opponent is over-betting. Then a target of 3 bets might become 2. Similarly, if your opponent is min-betting, you might call two or three bets with a 1-bet hand. You should not let a preconceived idea of bet numbers override what you believe is your best decision. The Number of Bets Framework is merely a guideline to get you thinking about how to control the pot, to the size you want, using "standard" bets.

Question No. 2: *What if my hand strength changes with new cards?*

Answer: Then you should modify your target number of bets. For instance, if your high card becomes top pair, then a "Maximum of 1 bet" might become "About 3 bets." If you flop top set and decide "As many bets as possible," you should rethink this decision if the board contains four cards to a low straight flush by the river.

Question No. 3: *What if my opponent prevents me from achieving my target number of bets?*

Answer: If your opponent does this by folding, there's nothing you can do. But ask yourself if you bet too aggressively or set an unrealistic goal. However, your opponent probably held a weak hand and was not willing to put chips in the pot.

On the other hand, if you cannot control the bet-number because your opponent is betting/raising beyond your target, this is generally a good indication you should fold. For instance, you flop bottom pair against a loose-passive opponent, and set a target of 2 bets. You bet the flop and get called. The turn comes a low card and you bet again. Your opponent raises. He is forcing you to play for at least three post-flop bets, a fact that corresponds with his raise indicating that he has you beat.

Question: No. 4: *How does the type of opponent you are facing affect the bet-number decision?*

Answer: The looser your opponent, the more willing you should be to play for more bets. And vice versa with tighter players. For instance, suppose you flop top pair with a weak kicker, a hand where 3 bets is generally a reasonable goal. Against a reckless opponent such as a maniac who might bet and raise each street with a draw or low pair you should be happy putting in many bets. But against a tight-passive opponent, 3 bets should be the most to play for because many tight-passive players will not call three standard bets without at least top pair, and if this opponent check-raised you on any street, you will generally be up against a higher top pair or better.

Now let us consider several variations on the same hand.

Your hand: A♠2♣

Action: You decide to limp during blinds of $10-$20. Your opponent checks in the big blind. The pot is $40.

Flop: A♣T♠5♦

Question: *How many bets do you want to enter this pot?*

Answer: With a weak top pair, three bets — one per street — is reasonable. You want value, which you are generally forfeiting by only putting in one or two bets. But if your opponent is willing to let 4 or 5 bets go into this pot, you'll usually find yourself facing a better hand at the showdown.

Here are possible betting sequences for your three bets:

Sequence No. 1: You bet all three betting rounds after your opponent checks.

Sequence No. 2: You bet the flop after your opponent checks. He leads out the turn and you call. He bets again on the river and you call.

Sequence No. 3: You bet the flop and your opponent check-raises. You call. You both check the turn. He bets the river and you call.

In Sequence No. 1, you are making straightforward value bets on each street. Perhaps you bet $30 on the flop, $75 on the turn, and $150 on the river for a final pot of $550. Your opponent is showing no sign he has your top pair beaten, so foregoing a bet on any of these streets will usually just win you a smaller pot.

In Sequence No. 2, if you raise the turn, your opponent will usually fold when he cannot beat your weak top pair, and call or reraise when he has you beat. Meanwhile, when playing heads-up, you need very compelling evidence you are beat to fold top pair, and an unexpected turn leadout does not qualify. For similar reasons, you call his river bet.

In Sequence No. 3, you call his check-raise with top pair, but you do not want to play a monster pot. So you gladly check behind on the turn, and calling the river is clear by process of elimination.

Now let us assume you bet the flop, and your opponent does indeed check-raise. The hand proceeds as in Sequence No. 3:

Flop: A♣T♠5♦

Action: Your opponent checks. You bet $30. He check-raises to $100 and you call. The pot is $240.

Turn: 8♥

Action: You both check.

River: Q♥

Action: Your opponent bets $150 and you call.

Suppose your opponent decides to bet the turn instead of checking. In this case, you will usually be playing a four-bet hand since an opponent who check-raises the flop and bets the turn is likely to bet the river as well. If he makes a pot-sized bet of $200 on the turn, and makes a bet of $600 on the river, you are then playing an $1,800 pot. Without a read on this player, his bets represent having at least a pair of aces, in which case any kicker above a five will beat you. Folding the turn (or river) now becomes reasonable since your opponent's insistence on playing a pot for more bets than your target is indicative of him having a stronger hand.

One exception is when your opponent is loose-aggressive. Here you should be willing to play for four bets. That's because the probability of him bluffing, or betting a weaker hand for value, is higher. If he raises any street and then bets the next round, this is not necessarily strong enough evidence to fold. Against a very loose opponent, be willing to play for four bets.

However, the opposite holds true against a tight player, who might not call 3 bets without at least top pair — be willing to settle for two bets and decline to play for 4 or more. One option against this opponent is to check behind on the flop. Now it will be easier to get in two bets because he might believe you are weak and either bluff or value-bet a marginal hand.

Question: *How might bet-sizes modify this play?*
   Answer: Suppose you bet $30 and your opponent check-raises to $400. Unless you have a read that this player is reckless, you should fold. By calling, you are pot-committing yourself to the hand. In addition, a weak top pair is rarely strong enough to play for your entire stack against an unknown opponent. Wait and choose a better spot. Similarly,

if he check-raises to $100 and you call, but his river bet is an all-in, be inclined to fold. Notice that due to the abnormal bet sizing, the number of bets criterion becomes less important.

Question: *What if the turn is the 2♥ rather than the 8♥?*

Answer: You want to maximize the number of bets that go into this pot, so go ahead and bet the turn after your opponent's check despite his flop check-raise.

Note that this analysis becomes more complicated with drawing hands, or when you are out of position. Playing in position allows you greater freedom to decide how many bets go into the pot. For instance, you can always increase the number of bets that enter a given street by betting or raising.

Meanwhile, drawing hands depend on the likelihood of your opponent folding when you semi-bluff, and the odds you get when he bets. In addition, the Number of Bets Framework is much more difficult to apply if you think you are behind, but may improve to a better hand.

One final consideration is that you should often try to put your bets in early or late in the hand depending on other factors. For instance, if you are playing the

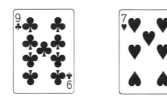

and flop top pair on a

board, then three bets would be a very reasonable target, but many turn cards could devalue your hand. Therefore, you want bets to go in as early as possible. So you should tend to bet or raise big immediately.

And with the full house example above, you would generally want to play the flop slower than the turn and river. Give your opponent a chance to catch up since you have the flop monopolized.

In summary, thinking in terms of "Number of Bets" is a valuable tool when playing made hands in position after the flop. Fundamentally, it is a tool designed to help you manipulate the pot size. But when competing factors override this guideline, don't cling to an inflexible bet-number decision.

An Extra Bet
for Value and Defense

Hellmuth has a slight chip lead against Men Nguyen.

Blinds: $200-$400

Hellmuth's hand: 3♣3♦
Nguyen's hand: K♠2♠

Action: Nguyen limps. Hellmuth raises to $1,600. Nguyen calls. The pot is $3,200.

Analysis: Hellmuth is correct to attack this button limp with a pocket pair. The safer play for Nguyen is to fold since many of the hands Hellmuth would raise with have Nguyen dominated.

Flop: K♣9♠9♦

Action: Hellmuth bets $1,500. Nguyen calls. The pot is $6,200.

Analysis: Hellmuth makes a standard leadout after raising preflop. Half the pot or just under is often a fine size, but a larger bet should work better since his treys are likely best, yet are vulnerable to bad turn cards. Nguyen's call is good strategy. He figures to be way ahead, and top pair, weak kicker is a good hand for three bets, but most players will not play for more than three bets with this flop holding worse than a pair of kings.

Turn: Q♣

Action: Both players check.

Analysis: Hellmuth checks looking to show down cheaply or be done with the hand. Nguyen should probably check a blank, such as the 7♥, but with two high straight flush cards on board, he should bet.

River: 4♠

Action: Hellmuth checks. Nguyen bets $3,000 and Hellmuth folds.

Analysis: Nguyen bets for value and Hellmuth folds even though the pot is offering him a little better than 3-to-1. Clearly Hellmuth does not feel his opponent would bluff more than 25 percent of the time. In addition, Hellmuth's turn and river checking is consistent with the goal of at most one post-flop bet, whereas Nguyen could go as high as three bets.

Position and the Check or Bet Decision

Let's return to the example of flopping a pair of aces with a weak kicker. Suppose your opponent is tight and you believe he will not put four bets into the pot with second pair or worse. When you flop top pair, your hand will usually be best at the showdown, but you must guard against those times your opponent has a better kicker or flops two-pair or better. Keeping careful control over the pot size is the best way to get value while not putting yourself at unnecessary risk.

We have seen that getting in exactly three bets is usually a straightforward process with position. But now suppose we are out of position.

Effective stacks: $1,500
Blinds: $10-$20
Note: Your opponent is tight-aggressive.

Your hand: A♣2♠

Action: Your opponent raises to $60 on the button and you call. The pot is $120.

Flop: A♥T♠5♣

Question: *Check or bet?*
    Answer: Be inclined to check. Doing so makes it more likely that the betting action will not go past three bets. If you bet and raise at every opportunity, however, when behind, you leave yourself vulnerable to playing an all-in pot.

Action: You bet $80 and your opponent calls. The pot is now $280.

Turn: 6♥

Action: You bet $200. Your opponent raises to $500. You call the extra $300. The pot is $1,280.

River: J♥

Action: You check and your opponent bets $650. You call and he shows A♦J♣ to win the pot. You have now fallen to a crippled stack of $210.

Question: *Did you get unlucky or could you have played this hand differently and lost less?*

Answer: You had top pair heads-up, a strong hand. On no one street did you make a particularly grievous error. Preflop you called getting 2-to-1 with a suited ace — folding is fine, but calling is certainly acceptable.

Then you bet your top pair on the flop, again reasonable. You bet the turn, and then called a raise getting approximately 4-to-1. At the river, you are getting 3-to-1, and you still have top pair with only a backdoor flush on board.

Even though you did not make a major mistake on any street, your overall strategy was flawed. The preflop call is fine as long as you are capable of getting away from the hand when you are up against a better ace or are able to keep the pot small. And the way to keep the pot small is to check the flop or the turn.

Question: *How else might the hand proceed now?*

Answer: Suppose you checked the flop and then called your opponent's $80 C-bet. (The pot is $280.) You then check-call a $200 turn bet. (The pot is $680.) Even if your opponent now bets two-thirds of the pot, say $450, rather than half of it as he did in the sample hand, you can call and still have over $700 remaining.

So now you have fallen to a 3-to-1 chip deficit (one double-up from even), rather than a 14-to-1 chip deficit (three double-ups from even). Clearly losing over half your stack hand is undesirable. But you cannot fold top pair readily in heads-up. If your opponent knows he can bluff you out of top pair by putting in one or two big bets, you will be bullied too easily.

So in this example, deciding on "At most 3 bets" is the decision that strikes the best balance between maximizing value and safeguarding against risk. If Villain did not have the A♦J♣ and had responded to your flop check by checking behind, then you would simply bet the turn and river for value. One additional benefit to this approach is that you might now get paid off by some weaker hands, such as T♣9♣, that would have folded had you simply bet each time it was possible. You might even get action from a hand that has missed entirely as your opponent will often interpret your check as weakness, rather than as an attempt to control the pot size.

Of course, checking the flop is not perfect either. There is a chance your opponent would call down three bets if you make them with a second best hand such as J♣J♠, and you will now win one less bet from him. And he could also fold a weaker hand to a flop bet, but after you check, he checks behind and outdraws you.

It is always difficult to play out of position. Your choices will be less favorable than if you had the luxury of acting second on each post-flop betting round. This is a major reason why you should often fold when facing a preflop button raise.

Bet-Number
Decisions from the Big Blind

This semi-final match features Antonio Esfandiari and Phil Hellmuth.

Blinds: $2,000-$4,000
Effective stacks: $100,000

Esfandiari's hand: 8♣7♣
Hellmuth's hand: A♥6♣

Action: Esfandiari calls on the button. Hellmuth raises to $19,000 and Esfandiari calls. The pot is $38,000.

Analysis: You should tend to raise mid suited connectors preflop but occasionally calling with them is also fine. After Esfandiari limps, Hellmuth's decision to attack is solid. His plan, if called, should be to bet the flop whether he hits or misses.

Flop: J♦7♥4♣

Action: Hellmuth bets $17,500. Esfandiari calls. The pot is $73,000.

Analysis: Esfandiari's call with 3-to-1 odds holding middle pair is correct. He wants no more than two bets to go into this pot, so calling is a good play.

Turn: A♠

Action: Both players check.

Analysis: Esfandiari's hand has strong showdown equity, but is not good enough to bet for value on two more streets. So he correctly checks, rather than force a pot with three bets.

Hellmuth's hand is strong enough for two more bets, but this goal is much harder to accomplish out of position because Esfandiari could raise a turn bet, putting him to a difficult decision. Instead, Hellmuth checks the turn, intending to call a bet or to value-bet the river if Esfandiari checks. Hellmuth might also get called by weaker hands after checking the turn, and then betting the river since his play can look like a bluff.

River: T♥

Action: Hellmuth bets $25,000 and Esfandiari calls.

Analysis: Hellmuth reasons that Esfandiari's actions are consistent with having some piece of the flop. Betting just over one-third of the pot, Esfandiari will probably call with a seven or a four since Hellmuth has shown weakness and is now offering him nearly 4-to-1 odds. So this is a well-sized value bet.

And indeed, Esfandiari calls with his fourth pair. This call will earn chips if Hellmuth is bluffing more than 20 percent of the time, and it is reasonable to think your opponent will bluff at this rate after you have shown weakness earlier in the hand.

Manipulating Bet-Number Decisions

As we have seen, one big advantage to playing a hand in position is having much greater control over the decision of how many bets enter the pot. One benefit when you do raise out of position is that you can sometimes limit the number of bets that go in after the flop.

Let's suppose you are playing a strong, loose-aggressive opponent. He routinely raises to 3 big blinds before the flop. You have a hand strong enough that you will at least call. However, if you reraise instead, you can sometimes win immediately. In addition, you limit your opponent's options post-flop when he does call because a greater portion of the effective stacks will have already been wagered, and so there is less that can be wagered after the flop.

In the extreme case, if you reraise all-in preflop, your opponent has no positional advantage since no more betting can occur. That is all betting actually takes place preflop where you act second, thus you are the one with the positional advantage for the hand.

You have $800 versus your tricky loose-aggressive opponent's $2,200.

Effective stacks: $800
Blinds: $25-$50

Your hand: 5♥5♠

Action: Your opponent raises to $150 on the button.

Question: *What is your play?*
    Answer: You should reraise all-in. A pocket pair figures to be ahead of a loose-aggressive player's button-raising requirements, and you should play this hand. So reraising all-in immediately reduces the potential number of post-flop bets to zero.

If you call, however, there could be up to two post-flop bets. For instance:

Flop: A♠9♥4♠

Action: You bet $200 and your opponent calls. The pot is $700.

Turn: 7♥

Action: You check. Your opponent bets all-in.

Question: *Does he actually have a hand, or does he interpret your turn check as weakness and is bluffing or semi-bluffing?*
    Answer: The point is that after you call the preflop raise, a good aggressive player can take advantage of his position. You deny him this option by reraising all-in immediately.

Now suppose that you and your opponent each have a stack of $1,500.

Effective Stack: $1,500
Blinds: $10-$20.

Your hand: 5♥5♠

Action: Your opponent from last hand raises to $60 on the button.

Question: *If you call, how many bets might enter this pot after the flop, when you lack position?*
  Answer: The number of possible post-flop bets ranges from zero to four or higher. For instance, one betting sequence is:

- **Flop:** Pot is $120. You each have $1,410. You bet $80, he raises to $200, you call. Post-flop bet count is two.

- **Turn:** Pot is $520. You each have $1,210. You check, he bets $300, you call. Post-flop bet count is three.

- **River:** Pot is $1,120. You each have $910. You check, he bets all-in.

Final post-flop bet count: four bets. And, regardless of what the hands are, your opponent has a major advantage in this battle because he gets to see what you do before he acts on each betting round.
  Now suppose you reraise to $210 preflop. Then normal bet sizes allow for at most two bets after the flop.

- **Flop:** Pot is $420. You each have $1,180. You bet $275 and he calls. Post-flop bet count is one.

- **Turn:** Pot is $970. You each have $905. You check and he goes all-in, which is just under the size of the pot.

Post-flop bet count is two bets.

So even with deeper stacks, reraising immediately greatly nullifies your opponent's ability to control the pot size.

> Against a solid opponent who raises his button preflop, strongly consider reraising immediately with any hand you will at least call with.

It is important to note how crucial each clause is to this statement. First, note that it says to "strongly consider" reraising rather than to go ahead and reraise. If a solid, perceptive button knows you will three-bet him widely, he can counter-exploit this tendency by four-betting all-in his stronger raising hands, calling more liberally, and so forth. Reraising preflop is one weapon in a strong no-limit heads-up arsenal.

Second, we specify that this principle applies to hands that "you will at least call with." If your hand does not compare favorably to your opponent's estimated preflop raising range, you should fold rather than call or reraise. Sometimes reraising will get your opponent to lay down a better hand, but normally you want to avoid raising big in the hope that your opponent may fold.

Lastly, the "solid opponent" clause is key. Suppose, for example, your opponent is loose-passive. Now you should not reraise as often. Against this weak player, wait until you are convinced you have a significant edge and then try to play a large pot. Tend to reraise only your strong hands (for value) against soft opposition.

Calling Versus Raising

Process of elimination (POE) is a very useful tactic in any poker variation. Even if you are uncertain what your optimal play is, you can often eliminate at least one option. This can be quite beneficial, especially when the option you eliminated is the only big mistake you could make.

For instance, suppose you have a short stack and a marginal hand on the button, and you are facing an aggressive opponent known to attack button limps. You may have difficulty deciding whether to shove or fold, but you know for sure you will not limp or make a small raise.

Or suppose you are playing heads-up with bottom pair on the river, and your aggressive opponent bets. You might not know whether calling is profitable over folding, but you know not to raise.

One common POE decision is when you have eliminated folding, and are debating whether to call or raise. Your hand is strong enough that you will at least call, so you might have any hand from the nuts to a strong draw. But it is unclear whether you should just call or raise immediately. We have already seen several benefits of both choices.

Raising can win immediately, whereas calling cannot. Calling does not add an extra bet into the pot on the current street, which raising does. Often you should raise out of position because you can win immediately and if you do not win you have limited the bet-number decision. Whereas, in position you are generally happy to have higher effective stacks to wager in the later betting rounds. And, the perceptive player also has access to more information when he calls in position.

Blinds: $15-$30

Your hand: 7♣6♠

Action: You limp on the button. Your opponent raises to $100 and you call. The pot is $200.

Flop: K♥5♣4♠

Action: Your opponent bets $140.

Question: *Fold, call, or raise?*
> **Answer:** With 8 outs to the nut straight, and six outs to an often-best second pair, you should not fold here. If you semi-bluff raise, you could win immediately without having to complete your draw. But if you call, you have access to much more information.
>
> For instance, suppose your opponent is tight. Based on his preflop raise, you believe he has a strong starting hand. However, he is also aggressive enough that it's likely he will bet the flop after his preflop raise whether he connected or not. So you call.

Action: You call. The pot is $480.

Turn: 4♣

Analysis: Based on his action here, you will know a lot more about his probable hand range. For instance, suppose he bets $450. Based on the turn card and his bet, you now have two additional pieces of information.

1. Your opponent feels he has a strong hand, most likely a pair of kings. Since he is tight, he would probably only make a second significant bet if he had at least top pair. So we can

further narrow his range from the collection of top starting hands to perhaps KK+, KTo+, K8s+, 55, and 44. He could also be bluffing. But the hand most consistent with his action on all three rounds of betting is a good starting hand containing a king.

2.   Your chance of making a straight by the showdown is now 17 percent rather than 32 percent since there is only more card to come. Furthermore, unless your opponent is on a bluff or possibly weak value bet, your partial outs to second pair are unlikely to be good.

Action: You fold (based on the turn card and your opponent's turn action).

Now suppose instead of betting $450, your opponent checks the turn. Since he will generally bet for value with kings, and also because there are straight and flush draws, his most likely hands are strong starting hands that do not contain a king, such as ATo, A8s, KJo, JTs, and 77.

So we bet. While our seven-high is unlikely to improve (although our outs to second pair are more likely to be good), our opponent should also be more inclined to fold.

So in both the turn-bet and turn-check examples, raising the flop probably does not help us. In the second example, when your opponent checks the turn, he will probably fold to a flop raise just as he will to a turn bet. And in the first example, we will simply be losing more chips against his strong hand when we raise the flop.

When we do make our draw with a turn such as the 8♦, then we can use Villain's action to decide what strategy is likely to extract the most value. For instance, if he bets, getting all-in by the river is a reasonable goal since he is likely to have top pair. And if he checks, a more manageable sum of perhaps one additional bet would now be a solid goal to aim for.

Sometimes the hand will play out such that raising would have gotten a better result, such as when your opponent is indeed making a routine C-bet with a missed hand, and he would fold to a raise but manages to spike a high pair or set on the turn. But calling the flop usually allows us to make a better decision on the turn, which tends to be worth the risk of being outdrawn.

> If you are confident in narrowing your opponent's hand ranges, and making clever use of further information, then this is a strong reason to call, rather than raise, in many situations.

The above statement applies primarily to hands where you have position. Lacking position, your opponent will generally be able to put further information to better use since you must act before him. So if two players have similar deductive ability for using additional information, the player with position should be much more likely to call and exploit his positional edge, whereas the player out of position should be more likely to raise and deny his opponent a positional advantage.

Raising the Turn for Value

In this third-round match-up, Antonio Esfandiari takes on Ted Forrest.

Effective stacks: $80,000
Blinds: $400-$800

Esfandiari's hand: 3♦2♦
Forrest's hand: A♠3♣

Action: Forrest limps on the button and Esfandiari checks. The pot is $1,600.

Flop: T♣8♦3♥

Action: Esfandiari bets $900 and Forrest calls. The pot is $3,400.

Analysis: Bottom pair is strong enough to bet for value on the flop.

Turn: 3♠

Action: Esfandiari bets $2,400 and Forrest calls. The pot is $9,000.

Analysis: Esfandiari bets his trip treys for value and to camouflage the routine jabs with weaker hands that constitute his aggressive style. Forrest, on the other hand, should raise. He wants to get his entire stack in with his trip treys and top kicker, and it will be tough to do so with a river pot of $3,400 and Esfandiari usually checking the river after Forrest calls a second large turn bet. Furthermore, Esfandiari could have a straight draw, in which case Forrest certainly wants to raise now. But the bigger reason to raise is that it is the only option that adds more to the pot immediately.

River: K♣

Action: Esfandiari bets $8,500. Forrest raises to $20,500. Esfandiari calls.

Analysis: Esfandiari makes a third substantial value bet, and Forrest raises for value as well. Esfandiari is correct to call rather than reraise since Forrest would probably call a third river bet here only if he held at least trip treys, in which case Esfandiari is at best splitting the pot with his bottom kicker.

Blinds: $100-$200
Effective stacks: $14,700

Note: Villain is tight-passive and has lost six small pots in a row.

Your hand: J♣9♣

Action: You raise to $600 on the button and Villain calls. The pot is $1,200.

Flop: Q♠T♠3♥

Action: Villain bets $600. You call. The pot is $2,400.

Analysis: Villain's small leadout bet is difficult to interpret. Is he betting a strong hand for value? Or perhaps he has tired of getting bullied and has decided to bluff? Raising now as a semi-bluff is a more aggressive play, and you should not be faulted if you chose to make it. But as previously, calling will give more information.

Turn: 8♣

Action: Villain bets $1,800. You raise to $3,800. Villain reraises all-in and you call. Villain shows 3♦3♣ and he rivers a full house to double-up.

Analysis: The turn raise is to build the pot. You have the nuts, and it looks like Villain was value-betting a strong hand on the flop since he fires again at a card that doesn't appear to be too dangerous. Not only do we want all the chips to be wagered by the river, but Villain may also slow down if the river comes a fourth card to our straight. Also note that in this particular hand, raising the flop could easily have cost us the opportunity to get all our money in if Villain had three-bet large enough that we were not getting the odds to call.

In summary, the most common reason justifying the more passive play of calling is when you have position and want to gain the information contained in the next card and the other player's action. But here we have an additional reason of not wanting to be raised off our nut draw.

Preflop Button Raising

Your preflop play sets up the rest of the hand, including the pot size going into the flop. Let us look at a few guidelines.

It is rarely a mistake to raise on the button because your opponent might fold, and if not, you are increasing the pot size when you will have position throughout the hand. We will discuss button-limping and button-folding below. For now, note that limping is acceptable, particularly when you hold a weak hand against a passive opponent who will require a strong hand to raise. Folding is also fine when you hold a weak hand against an aggressive opponent. But you should raise most hands on the button.

The normal button raise is a pot-sized 3 big blinds, which offers your opponent 2-to-1 on a call. But you can be flexible with this size, particularly in a fast-paced match where your opponent may not have the opportunity to pick up on your strategy. For instance, against a loose-passive opponent who is not perceptive, you should tend to raise in proportion to your hand strength. Make a large raise for value with your better hands, and call (or make a small raise) with your weak hands.

You should avoid raising to three big blinds or more with a junk hand if your opponent is loose and will rarely fold before the flop. You should also be much less inclined to raise weak face card hands relative to mid connectors, playable suited cards, and premium hands, because holdings like

and

play poorly after the flop. You are mainly playing these hands to hit a high pair, and when you do, your opponent may have the same pair, usually with a better kicker, if he is willing to play a large pot. It can be very tough to avoid going broke in these situations.

In each of the following hands, blinds are $10-$20 with $1,000 effective stacks and you are on the button. You do not have a read on your opponent.

Hand: 7♣5♠

Question: *What is your play?*

Answer: The only mistake is folding these two mid semi-connecting cards. Raising to $60 is the most common play, but limping and min-raising are not necessarily mistakes. The tighter your opponent has been, the more inclined you should be to raise.

Hand: J♥9♥

Question: *What is your play?*

Answer: You should raise to around $60. These mid-high suited semi-connectors play well after the flop, offering every reason to make the pot larger.

Hand: 8♣2♠

Question: *What is your play?*

Answer: The only mistake is a large raise. Folding is reasonable, as is limping against a passive big blind. If your opponent is a strong, aggressive player, tend to fold. If he is tight and passive, you can make a small raise with any two cards from the button.

This next hand features JC Tran and *World Series of Poker* Champion Johnny Chan in the *2007 National Heads-Up Poker Championship*.

Johnny Chan: $27,000
JC Tran: $13,000

Blinds: $200-$400

Chan's hand: Q♦T♣
Tran's hand: Q♥5♠

Action: Tran raises to $1,600 on the button and Chan calls. The pot is $3,200.

Analysis: A weak offsuit queen is not a good candidate for a large preflop raise for the reasons discussed above.

Flop: Q♠8♣4♦

Action: Chan checks. Tran bets $2,000. Chan raises to $6,000. Tran reraises all-in and Chan calls.

Final board: Q♠8♣4♦9♠9♦ and Chan wins a $26,000 pot and the match.

Analysis: Chan checks his strong top pair knowing that Tran is very likely to C-bet, so check-raising wins him an extra bet when Tran has missed and would fold to a leadout bet.

Question: *Can Tran now get away from the hand, or was he fated to lose all his chips?*

    Answer: In a deeper-stacked situation, you might fold top pair. But the pot going into the flop is $3,200, and the effective remaining stacks are $11,400. These stacks are too shallow to get away from top pair, which is strong in heads-up. So Tran cannot be faulted for getting all-in with his hand on the flop. His problem was building a large preflop pot with a weak face card hand. This seemingly innocuous preflop raise put him in a situation where he could lose a large pot even if he connected.

Thinking Multiple Moves in Advance

The good player anticipates future decisions and plans out how he will play a hand. Facing a flop bet, this player calls knowing if he will bet the turn if his opponent checks or if he makes his draw. After raising with a short stack, he already knows whether to call or fold if his opponent reraises. And so forth.

> If you cannot conclude how to act on later streets if you make a particular move, then you should probably make a different move.

Let's consider several examples of this idea.

Avoiding "Partial Pot Commitment"

Effective stacks: $1,300
Blinds: $50-$100
Note: Your opponent is loose-passive.

Your hand: A♠8♣

Action: Your opponent limps on the button.

Question: *What is your play?*

1. *Check behind?*
2. *Raise to $300?*
3. *Raise all-in?*

Answer: Raising to $300 is arguably the worst play. Suppose you make this raise and get called, as you often will against a loose-passive opponent. You act first in a $600 pot with $1,000 remaining. Roughly two times in three your hand on the flop will be ace-high. If you make a standard C-bet of around $400, then you have invested over half your stack. But checking essentially gives up on the hand. Ace-high will often be best, but the question of deciding whether to commit your remaining stack to find out will frequently be a difficult decision. This is particularly true with a positional disadvantage.

So your preflop raise sets you up for a tough post-flop decision, which is exactly what you want to avoid. Your best play is to raise all-in preflop due to your hand strength and because it reduces the post-flop bet-number possibilities to zero.

Checking after your opponent limps, while inferior to moving all-in, is better than the smaller raise since your post-flop decisions are easier. If you connect, make standard value bets. If you miss, try for a free showdown, or at most put in one bet with your ace-high. If your opponent puts up any resistance, you can fold without a significant loss.

Checking Behind with a Draw

Blinds: $10-$20
Stacks: $1,150
Note: Your opponent is aggressive.

Your hand: Q♠J♠

Action: You raise to $60 on the button. Your opponent reraises to $150. You call. The pot is $300.

Flop: K♣4♥2♠

Action: Your opponent checks.

Question: *Should you check or bet?*
   Answer: Be inclined to check. If you think your aggressive opponent will often check-raise, then betting may put you in a tough situation. (After all, why would an aggressive opponent three-bet preflop, and then decline what seems a clear betting spot?) Suppose you make a standard bet of $200, and he check-reraises to $600. Then what? Your opponent's small preflop reraise and flop check-raise indicate significant strength, so you will often be up against a pair of kings or other strong hand.

   But you would also be getting $1,100-to-$400 to call the raise, close to the odds you need for a flush draw. If you call and do complete your hand, you will often win all your opponent's chips. This is a tough decision, and one you will frequently face when you bet.

   But if you check instead of betting, your decision-making is greatly simplified since you now take a free card. If you hit, extract as much value as possible from your flush. And if you miss, you can bet if he checks the turn, or call a small bet offering you the odds you need to continue, but fold to a larger bet. Some of the time your opponent's flop check will be literal and you will miss out on an opportunity to win by not betting, but in general, your decision-making will be simplified by checking.

   Note that without the flush draw, this argument would no longer apply. With the Q♣J♣, for instance, you could make an easy fold to a check-raise. So you should often be more inclined to check behind on a draw than a total miss since the latter gives you an easy fold decision if raised, whereas the decision with a draw can be much tougher.

Reraising to Simplify the Turn Decision

Stacks: $90,000
Blinds: $1,000-$2,000

Hero's hand: K♣9♠

Action: Villain limps on the button and Hero checks. The pot is $4,000.

Flop: 9♣4♠2♣

Action: Hero checks. Villain bets $3,000. Hero calls. The pot is $10,000.

Analysis: Nines are a low top pair, and he should either lead out with a pot-sized bet or make a substantial check-raise after Villain's bet. It's true that top pair is generally a good hand for only 3 bets, but they should go in earlier when 20 possible turn cards make a higher top pair possible. If any of these cards hit, or possibly a card such as the 3♣, Hero may have a difficult decision. Raising the flop also allows the hand to end now which is preferable when your opponent has position.

Turn: 5♠

Action: Both players check.

Analysis: Hero's check is risky since the board now has multiple draws and Villain could easily check behind.

River: 3♠

Action: Hero checks. Villain bets $4,400 and Hero calls. Villain shows A♣2♦ and wins with his 5-high straight.

Analysis: A bad river card hits, but note that any ace, six, or trey would have put four cards to a straight on board, as well as the overcard with the ace and flush possibility depending on the suit. Hero should have anticipated this potential river trickiness and check-raised the flop or bet the turn.

Price-Setting the River

There is a rather well-known adage for playing the river in hold 'em: Bet your strong hands and some of your weak hands, but not your marginal hands. This is generally good advice. With a strong hand, you want to bet for value. With a weak hand, your only chance of winning may be to bluff. But there is generally less purpose in betting mediocre hands since weak hands that you are beating will tend to fold, and stronger hands are more likely to call.

In heads-up this is generally sound advice, although it is important to recognize that many hands which would be considered "marginal" in fuller games, such as second pair, are now often strong enough to bet for value. River play is an important topic and the subject of check-calling versus betting/raising will be discussed at greater length.

One reason to bet the river with a mid-strength hand is for "Price-Setting" purposes. This will be a small bet you make at the river when the following conditions hold:

1. You are first to act.

2. Your hand may or may not be best at the showdown.

3. If you check, you think your opponent might bet many hands. And,

4. If you bet, your opponent will only raise with strong hands.

These last two conditions are not uncommon. An aggressive player might bet many hands checked to him on the river, including bluffs and strong made hands, but his bet may also be large. So rather than let him choose the bet size, you can bet yourself. Unless your opponent is hyper-aggressive or knows your playing style well, he will tend to raise a river bet only with a strong hand. And since you are betting relatively small, usually one-third of the pot or less, you can still be called by worse hands.

Another way to look at such a "blocking bet" is as a pot size control measure. If you have a strong hand, your default should be to make a large bet for value. With a medium strength hand, you can often still get value because weaker hands than yours may call a small river bet, even if they would fold to a normal bet of around two-thirds the pot. And as usual, when your opponent prevents you from controlling the size of the pot such as raising your small river bet in this case, it's generally best to leave the hand.

Price-Setting the River with a Mid Pair

This hand features Lyle Berman and Phil Hellmuth.

Blinds: $800-$1,600

Berman's hand: K♦5♦
Hellmuth's hand: 9♦9♣

Action: Berman limps on the button and Hellmuth checks. The pot is $1,600.

Analysis: Berman should normally raise a suited king in position, but limping is acceptable. Folding this hand, getting 3-to-1 odds on the button, would be the only significant mistake. But Hellmuth's check is weak. You need a compelling reason not to attack a button limp with a strong hand. Winning immediately is a fine outcome when playing out of position.

Flop: Q♣T♦7♠

Action: Both players check.

Turn: 6♦

Action: Hellmuth bets $1,500 and Berman calls. The pot is $4,600.

Analysis: Berman plays this street passively. Any diamond or king figures to give him the best hand, but if he calls and misses, his king-high will probably not win. So semi-bluff raising this 12-out draw is a strong alternative to calling.

River: 4♥

Action: Hellmuth bets $1,200 and Berman folds.

Analysis: Now the price-setting bet. Hellmuth suspects his pair of nines is best, and he wants to see a cheap showdown. So he underbets the pot. Berman might call this small bet with a lower pair, and if he raises, Hellmuth can make an easy laydown. But suppose Hellmuth had checked instead. He would then sacrifice value when Berman does indeed have a lower pair and would have called a small bet, and he would also have a tough decision if Berman made a large river bet.

A short time later, Hellmuth makes this play again, but with a different result.

Berman's hand: Q♣5♣
Hellmuth's hand: 7♦6♠

Action: Berman limps and Hellmuth checks. The pot is $3,200.

Flop: 9♥7♠5♥

Action: Hellmuth checks. Berman bets $3,500 and Hellmuth calls. The pot is $10,200.

Analysis: Hellmuth's middle pair with a gutshot straight-draw is a premium hand on the flop. He should bet for value, plus many turn cards will devalue his hand if Berman checks behind.

Turn: 4♦

Action: Both players check.

River: 5♠

Action: Hellmuth bets $1,600. Berman raises to $7,600 and Hellmuth calls.

Analysis: Hellmuth makes another small price-setting river bet. This time Berman raises, and Hellmuth announces (out loud) that Berman either holds no piece of the board or has just made trip fives. The problem with Hellmuth's call is that if he finds it likely enough that Berman would put in a substantial raise as a bluff, then he should not have made a river price-setting bet to begin with. For this type of bet to be profitable, you must believe your opponent will only raise your small bets with his stronger hands. If Villain is just as liable to bluff-raise, then you should usually make the conventional play of checking mid-strength hands.

However, it could be that Hellmuth suspects his opponent realizes that he is making blocking bets, and believes Berman more likely to bluff-raise because of this. In general, however, you should not make a price-setting bet if you think your opponent could easily bluff-raise.

In a later match-up, Hellmuth finds himself on the receiving end of a river price-setting bet against Antonio Esfandiari.

Blinds: $2,000-$4,000

Esfandiari's hand: J♠6♥
Hellmuth's hand: A♣9♥

Action: Hellmuth limps on the button. Esfandiari raises to $17,500 and Hellmuth calls. The pot is $35,000.

Flop: A♥5♥4♣

Action: Esfandiari bets $18,500 and Hellmuth calls. The pot is $72,000.

Analysis: With top pair, Hellmuth is content to call and limit the bet-number to 3. He may also reason that the hyper-aggressive Esfandiari is more likely to bluff again facing a call instead of an immediate raise.

Turn: J♥

Action: Both players check.

Analysis: Esfandiari checks since his second pair has strong showdown value, but is not strong enough for two or three more substantial bets to go into the pot. Hellmuth declines to value bet his top pair and mid flush draw.

River: 7♥

Action: Esfandiari bets $24,000 and Hellmuth calls.

Analysis: On the river, Esfandiari makes a one-third of the pot price-setting bet with his weak one-card flush, a mid-strength hand. Esfandiari wants to get value if Hellmuth has a "Bluff-Catching" hand such as an ace without a heart, and Esfandiari can make a safe fold to a raise. But if Esfandiari checks, he might face a bet with a high heart, or as a bluff. So Esfandiari bets and Hellmuth correctly calls. A mid flush is too strong to fold to a bet, but if he raises, he figures only to be called when beat.

Question: *How high a heart would Hellmuth need to raise?*
    Answer: The nut K♥ is the only truly safe card for a raise here. Raising with the Q♥ would be marginal since Esfandiari might lay down even the third-nut T♥, figuring Hellmuth could not be raising with the 9♥ or below. If you raise with the Q♥ and your opponent makes a large three-bet reraise, this is a difficult situation because he would then be representing precisely the K♥, so you must choose between folding the second nuts, or calling with a hand your opponent is claiming he can beat.

    So Hellmuth only has a clear raise with the K♥, and raising any heart lower than the Q♥, such as the 9♥, would be an error.

Stacks: $24,000
Blinds: $150-$300

Hero's hand: J♣5♥

Action: Villain limps and Hero checks. The pot is $600.

Flop: K♣J♦2♣

Action: Hero checks. Villain bets $500 and Hero calls. The pot is $1,600.

Analysis: Middle pair is a good hand for 2 or 3 bets, so check-calling is reasonable.

Turn: 2♥

Action: Hero checks. Villain bets $1,500. Hero calls. The pot is $3,600.

Analysis: Hero can now beat close to zero non-bluffing hands. If Villain had any piece of the flop, he now either has top pair, trips, or the same pair (probably with a higher kicker).

River: T♥

Action: Hero bets $840. Villain raises to $3,900. Hero folds. Villain shows 6♦2♦.

Analysis: Villain does an excellent job building the pot with his trip deuces at the turn and river. While Hero makes a loose turn call, his river play is good. He believes that Villain will only raise this bet with a strong hand, and intelligently lays it down when this occurs.

Part Four

Crucial Heads-Up Concepts and Situations

Crucial Heads-Up Concepts and Situations

Introduction

This section will address many of the most important concepts in heads-up play. These situations and plays are vital to success because they arise so frequently, and improving your skills in these areas will greatly benefit your game. Crucial heads-up concepts and situations include:

- Betting Post-Flop in Unraised Pots
- Calling Button Raises
- Three-Betting Preflop
- Combining Reading and Odds to Optimize Call/Fold Decisions
- Attacking Button Limps
- The Call-Bluff (Floating)
- The Paired Flop Principle
- Bluffing the River
- Raising the River for Value
- Slowplaying
- Bluffing Multiple Streets
- "Finishing Off" an Opponent
- Playing the Short Stack
- The Stop 'n Go
- Calling All-In Bets
- Playing with a Significant Skill Difference

The first three chapters focus on common preflop and flop decisions, as do the chapters on "Attacking Button Limps" and the

146

"Paired Flop Principle." Crucial late-street decision-making is the focus of several chapters including "The Call-Bluff," "Bluffing Multiple Streets," and the dual chapters on river bluffing and value-raising. We then discuss short-stacked tournament play, and conclude with two chapters on playing against much stronger or weaker opponents.

Betting
Post-Flop in Unraised Pots

While the analysis in this section applies to decision-making in raised pots as well, the fundamental difference is that neither player "owns" an unraised pot. If the button raises and the big blind calls, then it is natural for the button to attack post-flop since he was the preflop aggressor. In addition, both players in a raised pot are representing a starting hand of some strength by virtue of putting additional money in the pot preflop.

By contrast, an unraised pot occurs when the button limps and the big blind checks. It's anyone's pot. The three primary factors when deciding whether to bet a flop in an unraised pot of two big blinds are:

1. **Position:** If you are in position on the flop with a two big blinds in the pot, then your opponent has necessarily checked preflop and on the flop. The combination of these checks and that most hands miss most flops should make you more inclined to bet.

2. **Your Opponent's Style:** The tighter and more passive your opponent, the more likely you should bet. Suppose you have missed the flop and are debating a bet versus a check against two different types of opponents: Opponent A is loose-aggressive and Opponent B is tight-passive. Clearly you should be more inclined to bet against Player B since he will tend to concede the hand more often when he has missed. But Player A might call with ace-high figuring you for nothing, raise with a weak draw, or otherwise play back with little or no piece of the flop.

3.   **Hand Strength:** Some players will bet any flop regardless of their holding, figuring their opponent is likely to have missed and wanting to be the aggressor. Others wait to connect with the flop so they can make profitable value bets. While you should indeed bet your good hands for value, and while you also do not want to bluff too often (particularly against loose opponents), taking small stabs at many uncontested pots is a strong style. Do not wait to hit a pair or better before you are willing to make a small bet in an unraised pot.

Let us consider some numbers behind this latter assertion. Suppose you bluff $30 into an unraised post-flop pot of $40. How much do you win if your opponent requires one pair or better to continue with the hand?

While it depends on the board, roughly two-thirds of the time your opponent will have no pair. The remaining one time in three you lose $30. So your expectation is $17.

$$\$17 = \left(\frac{2}{3}\right)(\$40) + \left(\frac{1}{3}\right)(-\$30)$$

Your actual expectation will tend to be lower since your opponent might raise or call with ace-high or bluff, particularly if you make these small bets routinely. Nonetheless, making small bets post-flop into unraised pots can be a source of small chip gains, particularly if not overdone.

Now let us return to the impact of hand strength on the decision of raising a previously unraised pot at the flop. We can categorize hand strengths into several basic groups: Weak high cards, decent high cards, mid-bottom pair, draws, and top pair or better.

Group No. 1: Weak High Card (WHC). Suppose you have no pair and no draw. Having a low high card, such as 7-high or below, is very different from having a good high card because while the latter may win at the showdown if checked down, the WHC will not win by itself (except in rare cases). So you should be more inclined to bet the WHC since it has no showdown value, and you can only win the pot by bluffing.

Group No. 2: Decent High Card (DHC). The DHC — any ace or face card, is often best at the showdown when playing heads-up. For instance, if you hold a queen-high on a paired, low card board, and each street is checked, don't be surprised if the chips come your way.

However, DHC hands are rarely strong enough to bet for value, so you generally want to keep the pot small and see a cheap showdown. You might make one bet yourself, particularly early in the hand, but realize that you can only beat a bluff if any real money goes in. So checking these hands down is often your best option.

Group No. 3: Middle-Bottom (M-B) Pair. You should assume that mid-bottom pair is good in heads-up. At the same time, you are still not looking to play a large pot. So tend to bet these hands early and be prepared to make a follow-up bet. However, M-B hands are rarely strong enough that you want three bets to go into the pot unless your opponent is very loose.

Group No. 4: Top Pair or Better. Top pair is a big hand in heads-up. It is likely to be best at the showdown, and is strong enough to bet for value on all three streets post-flop. If you flop a vulnerable top pair, such as

connecting with a flop of:

you should make large bets early in the hand because in addition to value, you also want to deny your opponent a profitable draw to a higher pair. With a pair of aces or kings you can spread your betting more gradually over the hand since your opponent will often make a smaller pair and pay off, plus it's less likely you will be outdrawn.

However, making strong value bets with high top pair hands will usually be your best option. If your opponent is a calling station, then playing it slow early may only limit the size of the pot you take down. The same principle applies to any hand better than top pair, such as two-pair or a straight or two-pair. If your hand will only rarely prove second best by the showdown, you should be inclined to make unrelenting value bets for the purpose of building a bigger pot.

Group 5: Draws. Tend to be aggressive with your draws. Not only can they turn into strong hands, but you can frequently get a lone high card to fold immediately. This will win you a pot when your draw would have missed and your opponent's high card would be best. Also, there is a larger chance in heads-up that your hand will actually be best at the time when you make your bet. For instance, if you bet a king-high flush, the unpaired king could be the current best hand.

In a game where aggressive play is paramount, you need a reason *not* to attack with a drawing hand, rather than a reason to attack. However, the two most common reasons to be passive are:

1. You have position against an aggressive opponent who will check-raise many hands, and your draw is too weak to call a large raise.

2. Your opponent is loose-passive, in which case you should often try to get free cards and not put money in the pot until you have connected.

Let's consider several examples of check-bet decisions. In each case, we are on the flop in an unraised pot of 2 big blinds with significant stacks behind each player. You will be deciding whether to check or make a standard bet of two-thirds to three-quarters of the pot.

Note: Your opponent is tight-aggressive.

Your hand: 5♥4♣

Flop: Q♦8♥2♥

Action: Your opponent checks.

Question: *Check or bet?*
> **Answer:** Bet. Your Weak High Card Hand has no showdown value, so your only value in this pot comes from your fold equity when you bluff. A bet of 1.5 big blinds will show a profit even if your opponent folds a little less than 50 percent of the time. This is a reasonable assumption facing a tight-aggressive player. Meanwhile, you have an easy check-fold decision if you are called or raised.

Now let us suppose you held A♥4♣ in the above hand.

Question: *Would you be more or less inclined to bet?*
    Answer: Less inclined because now your Decent High Card Hand might be good at the showdown. In addition, future cards may be to your benefit since you have backdoor straight and flush draws. Betting is reasonable, so long as you refrain from letting yourself get involved in a big pot without improving. But now you can win with a checkdown, so you no longer have to bluff to have a shot at taking this pot.

Note: Your opponent is loose-passive.

Your hand: 7♣3♠

Action: Your opponent limps and you check.

Flop: Q♥J♦8♥

Question: *Check or bet?*
    Answer: Check. Your loose-passive opponent will call with many hands, perhaps with a range as wide as any card eight or higher (giving him a pair, gutshot draw, or overcard). Since the only reason to bet is to get your opponent to fold, you should be inclined to check against this calling station.

Note: Your opponent is loose-passive.

Your Hand: 9♦5♣

Action: Your opponent limps and you check.

Flop: K♥9♣6♥

Question: *Check or bet?*
Answer: Bet. Your middle pair figures to be best, so you are betting for value.

Suppose instead the flop is: 9♠5♥2♦

Question: *Check or bet?*
Answer: Bet. Your top two pair is a monster hand, but you should still bet. Checking is a mistake; the only way to build a significant pot out of position against a passive opponent is to take the initiative and bet yourself. You *must* extract value from your strong hands.

If your hand was instead 8♣3♥, you would be correct to check since a loose and passive player will call bets in this situation with a wide variety of hands, and it is precisely for this reason that when you do hit a flop strongly you must bet. Value betting is always important in heads-up, but never more so than against an opponent who "can't be bluffed."

Your hand: 9♣8♦

Action: Your opponent limps and you check.

Flop: 7♥6♦3♣

Question: *Check or bet?*
Answer: Bet. You have a quality draw to the nuts. This merits a bet. Also, the three eights and three nines are likely outs if the hand goes to the showdown. So you will improve to beat a hand as strong as a pair of sevens a full 51 percent of the time.

In summary, you should pay close attention to these important factors influencing the check/bet decision in an unraised pot. If you are still unsure what to do, tend to make a small bet of 1 to 2 big blinds as you will often win immediately against a single opponent.

Failing to Bet an Unraised Pot

This hand occurs late in the match between Lyle Berman and Phil Hellmuth.

Blinds: $800-$1,600

Berman's hand: 3♥2♥
Hellmuth's hand: 9♣8♦

Action: Berman calls on the button and Hellmuth checks. The pot is $3,200.

Flop: K♣8♥8♠

Action: Both players check.

Analysis: Berman should bet his Weak High Card Hand since it has no showdown value, and Hellmuth should tend to bet his trip eights for value. This check-check sequence works best when Berman perceives Hellmuth as loose (i.e. likely to call his bluff), and Hellmuth perceives Berman as tight (i.e. unlikely to call his value bet). But the default for either player should be to bet in this unraised pot.

Turn: J♣

Action: Hellmuth checks. Berman bets $3,500 and Hellmuth calls. The pot is $10,200.

Analysis: Both players are correct to bet. Hellmuth should lead after Berman checked the flop because if Berman checks again, Hellmuth must then settle for a small pot with his trip eights. Unless Hellmuth has a very strong read that Berman will bet if he checks, there is no reason not to value bet now.

Meanwhile, Berman's 3-high has no showdown value, and so a bluff is his only chance to win the pot. Couple this incentive with Hellmuth's show of weakness on all streets so far, and he has a clear bet. A standard bet-size of $2,000 or $2,500 would probably work just as well as his slight overbet, and can succeed less often and still show a profit. The decision to bluff his WHC Hand is a good one.

River: 4♠

Action: Both players check.

Analysis: Hellmuth checks here to induce a bluff or value bet from Berman. But betting out is generally better. If Berman has nothing, he will often check rather fire a second bullet. And indeed, this is exactly what Berman does despite having no chance at an outright win. That's because you need a compelling reason to make consecutive stone bluffs in a hand, and a river four did not provide that reason. So again, Hellmuth's best approach is to probably bet.

Calling Button Raises

When you are out of position and your opponent raises, you should fold unless you are confident you can profitably play the hand. This is because you have a huge disadvantage on all subsequent betting rounds by being first to act. Even if you are a skilled post-flop player, it is difficult to outplay even a weak opponent who has position on you. This advantage is difficult to quantify; in *Harrington on Hold 'em, Volume II: The Endgame*, Dan Harrington and Bill Robertie reference Howard Lederer stating that two players can see a flop with the same hand and the player with position will have an advantage of nearly 2-to-1. Regardless of the exact magnitude of this edge, rest assured it is substantial.

We have discussed the benefits of reraising — you have a chance of winning immediately and are reducing the number of possible bets that can go in after the flop if called. But what about calling a button raise?

Reasons that you might call include some combination of the following:

- **Hand strength:** Obviously you should be more inclined to play stronger hands. Against an aggressive opponent raising perhaps 70 percent of his hands preflop, you should be looking to play at least the hands A8o+, A4s+, 98s+, 22+, or any two cards ten or higher. The narrower your opponent is raising, the fewer hands you should call (or reraise) with since you will on average be playing (out of position) against stronger hands.

    One common time that calling can be more attractive than three-betting is if your opponent is very passive and will frequently call three-bets and you believe you can win a large pot through straightforward value-betting when you flop a strong hand. A similar principle holds with loose-reckless opponents; these players will do the betting for you when you connect. So with a strong but non-premium hand you should often call his preflop raise if your opponent is a loose caller.

- **The button-raise is small:** If your opponent min-raises his button, then you are getting 3-to-1 odds on a call. Thus many more hands are worth playing than the 2-to-1 odds you have facing a three big blind raise. With a reasonable hand and moderately deep stacks, your implied odds will often be good enough to toss in the extra big blind with many non-junk hands.

- **Your opponent is weak:** You may call against a predictable opponent with high effective stacks relative to the blinds. For instance, if you have

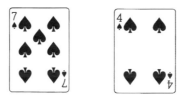

in the big blind against a maniac, then you can consider calling a three big blind raise if the effective stacks are deep with the plan of continuing on post-flop those times you flop a strong hand or a draw with high showdown equity.

The possible lines on the flop after calling a button raise are: check-calling, check-folding, check-raising, and betting out. Let us consider the best times to make each of these plays.

- **Check-calling:** Generally the weakest play you can make after calling a button raise because you have put more in the pot out of position with no chance of winning immediately.

The primary time to make this play is when your opponent is loose-aggressive and you have a hand strong enough to continue. You can let him bet and build the pot for you, often when he has a weak holding. Similarly, if your opponent is loose enough that he rarely folds after the flop, you can check-call with draws which you would normally semi-bluff. Betting or raising is unlikely to win immediately against these opponents, but if you do connect, you can win a large pot exploiting this player's unwillingness to fold. So there are certainly times when check-calling is good, and we will look at some examples below. But you need a compelling reason to do so.

- **Check/folding:** You should check-fold when your hand is poor, you do not have a good bluffing opportunity, and the pot odds to call are not worth while.

- **Check-raising:** When you connect well with the flop, a strong play is to check-raise since the preflop raiser will generally C-bet if you don't bet. So check-raising gives the "best of both worlds." You get more value for your hand, and you also give yourself the opportunity to win immediately. And as we have stated, unless you have a strong hand, you prefer to avoid late-street play when out of position.

- **Betting Out:** You should lead when you flop a strong, yet vulnerable hand, and think your opponent is liable to check behind if you go for a check-raise. For instance, during blinds of $15-$30, the loose-passive button raises to $90 and you call with

The flop comes

You prefer not to give a free card, so bet for value and protect your hand.

You can also bet out if you miss entirely and can make an easy fold if your opponent raises, so long as you think that bluffing is profitable in this spot. For example, if the flop comes paired or with three low cards, then it is unlikely to have connected with your opponent and you can bluff a hand with little showdown value (such as jack-high) if your opponent is tight with his post-flop calls. This play is best used sparingly.

A final reason to lead out with a bet is to build the pot in a deceptive manner when you flop a premium hand, such as a low set. This is a common play in no-limit ring games, made famous in *Super/System: A Course in Power Poker* by Doyle Brunson — "Lead into the raiser."

This play has the advantage of building the pot immediately, and your opponent may interpret the unexpected aggression as weakness. However, you will sometimes miss out on a bet when your opponent would have made a standard C-bet, but instead folds. This lost bet is more significant in shorter-stacked play where effective stacks rapidly become shallower and accumulating one more guaranteed bet is important.

Let's look at several examples of playing against a button raise out of position. In each case, the blinds are $15-$30, you have effective stacks of $1,500, and your opponent has raised to $90 on the button. We will specify any notes you have on the player and your hand. Your first job is to decide whether calling is indeed a good play. If so, you must then decide what line to pursue after the flop.

Blinds: $15-$30
Note: Your opponent is loose-aggressive.

Your hand: K♥T♥

Action: Your opponent raises to $90.

Question: *Should you just call?*
    Answer: Yes. You have a solid top pair hand with straight and flush potential. Three-betting is reasonable too, but you would prefer a stronger hand and a tighter opponent.

Action: You call. The pot is $300.

Flop: K♦7♣5♦

Question: *What is your move?*
    Answer: Usually to check-raise. Your loose-aggressive opponent will frequently bet this flop, so check-raising not only builds the pot with a near-certain best hand, but also earns you an extra bet (assuming he makes a standard C-bet).

Check-calling is not as good with possible straight and flush draws, but leading out is also okay. Be willing to play a large pot in this situation.

Blinds: $15-$30
Note: Your opponent is tight-aggressive.

Your hand: 7♣7♦

Action: Your opponent raises to $90.

Question: *Fold, call, or three-bet?*
  Answer: Usually three-bet. You want to play a loose-aggressive style against a tight-aggressive opponent. Any pocket pair is a big hand heads-up. Force your tight opponent to surrender immediately or commit to playing a big pot while your hand still figures to be best. The only big mistake here is folding your mid pocket pair, so let's assume that ...

Action: You call for another $60. The pot is $180.

Flop: A♠A♦9♥

Question: *What is your move?*
  Answer: Usually lead out. This flop is less likely to have hit your opponent since it is paired. Your hand will usually be best, and you want to give your opponent incorrect odds to continue with a hand such as the K♣J♠. Also, in this case, the turn and river cards not only have the potential to pair your opponent, but they may put a second pair higher than your sevens on board which would counterfeit your hand.

Blinds: $15-$30

Your hand: K♠6♣

Action: Your opponent raises to $90.

Question: *Should you call?*
    Answer: No. You have a weak face card hand, and you should fold against any opponent type.

Blinds: $15-$30
Note: Your opponent is loose.

Your Hand: A♠7♠

Action: Your opponent raises to $90 on the button.

Question: *Should you call?*
    Answer: Calling is fine. The more loose and aggressive the player, the better your implied odds when you hit.

Action: You call. The pot is $180.

Flop: 7♦3♦2♦

Question: *What's your play?*
    Answer: Bet. Your top pair is probably best, but the majority of turn cards devalue it. (This includes not only a fourth diamond, but any card eight or higher, particularly any card king down through ten.) Bet for value and to protect your hand. Even a maniac can decide not to C-bet, but he may also raise, in which case you should be willing to commit all your chips.

Blinds: $15-$30
Note: Your opponent is loose-aggressive.

Your hand: A♠5♣

Action: Your opponent raises to $90.

Question: *Should you call?*
> **Answer:** Probably not. While your hand figures to be ahead of the button's wide raising range, low offsuit aces play poorly post-flop when out of position. So in this spot against an aggressive opponent, most players are better off folding. If you play well post-flop, calling is fine, but this hand will never be a big money winner.

Blinds: $15-$30
Note: Your opponent is tight.

Your hand: K♠Q♠

Action: Your opponent raises to $90.

Question: *Should you just call?*
> **Answer:** Calling is reasonable, but three-betting is preferred. Your hand is too strong to fold, and while a tight player's raise should be taken seriously, you do have a strong enough holding to three-bet for value.

Action: You elect to call. The pot is $180.

Flop: A♥9♥2♠

Question: *What is your move?*
   Answer: Check and fold to a flop bet, but bet the turn if your opponent checks. Check-raising is too aggressive with no certain outs against a tight player's show of strength. Leading out is better since you risk fewer chips to determine whether your opponent has an ace, but the best play is to check. If your opponent also checks, then you can still bet the turn almost regardless of what hits.

Blinds: $15-$30

Your hand: J♠T♠

Action: Your opponent raises to $90.

Question: *Should you call?*
   Answer: Yes. Your hand is too strong to fold. You could three-bet, but against an unknown player calling works well. (Notice that in many of these hands we are using the Process of Elimination to decide on a play. For instance, here calling and three-betting are both fine plays — we eliminated the possibility of folding.)

Flop: 9♠7♥4♠

Question: *What is your move?*
   Answer: Bet. While you are almost certainly behind, you have six outs for top pair, nine flush outs, and an additional three outs for the gutshot straight draw. Therefore you are a favorite to improve by the river (see"Appendix B: Drawing Odds Chart" on page 377), and you should play this hand. You are happy to win immediately with your jack-high, and if not, you want chips to go into the center while you are probably a favorite. Betting also serves to disguise your hand.

If you do complete one of your draws it may be difficult for your opponent to realize what you have.

If raised, consider reraising. Your fold equity, plus your chance to draw out should give this play positive expectation.

Leading Out
with an Overbet

This hand features Billy Baxter and Doyle Brunson who has been aggressive and recently overbet-shoved a gutshot straight draw.

Baxter: $31,500
Brunson: $9,500

Blinds: $300-$600

Baxter's hand: 9♥8♠
Brunson's hand: T♠2♠

Action: Doyle raises to $1,500 from the button and Baxter calls. The pot is $3,000.

Flop: T♣8♣3♥

Action: Baxter shoves $8,000 and Brunson calls.

Analysis: Since Doyle raised preflop, Baxter knows he is likely to C-bet. Since mid-pair figures to be good, Baxter's best approach is to let Doyle pot-commit himself, and then check-raise all-in.

The problem with Baxter's unexpected bet is that Doyle is only likely to call this overbet with a better hand — namely any ten or strong eight. Meanwhile, he will fold hands that he would normally C-bet, such as a pair of treys, flush or straight draws, or overcards. So check-raising is the better play over leading out with an all-in overbet.

Final board: T♣8♣6♥3♥K♦ and Doyle's pair of tens holds up against Baxter's eights.

A similar leadout overbet arises in matchup featuring the late David "Chip" Reese, and Henry Orenstein.

Effective stacks: Less than $20,000
Blinds: $500-$1,000

Reese's hand: 9♦2♥
Orenstein hand: T♥9♣

Action: Reese raises to $3,000 from the button and Orenstein calls. The pot is $6,000.

Analysis: Reese has been aggressive recently and raised many pots. Televised footage shows him raising an earlier hand without seeing both cards. While an aggressive style is a winning one, you should usually stick to value raises when the stacks are this short since it is important to be quite sure your opponent's reraising range is narrow for this to be a good play. Having to fold to a resteal results in a relatively large chip loss.

Flop: K♣J♥3♣

Action: Orenstein bets $10,000. Reese folds.

Analysis: Normally, Orenstein's play is to check-fold since he only has a weak draw. Check-calling is the worst option since ten-nine has little showdown value on a double-overcard board, but

Orenstein elects to bet out, and his pot-committing overbet is a mistake. If he is willing to risk the remainder of his stack, check-raising is the better play since the aggressive Reese figures to C-bet widely. Suppose Reese bets $4,000. Then Orenstein is risking his stack to win $10,000 instead of $6,000 — a much better risk-reward ratio.

You rarely want to overbet the pot on a stone bluff unless you have a strong read that your opponent does not have a hand. That was not the case here since a king or jack are quite consistent with Reese's preflop raise.

Facing Tough Post-Flop Decisions after Just Calling Preflop

This next hand returns to the match between Billy Baxter and Doyle Brunson.

Baxter: $26,000
Brunson: $13,400

Effective stacks: $13,400
Blinds: $600-$1,200

Baxter's hand: A♠3♥
Brunson's hand: K♦5♦

Action: Baxter raises to $3,000 from the button and Brunson calls. The pot is $6,000.

Flop: A♦Q♦7♣

Action: Both players check.

Turn: 5♣

Action: Doyle shoves all-in for $10,400. Baxter calls.

Analysis: Preflop, Baxter can show an immediate profit by raising all-in. And if he doesn't, this is also a good time for Brunson to reraise all-in. There is $4,200 on the table, a healthy fraction of Brunson's stack and he puts himself in a very tough spot by calling since the pot is now $6,000 with only $10,400 remaining to be played. So by only calling, Brunson must play a pot for most of his stack, and he lacks position.

This is a situation where both players could have taken different preflop actions to simplify future decision-making. Rarely do you want to call a preflop raise that can easily lead to pot-commit where the decision for the remainder of your chips will also be when you are out of position post-flop.

Resolution: The river is the 8♠ and Baxter takes the match.

Facing a Button Min-Raise

This next hand features Todd Brunson and Erick Lindgren.

Brunson: $15,500
Lindgren: $24,500

Blinds: $200-$400

Brunson's hand: 5♦4♣
Lindgren's hand: K♦4♦

Action: Lindgren raises to $800 on the button and Brunson calls. The pot is $1,600.

Analysis: Brunson's call isn't too bad getting 3-to-1 odds with low connecting cards, but facing a normal three big blind raise, you should probably fold this weak hand before the flop.

Flop: T♦3♣2♣

Action: Brunson checks. Lindgren bets $600. Brunson raises to $1,900 and Lindgren calls. The pot is $5,400.

Analysis: Brunson's flop play is excellent. If Lindgren checks, he gets a free card. And when Lindgren bets, his check-raise semi-bluff gives him a good chance to win immediately.

Lindgren's flop C-bet of $600 is small. When you offer your opponent nearly 4-to-1, he is correct to call with many weak hands. Lindgren's decision to call the check-raise is strange since he is getting around 3-to-1 pot odds, but he is a full 10-to-1 underdog to improve (assuming he has three king outs to improve to top pair, and one out each for the backdoor flush and straight draws).

Turn: A♦

Action: Brunson bets $2,400. Lindgren calls. The pot is $10,200.

Analysis: Correctly, Brunson elects not to slowplay his low straight. Many players would check, but betting is the superior play for three main reasons.

1. Brunson has a strong hand and he wants to play a big pot.

2. Betting also charges draws, and there are two possible flush draws.

3. Betting might look like a bluff. Even if Brunson liked the flop, he could now be losing to aces.

Lindgren now has nine outs to the nut flush and three outs to a probable-best straight, so he will show a profit on this call getting better than 3-to-1 pot odds. (See "Appendix B: Drawing Odds Chart" on page 377.) Since Lindgren will often win more money on the river when he completes his draw, the implied odds make staying in mandatory. Lindgren could also raise, giving him the opportunity to win immediately, but since this leaves him vulnerable to a reraise, calling is a good decision.

River: 5♥

Action: Brunson shoves $10,400. Lindgren calls.

Analysis: The river five makes both players happy to get it all-in with their straights, and the pot is split.

The next televised hand in this match shows how to build a big pot, and when to walk away from one.

Brunson: $15,500
Lindgren: $24,500

Blinds: $200-$400

Brunson's hand: 7♦6♣
Lindgren's hand: 8♣7♣

Action: Brunson limps on the button and Lindgren checks. The pot is $800.

Flop: K♣7♥6♠

Action: Lindgren bets $400. Brunson raises to $1,900 and Lindgren calls. The pot is $4,600.

Analysis: Lindgren bets for value with mid-pair. Brunson's overbet raise is much stronger than just calling. He wants to build a large pot with a very strong (yet vulnerable) made hand. Notice that any king counterfeits his two-pair, and there are multiple straight draws.

Lindgren is getting better than 2-to-1 odds to call with mid-pair (and a backdoor straight and a backdoor flush draw). However, he is also out of position facing an overbet. This is generally a good time to fold because even if you are ahead, future decisions can be difficult in this large pot.

Turn: 3♠

Action: Lindgren checks. Brunson bets $4,000 and Lindgren folds.

Analysis: Brunson makes a pot-sized bet for reasons similar to his flop bet. There is now also a possible spade draw, and a five or four put four cards to a straight on board, so betting is necessary.

Faced with another large bet, Lindgren needs to fold. It's unlikely Brunson would make a follow-up pot-committing bet without a quality hand, and Lindgren should not commit the rest of his stack with middle pair.

We conclude this chapter with a hand from an $11 online match showing difficult late-street decisions after calling a button raise before the flop.

Effective stacks: $1,240
Blinds: $10-$20
Note: Data-mining shows Villain to be a winning low-stakes player.

Hand: A♦6♦

Action: Villain raises to $60 from the button and we call. The pot is $120.

Flop: 9♣5♥4♦

Action: We bet $75 and Villain calls. The pot is $320.

Analysis: An ace-high coupled with two backdoor draws (straight and flush) is a good hand. Check-calling is too passive. Check-raising commits a lot of chips, and if Villain calls it leaves us out of position in a big pot which is a bad spot. Check-folding is tight, but not unreasonable. However, leading out gives us the possibility of an immediate win. If Villain does call, we might improve on the turn, and if he raises, we will fold.

Turn: 6♥

Action: We bet $200 and Villain calls. The pot is $720.

Analysis: The turn improves us significantly, and we bet both for value and to give insufficient odds to 5 or 6 out hands. Villain would most likely have raised with a pair of nines on the flop, and we have the highest kicker with our second pair. Likely hands for him are a pair with a draw, such as seven-five, a pair with an overcard to the flop, or possibly two overcards.

River: 2♣

Action: We check and Villain bets $440. We …?

Analysis: Villain's bet could mean one of two things:

1. A bluff with a missed draw, or

2. A value bet with a better hand.

Since we know he is a winning player, it is unlikely he would bet with a mediocre hand such as A♥4♥ that could win a showdown.

What better hands could Villain have here? The turn has three connecting cards and a double-flush draw. If Villain holds the nine, he would almost certainly raise on fourth street (if not the flop). Overpairs and sets are rare in heads-up, and when Villain does hold a such a hand, he will probably raise the turn.

The pot is $1,160 and it costs us $440 to call, so we are getting approximately 2.6-to-1 odds. If we win more than two times in seven, this call will show a profit. Considering that we have second pair and very few holdings that beat us are consistent with Villain's actions, we make the call. He indeed shows a stone bluff with the J♥8♥, and our mid-pair wins the $1,600 pot.

While Villain's flop call of our lead bet is loose, the rest of Villain's actions were quite reasonable. His hand is strong enough to raise preflop. He has a flush draw, overcard, and gutshot straight draw on the turn. At the river, he knows his jack-high can only win if he bluffs.

Three-Betting Preflop

To continue our discussion facing button raises, we now address three-betting in more detail. This first section discusses an advanced play that works well against thinking, aggressive opponents, particularly those who raise liberally from the button preflop. It requires having already played tightly from the big blind, which if you follow the advice given so far you will be doing.

Suppose you are facing an aggressive player's button raise. You know it could mean many different hands, but you don't have a hand that figures to be a favorite, or at least a significant enough favorite to build a large pot out of position. But it has potential. In particular, good candidates include T9o, T8s, 54s, or a small pair.

You have been folding to most button raises, and you now make a small reraise. Against such a small reraise, it is unlikely your opponent will fold preflop. If he plays back before the flop, you fold. When he calls, you lead out on any flop for a one-half to two-thirds pot bet. If you miss the flop and he calls or raises, you are done with the hand (unless you improve to a strong holding on the turn).

The reasoning behind this play is that an intelligent player will tend to think that someone who has been tight from the big blind and unexpectedly makes a small reraise may be doing so because he wants action with a strong hand. Unless your opponent connects with the flop in some way, he will usually concede the hand.

This play is a way to be the one showing the greatest strength preflop, and therefore the natural one to take it down after the flop, without committing a lot of chips. Plus, you can always win a big pot when you flop a strong hand and your opponent connects as well.

Effective stacks: $1,500
Blinds: $10-$20

Note: Your opponent plays a solid tight-aggressive style, raising about 50 percent of his hands preflop, and you have been inactive facing button raises.

Your hand: T♠8♠

Action: Your opponent raises to $60 from the button. You reraise to $115 in the big blind and he calls. The pot is $230.

Flop: K♦7♥2♥

Action: You bet $130 and your opponent folds.

Analysis: Unless your opponent has a king, it will be difficult for him to stay in this hand. You have shown significant strength, and, due to your earlier tightness, there is no reason for him to believe you are bluffing.

When your opponent does play back, you need to be careful. For instance, if the flop had been J♣8♥2♥, and he raised your post-flop leadout bet, then more often than not, you will be facing at least top pair or perhaps second pair with a higher kicker. You have shown significant strength on two betting rounds, yet your tight-aggressive opponent still wants to build a big pot. So it is likely he has the best hand. You might call if the raise was small and the stacks deep enough that the implied odds to draw to your five-outer (the three tens and two eights) were there, but generally, when an opponent plays back at you in this situation, give him credit for a real hand and fold.

And finally, remember that the small three-bet is an advanced play to be used sparingly against players who are both aggressive and perceptive. But against a different type of opponent, this play can and should become a money loser.

Another variation on three-betting is the three-overbet. Sometimes when you are the big blind and the button raises, you should make a larger-than-normal reraise to simplify further decision-making. By "larger-than-normal," I mean at least five times the button's raise. There are several conditions that make this play particularly beneficial:

1. You have a robust yet non-premium hand.

2. You do not feel that you can significantly outplay your opponent with conventional strategy. And,

3. Your stack does not significantly exceed 10 times the button's raise-size.

Let us look at an example where all these criteria are optimal, and then change the conditions to see how they affect our willingness to make a three overbet.

Villain: $2,100
You: $900

Blinds: $25-$50
Note: Villain is an online professional heads-up player.

Your hand: 4♠4♣

Action: Villain raises on the button to $150.

Analysis: This is an excellent time to execute a three-overbet by reraising all-in. A smaller raise will tend to pot-commit us, and pocket pairs play well in case of a call since two high cards significantly outnumber pairs from a hand combination perspective.

Action: We reraise all-in for $900 and Villain folds.

Now let us modify each of the criteria and consider their effects on our decision. First, suppose our hand was A♣2♠ rather than 4♠4♣. When our opponent folds, we win the hand regardless. But when he calls, the pair will often be a slight favorite. By contrast, unless he perceives us as being hyper loose-aggressive, his calling hand range consists primarily of hands that have us behind as a 70-to-30 underdog — stronger aces and pocket pairs. And we are only a slight favorite against the remainder of his possible calling hands, such as king-ten suited or king-queen offsuit.

Similarly, hands such as

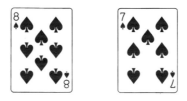

are more favorable than Weak High Card Hands such as

simply because the mid suited connectors will tend to be live, whereas a kicker-less king will often be dominated. So with K♦2♣, we should be inclined to fold rather than three-overbet.

Next, suppose our opponent was much weaker, perhaps tight-passive. Then not only might we worry about the strength represented by a passive player's raise, but folding leaves us with an excellent opportunity to regain a stack by chipping away at this player. In particular, simply by playing a standard loose-aggressive style, you will have a considerable edge if the match progresses normally. So you would be much less inclined to go for a potentially match-ending three-overbet.

Lastly, suppose we again have a small pair against a much better opponent, but the money is significantly deeper with a shorter stack of $4,000. Raising $4,000 to win the $200 on the table risks too much for a small reward. We could instead make our three-overbet a more conventional $750, which indeed works well when we get an immediate fold, or when he calls and we spike a set. But those times our opponent four-bets us all-in, or calls and we miss, creates a difficult spot for us. In the first case, we must either forfeit our large chip investment, or call another $3,250. And against a flat-call and missed flop, we will be playing a huge pot, out of position, generally facing three overcards. This is clearly a situation to avoid.

Combining Hand Reading and Pot Odds to Optimize Fold-Call Decisions

Should you call an opponent's all-in? Answering this question is a matter of assessing how your opponent's possible hands match up against yours, and then seeing whether the pot odds justify a call. Here's an example.

You are down to the final two in a multi-table tournament.

Effective stacks: $400,000

Blinds: $6,000-$12,000 ($2,000 ante)
Note: Your opponent is loose-aggressive.

Your hand: 9♠8♠

Action: You call on the button. Your opponent raises to $40,000 and you call. The pot is $84,000.

Analysis: Folding preflop is out of the question with mid suited connectors in the small blind. Raising is generally the best play, but limping against a loose-aggressive player likely to raise or reraise with many hands is a reasonable alternative.

Flop: 7♠4♣4♦

Action: Your opponent leads out for $50,000. You raise to $150,000. He reraises all-in.

Question: *Should you call or fold?*

 Answer: The pot is just under $600,000 and it costs you $210,000 to call, so your pot odds are 2.83-to-1. You should call if you believe your winning chances are greater than 26 percent.

$$.26 = \frac{1}{3.83}$$

(Have a calculator if playing online to get these figures quickly and exactly. If playing live, approximating is fine.)

Question: *Do you have the 26 percent showdown equity you need to make this a profitable call?*

 Answer: Your nine-high is unlikely to be best at the moment, in which case you have six outs for top pair, and roughly another two outs for your backdoor straight and flush draws. So you will improve around 32 percent of the time by the river, but is this improvement enough? For instance, if your opponent holds a pair of jacks, your pair outs are dead — similarly if he holds a four. If he holds a mid pocket pair or the seven, all your outs are good (unless he has nine-seven or eight-seven). If your opponent holds two higher cards, the turn or river pairing your hand may still result in a loss if he also pairs one of his cards for a higher two-pair.

 We ask the freeware program *PokerStove* to determine our equity against various hands, and we also estimate, using our best judgement, the likelihood of such hands.

Opponent's Hand	Estimated Likelihood	Your Equity
Sevens: A♥7♣	25%	30%
Trip Fours: A♥4♣	12%	8%
Full House: 7♦7♠	3%	1%
Overpair: J♣J♥	10%	7%
One Overcard: A♣2♦	20%	33%
Two Overcards: K♥Q♥	20%	31%
Bluff: 6♣3♠	10%	65%

Based on this table, your expected equity would be just above 26 percent at 28 percent,

$$.28 = (.30)(0.25) + (.08)(0.12) + \ ... \ + (.65)[0.10]$$

and since our calculation will not be exact to within two percent, calling and folding are similar in value.

So in a situation like this, your decision doesn't matter. On the other hand, if your opponent is a maniac, and would blindly shove any two cards on this raggedy board, then random hands such as a bluff or one or two overcards deserve considerably higher weight, and you should call.

But suppose your opponent is not so loose. He might raise your preflop limp widely, and then bet almost any two cards at a paired flop where he knows you are unlikely to have connected, but when you make a substantial raise, he would need a strong hand to continue. If this more accurately describes your opponent, then hands such as pocket pairs, sevens, and fours rise significantly in likelihood relative to overcard semi-bluffs or the "any two card" mentality. Now you should fold since it is much more likely you are only drawing to your backdoor hands.

In the actual hand where this occurred, the player laid his hand down dismissing outright the possibility of calling an all-in reraise when he almost could not be ahead at the moment. The other player's cards were never shown, and folding is not necessarily wrong here. But not considering a call is a mistake; if the odds are there, you can be correct to call with almost no chance of having the best hand at the time. Keep in mind though that if you feel you play much better than your opponent, it still may be worth passing on a small edge.[8]

In the hand above, both pot odds and your read on your opponent are important in making this decision. Sometimes, however, one of these criteria is more important.

For instance, with effective stacks of $1,500 and blinds of $25-$50, you raise on the button to $150 with the A♦9♣. Your opponent reraises all-in. Now you are getting just better than 6-to-5, but the question really comes down to how wide your opponent would make this play. If he has shoved the last four hands, you have an easy call. If he has yet to three-bet your button raise, then you have a clear fold. The primary criterion in making this decision is your read on your opponent.

Conversely, pot odds alone can also sometimes tell you all you need to know. Here's an example.

You are three hands into a turbo online sit 'n go with no read yet on your opponent.

Effective stacks: $1,400
Blinds: $10-$20

Your hand: J♦6♦

Action: Your opponent raises to $40 from the button. You call. The pot is $80.

---

[8] See *Tournament Poker for Advanced Players: Expanded Edition* by David Sklansky for more discussion.

Flop: 4♦3♦2♠

Action: You check. Your opponent bets $80. You raise to $200. Your opponent reraises all-in to $1,360.

Question: *Call or fold?*

Analysis: Pot odds alone can answer this question. The pot is $1,640 and it costs us $1,160 to call, so we are getting 1.4-to-1 on our money, or just worse than 3-to-2.

Our jack-high is almost certainly beat at the moment, so we must count our outs. Against any one-pair hand (4X, 3X, or 2X), we are drawing to:

- **Top Pair:** Six outs — the three jacks and the three sixes

- **Gutshot Straight:** The 5♣, 5♥, and 5♠

- **Flush:** Nine diamonds give us a flush

So with 18 outs, we will improve by the river over 60 percent of the time and would gladly call even if the pot was not laying us any odds.

Now suppose your opponent has a much better hand, perhaps A♠A♣. In this case, we lose our six top-pair outs leaving us with a total of twelve outs. The odds against us hitting are now 1.2-to-1, so we are still getting the odds to call.

There are very few hands your opponent could have that deny us the odds we need to improve. In particular, he would need to have a set, a straight, or a better mega-draw such as A♦5♦. Even against the nut straight, we are only a 40 percent underdog. Furthermore, the likelihood of your opponent flopping such monster hands is much lower in heads-up relative to fuller games since players are more selective about the hands they play at a full table. Here, for instance, you will often be up against a hand such as ace-four or a pair of sevens.

Even if we take doom-and-gloom estimates that our opponent is equally likely to have a set or straight, a high overpair, or a pair with an overcard and never bluffing or betting a naked draw, then our showdown equity, again using the *PokerStove* program, is still 46 percent.

$$.46 = (.33)(.36) + (.33)(.41) + (.33)(.61)$$

which is equivalent to pot odds of 1.2-to-1.

Since the 1.4-to-1 odds we are getting more than qualifies, our expectation for calling, based on these assumptions, is $125.

$$\$125 = (.46)(\$1,640) + (.54)(-\$1,160)$$

So we call, and our opponent flips the A♦4♠. His draws devalue our hand slightly, but we are still a 55 percent favorite and in a chip-favorable situation.

Committing All
Your Chips with Ace-King

This next hand features actor James Woods and Johnny Chan.

Chan: $20,500
Woods: $19,500

Blinds: $600-$1,200

Chan's hand: A♣K♥
Woods' hand: A♠J♦

Action: Woods limps from the button. Chan raises to $5,200 in the big blind. Woods reraises to $9,200 and Chan calls. The pot is $18,400.

Flop: 9♦7♦4♣

Action: Chan checks. Woods shoves $10,300 and Chan folds.

Analysis: A strange hand. First, we note that with shallow effective stacks, both Chan and Woods should be willing to commit all their chips preflop holding such strong hands. Woods's willingness should stem from his hand strength and desire to play large pots early in order to negate Chan's superior post-flop experience. Meanwhile, Chan is out of position with a premium hand so a conventional route for this hand would be for Woods to raise his button, Chan to make a pot-committing reraise, and all the chips to go to the center preflop. Instead, we have this peculiar maze of bets and raises, culminating in a huge laydown.

Woods attempted a variety of psychological tricks throughout the match, and since he ended up succeeding in getting Chan to lay down his monster hand, let's give him the benefit of the doubt and look at this hand from Chan's perspective.

After Woods reraises Chan's raise, Chan knows that Woods likely has a strong hand, and is unlikely to lay it down preflop, but ace-king is simply too strong to fold, particularly with an already-large pot. Chan's two options are to reraise all-in now, often coin flipping against an underpair, or to shove all-in on the flop.

After calling preflop, even if Chan were the one to call an all-in bet rather than shove himself, he would be getting nearly 3-to-1 pot odds, and two overcards are 3-to-1 to improve. Since Chan is already ahead of any other two unpaired overcard hands, he should be quite willing to play for an all-in. He is not getting proper odds only if Woods has a set or pair of kings or aces.

Let's look at a sample hand distribution that Woods might reasonably be on:

Chan's Equity
Against Woods Hands Distribution

Hand	Combi-nations	Estimated Likelihood	Equity
Aces or kings	6	30%	6%
Queens, jacks, or tens	18	30%	24%
Ace-king or ace-queen	21	30%	67%
Bluff	Multiple	10%	50%

A couple of notes on this table. First, while aces or kings are certainly very consistent with Wood's limp-reraise before the flop, these hands are the least consistent from a hand combination perspective. Since Chan holds one ace and one king already, there are particularly few of these monster hands left in play, so weighting aces or kings with 30 percent likelihood is worst-case.

The "bluff" category is inclusive of every single hand, and so it includes all underpairs, as well as strong hands such as Woods's actual holding. This minimal weight to the bluff category, coupled with the aces or kings getting fully equal weight to the much more prevalent overcard and smaller pair hands remaining in the deck, make this about the most unfavorable distribution for Chan to place Woods on. And using this hand distribution, Chan's equity is 34 percent.

$$.34 = (.30)(.60) + (.30)(.24) + (.30)(.67) + (.10)(.50)$$

Even if Chan assumes that Woods will lay down 0 percent of his range to a shove, and that he will hold aces or king a full 50 percent of the time, never have a "bluff," and hold the remaining hand categories 25 percent each, he is still getting slightly better than the 3-to-1 odds he needs to play an all-in here, and it is always possible that Woods will fold if Chan shoves first.

Most likely Chan's check-fold is due to a combination of three reasons:

1. He does indeed place a heavy weight on aces or kings. (Probably because Woods reraise was so small.)

2. He wants a significant advantage before committing all his chips. And,

3. He has limited time to act in front of a large audience, and the assessment he makes of these numbers in his head differs from the methodical approach we can outline here with unlimited time and resources.

Calling or Folding the River: The Pot Odds Approach

Huck Seed and Phil Hellmuth get involved in a large pot with deep stacks.

Blinds: $300-$600

Hellmuth's hand: A♦4♠
Seed's hand: 4♦3♦

Action: Seed calls from the button and Hellmuth checks. The pot is $1,200.

Flop: A♠T♦8♦

Action: Hellmuth checks. Seed bets $1,100 and Hellmuth calls. The pot is $3,400.

Analysis: Hellmuth has the A♦, so if a third diamond falls he will have a redraw to the nut flush. Without the redraw, he should play this hand aggressively. After Hellmuth checks, Seed could check for a free card, but instead semi-bluffs his flush draw.

Turn: 2♦

Action: Hellmuth bets $2,000. Seed raises to $9,000 and Hellmuth calls. The pot is $21,400.

Analysis: A third low diamond hits. Hellmuth bets, figuring his top pair is probably best, and if not, he holds a nut flush draw as well. Seed makes an excellent overbet raise since he wants maximum value for his premium hand, and also because a fourth diamond will either cost him the pot (if Hellmuth has any diamond in his hand), or severely limit how much he can win (since Hellmuth is unlikely to play a large pot without a diamond if four diamonds are on board).

Hellmuth now makes a smart call. Folding is a clear mistake since he holds top pair and the nut draw against a single opponent, but he must reason that Seed likely has one of two categories of hands:

1.   A better made hand, such as two-pair, a set, or a flush.

2.   A semi-bluff, such as J♦7♠ or K♦8♠.

Therefore, Hellmuth is correct to call rather than reraise. It is unlikely he will get a better made hand to fold, and since he holds a higher pair and higher draw if Seed is semi-bluffing, going to the river is a fine result.

River: Q♣

Action: Hellmuth checks. Seed bets $16,000. Hellmuth folds.

Analysis: Hellmuth checks, looking to show down without a river bet. Seed then makes a large value bet with his low flush. Given that Seed's turn bet is consistent with a better made hand or semi-bluff, and no obvious draw hit on the river, Hellmuth knows that Seed should be glad to check behind with most semi-bluffing hands such as K♦8♠. His bet indicates that he either had a better made hand on the turn, or he had a draw that missed entirely and is now bluffing a weak high card (e.g., the J♦7♠).

Getting pot odds of 2.3-to-1, Hellmuth can make a profitable call if and only if he believes Seed is bluffing at least 30 percent of the time. Thus Hellmuth's fold indicates that he weighed the latter category high enough that he folds his top pair. So while this decision is largely understanding how an opponent plays, the math is important. Getting 9-to-1, for instance, Hellmuth could be equally convinced that Seed is bluffing at the exact same frequency, yet still call because he now must be correct only 10 percent of the time to show a profit.

Attacking Button Limps

Most good players raise the majority of the hands they play from the button so someone who frequently limps from this spot is unlikely to be playing well and you should take advantage of this. While there are exceptions and some strong post-flop players prefer not to build the pot preflop, it is more common that such serial button-limpers are simply passive and unaware.

How do you exploit this weakness? By raising from the big blind you are quite happy to win the blinds immediately, so tend to make a solid raise to four or five big blinds to discourage action. Force your opponent to surrender a pot of two big blinds immediately, or play a larger pot with a generally inferior hand. What hands should you raise a button limp with? If your opponent is limping often, and he is not a calling station, then you can raise with hands as weak as Q♠8♥, J♣8♣, T♠9♣, 8♠6♠, and 6♦5♦.

However, even if your opponent limps every hand, you should generally not bluff-raise with trash hands. You will be dealt enough hands with showdown value that you do not need to force plays. For one thing, your opponent is much more likely to understand what you are doing if you raise his button limps constantly, and even weak players will begin to play back at you.

In addition, when you do get called you can still connect with the flop holding a hand such as

But with a trash hand such as

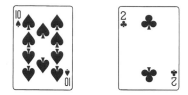

the opportunity to take the blinds without a fight may not compensate for the many times you will have put yourself in a large-pot situation while holding a weak hand out of position. This is particularly true against loose-passive opponents who will often call down. Now you will require a stronger hand relative to a tighter player since your raise is almost entirely for value.

When you do attack a button limp, you should lead out betting just as often as you would C-bet after raising on your button and your opponent checks on the flop. This sequence of attacking a button limp and then leading on the flop can be quite profitable, independent of cards, if your opponent is sufficiently tight. Suppose, for instance, he will fold the bottom third of his limping range when you raise preflop, and then requires at least bottom pair to continue after your flop bet.

Even if you never connected with a flop, your expectation on this betting sequence would be positive. Assuming you raise to four big blinds preflop, bet two-thirds the pot after the flop, and your opponent misses the flop 65 percent of the time, your expectation is to win .22 BB.

$$.22 \text{ BB} = \left(\frac{1}{3}\right)(2 \text{ BB}) + \left(\frac{2}{3}\right)\left[(.65)(4 \text{ BB}) - (.35)(9.33 \text{ BB})\right]$$

Effective stacks: $1,320
Blinds: $15-$30
Note: Villain is tight-passive.

Your hand: A♥6♥

Action: Villain limps on the button. You raise to $130. He folds.

Analysis: Your mid-suited ace is strong enough to attack a button limp from even a loose opponent. Facing a tight-passive opponent, you should make this play unhesitatingly.

Blinds: $25-$50
Note: Villain is loose-passive.
Your hand: J♠7♣

Action: Villain limps on the button.

Question: *What is your move?*
   Answer: Check. Your hand is not quite strong enough to value-raise against an opponent who will be calling this raise with almost any two cards. Take a free flop and value-bet if you connect.

Question: *What would be the weakest hands with a jack or ten that you should raise here?*
   Answer: Roughly jack-nine offsuit or ten-eight suited. Ten-eight offsuit is a little weak, while king-ten or queen-ten are certainly strong enough.

Effective stacks: $1,500
Blinds: $25-$50
Note: Villain is tight-passive.

Your hand: J♠9♠

Action: Villain limps on the button.

Question: *What is your move?*
> **Answer:** Raise to $200. You could take the $100 on the table by raising the tight-passive Villain, and your hand has potential to connect solidly with the flop.

Action: You raise to $200 and Villain calls. The pot is $400.

Flop: K♥T♠2♣

Question: *Do you check or bet?*
> **Answer:** Bet around $250. This should win the pot immediately if Villain has missed. If he raises, you can make an easy fold. And if he calls, while you are almost certainly behind at the moment, your gutshot straight draw and three-flush offer you approximately five outs.

Question: Suppose your opponent has been playing aggressively preflop and he now makes an uncharacteristic button limp. *What should you do?*
> **Answer:** Your opponent could be trapping or he could have a junk hand and want a cheap flop. Since you know little, base your decision primarily on the strength of your hand. Tend to raise with any well above-average hand such as 4♣4♥, A♠7♣, Q♥T♦, or 9♠8♠.

Attacking for Value

With approximately even stacks, the following hand arises in the match between Phil Hellmuth and Lyle Berman.

Blinds: $400-$800

Berman's hand: Q♦T♣
Hellmuth's hand: A♣T♦

Action: Hellmuth limps on the button. Berman raises to $3,300 and Hellmuth calls. The pot is $6,600.

Flop: K♥7♥5♠

Action: Berman bets $5,000 and Hellmuth folds.

Analysis: This hand is a fine example of aggressive play from the big blind. Berman has an excellent hand, so he raises to just over four big-blinds after Hellmuth limps. He makes a substantial leadout bet knowing that Hellmuth will be inclined to fold the majority of times when he has missed the flop. If Hellmuth stayed in and Berman did not improve, he could simply cut his losses. The weaker hand wins through aggressively attacking a button limp and following this raise with a bet at the flop when both have missed. (Notice that Hellmuth probably cost himself the pot by not making the recommended preflop raise.)

Attacking with a Marginal Hand

This next hand features Antonio Esfanidiari and Scott Fischman.

Blinds: $300-$600

Esfandiari's hand: Q♦6♠
Fischman's hand: K♣J♠

Action: Fischman limps on the button. Esfandiari raises to $3,000 and Fischman calls. The pot is $6,000.

Analysis: Fischman has button-limped previously in this match, and while Q♦6♠ is generally too weak to raise from the big blind, Esfandiari decides to aggress on his button-limping opponent.

Flop: 8♠6♦2♥

Action: Esfandiari bets $4,600. Fischman folds.

Analysis: Esfandiari is prepared to bet any flop after his preflop raise, and second pair makes this a value bet. Fischman has no choice but to fold his strong preflop hand, having failed to show strength before the flop and having missed the flop. It is a routine occurrence for both players to miss the flop, and the pot goes to the aggressor. This hand is another example of the betting sequence:

1. Attack button limp, and

2. Bet the flop if called.

Later in the match, Esfandiari attacks a button limp again, but this time, he elects to do so with a trash hand.

Blinds: $1,000-$2,000

Esfandiari's hand: 9♣4♥
Fischman's hand: K♣8♦

Action: Fischman limps on the button. Esfandiari raises to $8,600 and Fischman folds.

Analysis: When a player limps his button, you should not be afraid to attack preflop with a raise of four to five big blinds. However, you should normally choose a hand that has some potential to connect with the flop, even low offsuit connectors such as the 5♥4♦, because your raise has much more value when you can reasonably flop a good hand if called. (Again, the exception would be against a player quick to reraise but reluctant to call.) Nonetheless , Esfandiari could believe that Fischman is limping weak hands on the button, and so attacking with any two cards will not be a significant mistake. This is the power of aggression in heads-up poker.

In the next hand, Fischman, presumably frustrated with Esfandiari taking away pot after pot with preflop aggression, decides to set a trap.

Blinds: $1,000-$2,000

Esfandiari's hand: 9♦8♥
Fischman's hand: T♣T♠

Action: Fischman calls on the button and Esfandiari checks. The pot is $4,000.

Analysis: This would be a weak slowplay with pocket tens against a less aggressive opponent, but we have just seen that Esfandiari is capable of attacking button limps with a wide range of hands. Most likely Fischman understands this and wants to trap Esfandiari, or at least get him to realize he is capable of limping his stronger hands as well.

Question: *Why does Esfandiari suddenly decide to check now that he has a playable hand?*
  Answer: You should not make this limp-attack play every time, particularly against a solid opponent who will adjust his actions based on prior hands.

Flop: 9♥6♣5♦

Action: Esfandiari bets $2,200. Fischman raises to $8,000 and Esfandiari calls. The pot is $20,000.

Analysis: Both players play the flop well. Esfandiari could also three-bet here with top pair and a draw, but he is content seeing another card and possibly filling his straight.

Turn: 7♣

Action: Esfandiari bets $9,400 and Fischman calls. The pot is $38,800.

River: A♣

Action: Esfandiari bets $13,400 and Fischman calls.

Analysis: Fischman is ahead of few holdings that Esfandiari could logically have putting in this fourth bet with an overcard and four to a straight on board. However, Fischman is getting nearly 4-to-1 with a hand that beats a bluff, and his opponent is aggressive. Therefore, Fishman's call indicates he believes his opponent is making a play more than one time in five, which is not an unreasonable assumption.

Attacking, and then Checking

We return to another hand between Phil Hellmuth and Huck Seed.

Blinds: $600-$1,200

Hellmuth's hand: 9♠5♠
Seed's hand: T♥T♦

Action: Hellmuth calls on the button. Seed raises to $3,700 and Hellmuth calls. The pot is $7,400.

Analysis: Seed is attacking Hellmuth's button limp for value.

Flop: J♣7♦7♣

Action: Seed checks. Hellmuth bets $2,000 and Seed calls. The pot is $11,400.

Analysis: Strange plays by both players. Not only is Seed's hand likely best, but as the preflop raiser he is expected to bet. The reason Seed probably elects to check is that a pair of jacks or better will not fold, and most weak hands will not call. So while this is reasonable, a turn overcard could put Seed in a much more difficult position.

Even though Seed's check is suspicious, the combination of a raggedy board unlikely to help most hands and the lack of showdown value in his own hand makes this a reasonable stealing opportunity for Hellmuth. The problem is that his bet is so small that Seed is correct to call with almost any hand strong enough to raise preflop, as he is getting nearly 5-to-1 odds.

A good follow-up betting sequence for Hellmuth after this odd flop bet is to continue to represent a seven or a jack, making a larger turn or river bluff if his opponent checks the turn. Nonetheless, building the pot when you are way behind is risky, and you need a good reason to do so.

Turn: 9♥

Action: Seed checks. Hellmuth bets $4,000 and Seed calls. The pot is $19,400.

Analysis: Since Seed's hand still figures to be either way ahead or way behind, and he is now drawing to a gutshot straight as well, he correctly check-calls.

Hellmuth pairs and makes another underbet, this time for value, and possibly to see a free showdown. Betting larger for value and to protect against an unfavorable river is usually the better alternative.

River: 3♠

Action: Seed checks. Hellmuth bets $3,000 and Seed calls.

Analysis: Seed check-calls for reasons similar to the turn play. Hellmuth's nines are strong enough to possibly collect a few chips, and he makes another value underbet.

One particularly lucrative type of flop for follow-up betting after attacking a button limp is the type of paired flop that appears in this last hand. Such flops represent a unique opportunity for aggressive plays to succeed.

The Paired Flop Principle

When the flop comes paired, everything changes. Consider the following two examples.

Flop A:

Flop B:

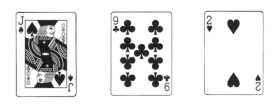

The texture of Flop A is much more conducive to a bluff because if your opponent does not have a pocket pair, as will be the case the vast majority of the time, he can only have connected if he holds one of the three remaining deuces or two remaining jacks, i.e., the five cards: J♦, J♥, 2♠, 2♣, 2♦.

Meanwhile, not only is there a third jack to connect with Flop B, but there are also three more nines that can make a pair. So nine potential hole cards help your opponent rather than five. Also, there are possible draws with the unpaired flop.

You should take advantage of this decreased probability of your opponent connecting. Do this by betting more often since you are more likely to catch your opponent with no hand.

201

> On a paired flop, fewer hand combinations help your opponent, so he is less likely to have improved his starting hand. Exploit this knowledge by betting or raising aggressively.

The one time a paired flop helps you less is against a calling station who does not need to connect to call a bet. Now you should be more likely to bet ace-high or king-high for value, but do not bluff against loose-passive opponents. You should only bet when you can do so for value. Now let us look at an example of a paired flop facing an unknown opponent.

Blinds: $50-$100
Your hand: J♣8♠

Action: Villain limps on the button and you check. The pot is $200.

Flop: T♠T♦7♣

Question: *Check or bet?*
> **Answer:** You should bet the standard $100-$150 since the paired board gives you higher fold equity because your opponent is less likely to have connected. Furthermore, you have a gutshot straight draw which gives your hand a little more value if called.

When playing a paired flop, realize that a smart opponent will know that the paired flop is less likely to have helped you as well, and that you are aware of this information. A smart player might reason, "I have missed the flop, but this guy I'm playing is smart enough to know that I'll miss more often on this paired flop. He is more likely to be bluffing or betting a weaker-than-normal hand for value." He might then counter by bluff-raising more often in these situations, or even calling you with weak hands, possibly looking to see a cheap showdown with a good high card or take the pot away from you on a later street.

The following hand, featuring Phil Hellmuth and Paul Phillips, is a good example of multiple-leveling thinking on a paired flop.

Hellmuth: $45,000
Phillips: $35,000

Blinds: $1,000-$2,000

Hellmuth's hand: 9♣5♣
Phillips' hand: J♥2♥

Action: Hellmuth limps on the button and Phillips checks. The pot is $4,000.

Flop: J♠J♦2♠

Action: Phillips checks. Hellmuth bets $2,000. Phillips raises to $5,000. Hellmuth reraises to $10,500. Phillips raises again all-in to $33,000 and Hellmuth folds.

Analysis: Phil Hellmuth, normally one who sticks to a small pot strategy, makes a three-bet bluff with nine-high.

Question: *Why did he do this?*
　　Answer: Because the flop is paired. Hellmuth knows that Phillips most likely can only have a good hand if he holds a jack or a deuce. Phillips happens to have one of each, but Hellmuth can only go by the odds. It is also possible that Phillips would fold a weak deuce facing this strength. The jacks are of biggest concern for Hellmuth and there are

already two jacks accounted for. So he reasons that Phillips is not likely to have anything, hence his uncharacteristic bluff three-bet.

The other interesting aspect of this hand is Phillips's decision to go all-in on the flop rather than call Hellmuth's reraise. The main reason to raise and reraise with strong hands is to play a big pot, but if Phillips calls, the pot will be a full $25,000 with $22,500 left to be bet. Getting in a sub pot-sized amount into the pot, with two full betting rounds to go, is more likely to succeed in winning the most chips possible than simply reshoving the flop.

In addition, there is effectively no chance of Hellmuth drawing to a better hand. If Hellmuth is significantly behind, as is likely, then he might catch up to a hand he thinks is worth putting in more chips. For instance, if Phillips calls and the turn comes a nine or a five, Hellmuth could go broke. So this is a situation where Phillips would do well to slow down after getting in three bets on the flop with a made full house.

Playing the
River: Check or Bluff?

Assume you have position on the river, and your opponent checks. When should you bluff? And before we consider a general answer to this question, what does it mean to bluff in heads-up? Suppose the pot at the river is $200 and the final board is

You raised preflop and get called. You C-bet the flop and get called again. You both checked the turn. Now your opponent checks one more time and this is the first hand so you have no reads.

Question: *Which of the following hands would you be most inclined to bluff?*
1. Ace-high?
2. 8-high?
3. A low pair?

Answer: No. 2. 8-high.

Notice that this is the only possible correct answer, since Nos. 1 and 3 are not bluffs. It is likely that any pair or good high card will win you this pot if you also check behind. More importantly, it is unlikely that a better hand will fold if you bet.

Question: *What are you opponent's most likely holdings?*
Answer: Lacking a read, we take his actions at face value. He has a non-trash hand preflop, liked his hand enough to call the flop, and then wanted no further action from the turn onward. This is most consistent with a busted heart draw (like Q♥J♥), ace-high, or possibly a low or mid pair (e.g. A♣4♣ or 7♥7♦).

So when you hold ace-high or a hand like Q♣2♣, you are not bluffing. Your hand may legitimately be best, and your opponent will usually fold worse hands and call with better hands. This is particularly true with the ace-high. Single high cards are often enough to win at the showdown in heads-up play, particularly when your opponent has shown weakness by checking two consecutive streets. So just check them down.

But with 8-high, perhaps you hold 8♦7♦, your opponent almost cannot have a worse hand because there are few weaker hands that have not made a pair or straight at this point. Since your opponent will generally fold ace-high or a busted heart draw with a better high card than yours if you bet the river, bluffing is a solid play.

Suppose you bet around half the pot, $150. If he folds more often than one time in three, you show a profit. Considering the weakness he showed by checking the last two streets, he could certainly fold one time in three. Therefore, you should bluff.

Note that these bluffs are harder to accomplish when playing out of position. In the above hand, your opponent has checked twice while you have only checked once. If you were out of position, you would be forced to act before his river check. Having seen him check only once, you could not narrow his hand range as much. Your opponent might even be slowplaying three kings or a full house.

In summary:

1. Bluffing is best accomplished when you have position against an opponent who has shown significant weakness and your hand has no showdown value if you check.

2. Bluffing is more difficult to pull off out of position. And,

3. You should rarely "bluff" when your hand may actually be best, such as a lone high card on a raggedy board.

Bluffing the River with 7-High

James Woods and Johnny Chan have similar stacks in this hand from their round one match.

Blinds: $300-$600.

Chan's hand: A♠8♠
Woods' hand: 7♠3♦

Action: Chan limps on the button and Woods checks. The pot is $1,200.

Analysis: You should tend to raise a mid-suited ace preflop for value.

Flop: Q♣J♥5♦

Action: Both players check.

Turn: T♦

Action: Both players check.

River: 2♣

Action: Woods bets $1,200 and Chan folds.

Analysis: Woods has almost no chance of winning the pot without a bluff on one of the post-flop streets. With even a 9-high, Woods could check and hope to win the pot at the showdown, but his 7-high is too weak, so his decision to bluff is good. If Woods wins at least fifty percent of the time betting the pot here, then he will show a profit. Since Chan has shown weakness on each street, this is a very reasonable assumption.

Bluffing
the River without Position

Here's another hand between Antonio Esfandiari and Phil Hellmuth.

Effective stacks: $320,000
Blinds: $800-$1,600

Esfandiari's hand: J♣3♠
Hellmuth's hand: T♦6♦

Action: Esfandiari raises to $4,200 on the button. Hellmuth calls. The pot is $8,400.

Flop: 9♦8♦2♠

Action: Both players check.

Analysis: Hellmuth's gutshot straight flush draw with an overcard is strong enough to bet. Leading out is normally the best play, but Hellmuth expects the aggressive Esfandiari to C-bet this flop if he checks and check-raising is a strong option.

Turn: J♥

Action: Hellmuth bets $5,000 and Esfandiari calls. The pot is $18,400.

River: 9♠

Action: Hellmuth bets $7,000 and Esfandiari calls.

Analysis: This is a clever bluff by Hellmuth with his ten-high. If Esfandiari has another ten with a higher kicker, or overcards, he will almost certainly fold a better hand to this small bet. Esfandiari can call over two times in three and Hellmuth will still show a profit. This bluff is designed to get Esfandiari to fold a better high card.

With blinds of $600-$1,200, Chan and Woods both face another check or bet river decision.

Chan's hand: K♣J♠
Woods' hand: 4♦3♦

Action: Woods limps on the button and Chan checks. The pot is $2,400.

Flop: T♠5♠4♣

Action: Both players check.

Turn: 5♥

Action: Both players check.

Analysis: Woods could have bet the flop and he should bet here. His bottom pair figures to be best, particularly since Chan has checked twice. Not only could any card six or higher pair Chan, but a river ten would counterfeit Woods's low pair.

River: 2♣

Action: Both players check.

Analysis: Chan's check is good since his king-high could certainly be the best hand given the raggedy board and weakness shown by Woods. From Woods's perspective, Chan would not have checked a five or ten on multiple streets, so betting would be for value. Woods could make a small bet of $1,200 or $1,500 hoping to get paid off by a high card or pair of deuces, but checking behind for a free showdown is reasonable and better than making a large bet with the aim of taking Chan off a stronger hand.

In our next hand, however, Woods' decision not to value-bet the river is a clear error.

Effective stacks: $15,000

Blinds: $1,000-$2,000

Chan's hand: T♠7♠
Woods' hand: K♦J♦

Action: Chan limps on the button. Woods checks. The pot is $4,000.

Analysis: Woods should shove before the flop. He is out of position with a strong hand and over 25 percent of the effective stacks is already in the pot.

Flop: K♥8♦8♣

Action: Woods checks. Chan bets $2,000 and Woods calls. The pot is $8,000.

Turn: 3♦

Action: Both players check.

River: 2♥

Action: Both players check.

Analysis: Chan makes a min-bet at this paired flop knowing that Woods is likely to have missed. When Chan is called, he gives up on the hand.

Meanwhile, Woods checks his top pair every round of betting. This check is reasonable on the flop, where Chan will often bet.The turn check is reasonable since Chan might bet again, and if Chan checks, the river card might improve Woods's hand since he has picked up a flush draw. However, Woods failing to bet the river for value is a mistake. Chan will often check behind since he has just checked the last street. It is rare that top pair is not strong enough to bet the river, particularly after your opponent checks the previous round.

In the first hand of Eric Lindgren's match against Todd Brunson, Lindgren does not emulate Woods's error and value-bets his top pair after all the cards are out.

Effective stacks: $20,000
Blinds: $100-$200

Brunson's hand: 7♦6♥
Lindgren's hand: Q♣7♣

Action: Lindgren min-raises to $400 on the button and Brunson calls. The pot is $800.

Flop: 6♣5♦3♦

Action: Brunson bets $600. Lindgren calls. The pot is $2,000.

Analysis: Brunson makes a solid bet holding top pair and a gutshot straight draw. He is out of position and many turn cards significantly devalue his hand — any card ten and above, so he leads for value, content to win immediately.

Lindgren's hand is modest, and a major component of this call is having position. Even if he does not hit a pair or a draw, Lindgren could have a chance to win the pot by bluffing if Brunson checks a later street.

Turn: Q♥

Action: Brunson bets $1,300. Lindgren calls. The pot is $4,600.

Analysis: Brunson makes a follow-up turn bet because his hand still figures to be best against a single opponent, and if he checks, his hand is strong enough to call, and betting out gives Brunson the chance to win immediately. If the turn had been the K♥ or J♥, rather than the queen, then Brunson's follow-up bet would probably have taken this pot.

Lindgren would have to bet his top pair if Brunson checked, but after Brunson bets a significant fraction of the pot, calling is proper strategy. This line will tend to result in a pot with three total bets. Brunson might improve with another card. If Lindgren raises, Brunson will probably discard most low pair hands, but if Lindgren just calls, he will often win another bet on the river.

River: J♦

Action: Brunson checks. Lindgren bets $1,200 and Brunson calls.

Analysis: Both players understand what is happening at this river. Brunson's hand is not strong enough to value-bet due to the two overcards on board and Lindgren having called his two post-flop bets. Brunson checks, hoping for a free showdown.

Lindgren makes a small bet. Brunson realizes he is likely facing a value bet from a better hand. Getting nearly 5-to-1 pot odds, Brunson will show a profit if Lindgren is bluffing more than 1 time in 6, and so he should call.

Calling the River
or Raising for Value

You must relentlessly bet your strong hands at the river, but a difficult value decision often arises on this last betting round when your opponent bets first. You have a strong hand, but not the nuts. Your opponent bets. If you call, you will often miss out on substantial value relative to the raise. But if you are beat, you will lose much more.

When deciding whether to value-raise or just call, here are the relevant factors:

1. **How strong is your hand?** Obviously, the stronger your hand, the more likely you should be to aggressively seek value from it.

2. **Is it possible your opponent will call with a worse hand?** If, for instance, you have top set on a board where any card of a particular rank makes a straight, you will generally only get action when your opponent holds the straight. So your set is really just a bluff-catcher.

3. **Would you have an easy decision if your opponent three-bets?** If not, then you should be more inclined to call rather than raise.

Let us consider several examples of this call-reraise decision.

Effective stacks: $1,320
Blinds: $10-$20
Note: Your opponent is loose-aggressive.

Your hand: T♠9♥

Action: You raise to $50 on the button and your opponent calls. The pot is $100.

Flop: 8♣7♦3♦

Action: Your opponent checks. You bet $75 and he calls. The pot is $250.

Turn: 6♣

Action: Your opponent checks. You bet $150 and he calls. The pot is $550.

River: A♣

Action: Your opponent bets $300.

Question: *What is your move?*

> **Answer:** You should raise. Letting the third flush card scare you into calling is timid since your loose-aggressive opponent would lead here with many hands other than a backdoor flush. Your top straight is strong and your loose opponent could call with a variety of inferior hands, such as A♥3♣ or 9♣8♥. If you made a non all-in reraise and your opponent shoved in his remaining chips, you would call.

Blinds: $25-$50
Note: Your opponent is solid.

Your hand: 3♣2♥

Action: Your opponent limps his button and you check. The pot is $100.

Flop: K♥K♦5♥

Action: You both check.

Turn: 2♣

Action: You bet $70 and your opponent calls. The pot is $240.

River: 2♦

Action: You bet $150. Your opponent raises to $400.

Question: *What is your play?*

Answer: You should just call. Getting 2-to-1 odds with a full house, you cannot fold, but if you reraise, your opponent will only call when he also has a full house. He will probably discard his bluffs and other losing hands knowing that you could only three-bet with a full house on this double-paired board. So you will be called only when he holds a king or two fives, or the case deuce for a split.

Calling his raise is good strategy because he might be bluffing, or you might split. If you reraise, again you will only be called when he will at least split the pot. Therefore you cannot three-bet this river raise for value, and you should flat-call.

Calling vs Raising the River with Two-Pair

This hand from the quarter finals features Lyle Berman and Phil Hellmuth.

Blinds: $1,000-$2,000

Berman's hand: K♠9♥
Hellmuth's hand: T♦5♦

Action: Hellmuth limps on the button and Berman checks in the big blind. The pot is $4,000.

Flop: K♣T♥8♦

Action: Berman checks. Hellmuth bets $2,000 and Berman calls. The pot is $8,000.

Turn: J♥

Action: Both players check.

Analysis: Berman should bet his top pair (plus gutshot draw) to get value from a strong hand.

River: 5♠

Action: Berman bets $3,000 and Hellmuth calls.

Analysis: Berman makes a fine value bet with top pair when it appears that Hellmuth has little. Clearly Hellmuth will not fold his two-pair, but the question is: Should he just call or can he reraise for value?

There are only a few possible straights, and Berman has not shown much strength. It is true that he might make a small bet with hands stronger than Hellmuth's, and he would certainly call a raise with a strong two-pair or better. Berman could also make this playing sequence with a pair of kings, or possibly jacks. Hellmuth has shown no strength so far, and the pot is small. So this is a reasonable time to raise any two-pair hand. And with only the weakest possible two-pair, Hellmuth could fold facing most three-bets which would tend to come only from straights or higher two-pairs.

Nonetheless, calling with a low two-pair does not forfeit much value. A high two-pair, such as kings and tens, would be a mandatory value-raise because not only might a high pair call, but you are ahead of almost all two-pair hands — all of which will certainly call. In summary: Hellmuth should raise with a high two-pair or better, call with a good one-pair hand, and cannot make a big mistake either way with a weak two-pair.

The Call-Bluff

Suppose you bet into a board of

and your opponent calls on the button. Assuming he is not a calling station, what hand would you put him on?

Most likely a queen or a nine. Or more accurately, you would be sufficiently concerned by this possibility that you would need a decent hand to put more money into this pot on a future street.

The call-bluff is an advanced play used to exploit positional advantage when you have the button. The idea is that you call on the flop, intending to win the pot by betting the turn if your opponent checks. The board should be one that is unlikely to have helped your opponent, such as a paired flop, or three low cards (without significant draw potential) in a raised pot.

This play works best against aggressive, thinking opponents. If your opponent is passive, his aggressive lead-out is likely to indicate strength. If your opponent is a maniac, then he may proceed to follow-up bet the turn with a wide range of hands. But a smart, aggressive player may be worried by your flop call, and if he indeed lacks a hand, will tend to give it up to your turn bet. However, this play is easily overused, and if you are routinely "floating" these uncoordinated flops without a hand, your opponent is much less likely to interpret your call as strength.

Effective stacks: $200
Blinds: $1-$2

Note: Your opponent is a smart, aggressive player.

Your hand: 6♥5♥

Action: You raise to $6 on the button and your opponent calls. The pot is $12.

Flop: T♠T♦9♣

Action: Your opponent bets $8 and you call. The pot is $28.

Analysis: Your 6-high is certainly inferior now, and you are not drawing to anything. What does your opponent have? Most likely two unpaired high cards since he would reraise many pocket pairs before the flop, and the flop is paired, so there are relatively few hands he would call with preflop that connected. You suspect your opponent is weak, but you can't even beat a bluff.

However, if you raise:

1. Your opponent may have two high cards, but be unconvinced by your raise which looks like it might indeed be a move. And,

2. You will commit a lot of chips on a bluff without much information.

So folding is reasonable because you do not have to make an elaborate play. But suppose you elect to call.

Turn: 4♦

Action: Your opponent checks. You bet $15 and he folds.

Analysis: The turn blank is exactly what you wanted. Any ace or face card could make your opponent top pair, or possibly a straight, but a four is unlikely to have helped him. Meanwhile, his check probably indicates genuine weakness. If you bluff now, you will often take down the pot. Your opponent will almost certainly fold two high cards, and with your position and significant remaining stack a looming threat for the river, he might even lay down a hand of modest value such as a small pocket pair.

The key point about call-bluffing, however, is that it is a fancy play and requires a confident read of your opponent to employ it. If he is loose-reckless, then he may call or raise liberally and you have thrown away chips for no reason. However, against a thinking, aggressive foe, this play can be used sparingly to mix up your game.

Call-Bluffing without Position

We return to the *2005 National Heads-up Poker Championships* where Antonio Esfandiari tries a high-risk variant of the call-bluff against Daniel Negreanu.

Effective stacks: $40,000
Blinds: $200-$400

Esfandiari's hand: 7♥2♠
Negreanu's hand: 8♠6♦

Action: Negreanu limps on the button and Esfandiari checks. The pot is $800.

Flop: 9♦4♣4♥

Action: Esfandiari checks. Negreanu bets $600 and Esfandiari calls. The pot is $2,000.

Analysis: Negreanu's eight-high has little showdown value (even though it is actually the best hand at the moment, but Negreanu cannot know this), so he makes a bet to try to win immediately. Negreanu knows it is unlikely Esfandiari has connected with this flop since it is paired and only five cards in the deck can help him. Esfandiari is actually sitting on an even weaker hand than Negreanu with his seven-high. Why, then, does he call out of position with a trash hand?

Esfandiari decides to call-bluff because he knows Negreanu is equally unlikely to have hit this flop. Esfandiari is out of position, so his plan is to check-call the flop and then bet on the turn or river.

The default play in Esfandiari's situation is to fold. But if you are going to bluff, calling lowers the chip fluctuations relative to raising immediately which may appear more suspicious to Negreanu since an opponent with trip fours would usually check-call.

Turn: A♥

Action: Both players check.

River: Q♠

Action: Esfandiari bets $1,100 and Negreanu folds.

Analysis: After each player checks the turn, Esfandiari's belief that Negreanu does not have a hand is pretty much confirmed. Furthermore, Esfandiari cannot beat the board (and amusingly, neither can Negreanu). So he executes the bluff component of his call/bluff and indeed wins the pot.

After the hand, Esfandiari says, "I made it on the turn." Negreanu replies, "You had it all the way." Unless Negreanu is lying about his perception of Esfandiari's hand (as Esfandiari is lying to Negreanu, suggesting he was playing an ace), then

Negreanu's comment indicates Esfandiari's flop call at the paired flop did indeed convince him that his opponent flopped trip fours.

This out-of-position call-bluff is a risky play as Esfandiari discovers in his later match-up facing Scott Fischman.

Blinds: $400-$800

Esfandiari's hand: J♥5♥
Fischman's hand: K♣Q♠

Action: Fischman limps and Esfandiari checks. The pot is $1,600.

Analysis: We have already seen the complicated button-limping dynamic between these two players, but normally you should raise with king-queen.

Flop: A♣K♦2♣

Action: Esfandiari checks. Fischman bets $800 and Esfandiari calls. The pot is $3,200.

Analysis: With no hand and no draw, it is strange that Esfandiari calls this bet. Folding would be the standard play, and raising might allow Esfandiari to win immediately. Call-bluffing is a lot easier with position. Lacking any hand, any draw, and position, you should almost always fold here.

Turn: 5♠

Action: Esfandiari bets $1,200. Fishman calls. The pot is $5,600.

Analysis: Esfandiari catches a low pair and bets. The problem is that his bet is so small that Fischman will fold few hands getting nearly 4-to-1 odds. Meanwhile, Fischman's second pair lends itself to at most three bets entering the pot post-flop, so he calls.

River: 8♦

Action: Both players check.

Analysis: Both players elect to show down cheap. Esfandiari would probably have fired a larger turn or river bullet if he had not paired for the purpose of completing his call-bluff sequence. But with a pair that could win a showdown, Esfandiari correctly checks.

When the Turn Brings an Overcard

One common situation in heads-up occurs when the flop is bet and called, and the turn comes an overcard. What makes this interesting is the best hand the flop bettor is representing, top pair, is now second pair. If you were the flop bettor, then the presence of an overcard will often change your turn decision.

If you bet the flop as a bluff or C-bet without any piece you should be more inclined to bet again than had a blank fallen. Compare the following two situations.

Blinds: $15-$30

Your hand: A♠7♣

Action: You raise to $90 on the button and Villain calls. The pot is $180.

Flop: 9♣4♥2♠

Action: Villain checks. You bet $120 and he calls. The pot is $420.

Turn: 5♥

Action: Villain checks.

Question: *What is your play?*
> **Answer:** You should generally check. Villain's call on the flop indicates he likes his hand, and the turn card changes little. Any pair he believed good enough to call a bet on the

flop is probably good enough for him to call another bet at the turn.

Meanwhile, with the same preflop and flop action, suppose the turn instead is ...

Turn: K♥

Action: Villain checks.

Question: *What is your play?*
> **Answer:** You should strongly consider a follow-up bluff of around $250. Villain will be much less inclined to play a large pot with a low pair now that a king has hit. In addition, your action so far is consistent with many hands that hold a king. Multiple king-high hands are strong enough to merit a raise preflop, and you would still probably have bet the flop with just overcards. So even if you missed the flop, you could very well have just made top pair. So unless Villain is trapping with a strong hand, or he is a calling station, it will be difficult for him to call another sizeable turn bet with just a low pair or weak draw.

But if you have actually connected with the flop, the opposite principle will tend to hold. For instance:

Blinds: $15-$30

Your hand: 9♦8♦

Action: You raised your button to $90 and Villain calls. The pot is $180.

Flop: 9♣4♥2♠

Action: Villain checks. You bet $120 and he calls. The pot is $420.

Turn: 5♥

Action: Villain checks.

Question: *What is your play?*
>   **Answer:** You should bet. You have top pair, and you need to bet for value. You are fine with an immediate win, as a pair of nines can be cracked.

And if the turn instead is an overcard...

Turn: K♥

Action: Villain checks.

Question: *What is your play?*
>   **Answer:** Consider checking behind. Betting is often correct, such as if Villain is loose-passive. But you should be much more inclined to check this turn than the 5♥ because not betting keeps your decision-making simple.
>   Your second pair hand is good for two post-flop bets against most opponents. If you check behind, then on the river you can bet if Villain checks, and call if he bets. If you had bet the turn and Villain check-raises, or even calls and then leads on the river, you will have a difficult decision to make. Do you play a much larger pot than you would like with second pair, or do you lay down a strong hand? Checking simplifies this decision considerably and when

faced with a difficult decision, it becomes easy to make a mistake.

Yes, sometimes the free card you give Villain by checking will let him outdraw you. But nonetheless, the ability to play exactly the size pot you want tends be worth this risk and in the long run should maximize your expectation.

We now return to the dynamic match-up between Antonio Esfandiari and Scott Fischman to look at a hand whose flow changes entirely when an overcard hits the turn.

Blinds: $800-$1,600

Esfandiari's hand: A♦T♦
Fischman's hand: A♥9♦

Action: Esfandiari raises to $4,100 on the button and Fischman calls. The pot is $8,200.

Flop: T♣7♣5♠

Action: Fischman checks. Esfandiari bets $5,400 and Fischman calls. The pot is $19,000.

Analysis: Fischman should either fold or reraise. Folding would be the standard choice since he only has ace-high and lacks position. Out of position, it is difficult to steal the pot later in a hand, so calling is the worst option. He may be doing this to remain unpredictable, or as a call-bluff, but normally check-calling a substantial bet with ace-high on this coordinated flop is a losing play.

Turn: K♥

Action: Fischman checks. Esfandiari bets $11,000. Fischman raises to $30,500 and Esfandiari folds.

Analysis: The flop is one where Esfandiari wants three bets to enter the pot with his top pair and top kicker, but with second pair, two bets are better. So when Fischman checks, Esfandiari should check as well to ensure the pot is played for exactly two post-flop bets. He can achieve this by betting the river if Fischman checks again, and otherwise calling a bet. The only downside to this strategy is a free card might improve Fischman to the winning hand, but unless the board is very draw-heavy, this risk is usually worth it for the full ability to control the pot size.

    If the turn had come the 2♦ or another blank, Esfandiari would be correct to fire again, but an overcard should often be checked. Meanwhile, Fischman's preflop and flop calls are fully consistent with two unpaired high cards. He could certainly have a hand such as K♣Q♦ or K♠J♠, and his check-raise represents precisely such a holding. Fischman's strategy in this hand is very risky, but pulling the trigger on a turn overcard is a powerful play, and he gets Esfandiari to lay down a strong hand since Fischman is representing a hand that's even stronger.

Checking the Turn when You are Strong

One theme of this book has been to value bet your strong hands. But against a perceptive opponent, you must sometimes check when strong. Otherwise, this player can exploit your straightforward betting patterns by betting when you check, even if he is weak. If your opponent has position, he could make a habit of call-bluffing the flop with a wide range of hands. For instance, suppose Hero has always bet the turn when he has held a strong hand earlier in the match.

Effective Stacks: $1,500
Blinds: $10-$20

Hero's hand: A♠2♠

Action: Villain limps on the button. Hero raises to $80 and Villain calls. The pot is $160.

Flop: K♥4♦4♣

Action: Hero bets $120 and Villain calls. The pot is $400.

Turn: 6♥

Action: Hero checks. Villain bets $250 and Hero folds.

Analysis: Villain could hold any hand with which he would limp and call pre-flop because he knows most hands do not connect with a paired flop, and if Hero did indeed miss, then he can win by betting after Hero checks the turn.

Clearly, Hero does not want Villain to have this knowledge of how to exploit his play. An unimproved ace-high will often be the best hand at the showdown, so letting Villain claim the pot at the turn with a weaker hand is undesirable.

The way to avoid getting exploited in this fashion is to occasionally check your strong hands on the turn. You may then check-raise a turn bet, or value bet the river if your opponent also checks. Adding this randomizing component to your turn check/bet decision will make it difficult for your opponent to attempt exploitative turn plays.

Effective Stacks: $2,800
Blinds: $30-$60

Hero's hand: T♠6♠

Action: Villain limps on the button and Hero checks. The pot is $120.

Flop: K♥T♣6♣

Action: Hero bets $100 and Villain calls. The pot is $320.

Turn: 5♥

Action: Both players check.

River: 9♦

Action: Hero bets $200. Villain raises to $750 and Hero folds. Villain voluntarily shows 8♠7♣ for a rivered straight.

Analysis: Normally, Hero should bet the turn. But when he checks instead, Villain may check behind on a board with multiple straight and flush draws. If any of these draw cards hit, or a king or a five comes, Villain might shut down if he holds a one-pair hand. Furthermore, Villain might be willing to call turn and river bets with a weak hand, yet might not bet himself if he is checked to.

So these are compelling reasons for Hero to bet the turn. However, if he always bets for these reasons, then Villain would know that he could probably win the pot by betting when Hero checks. Therefore, Hero should sometimes not bet with the intent of check-raising and/or value betting most river cards.

Slowplaying

Only rarely do you not want to bet or raise when you have a hand that strongly figures to be best. The two most important reasons not to "slowplay" are:

1. You may not succeed in building a bigger pot. And,

2. A card may hit that either improves your opponent to a better hand than yours, or alternatively scares him away from playing a large pot.

Slowplaying is deceptive since you are representing a weak hand when you are actually strong, but deception is not necessarily beneficial. For instance, suppose you start with

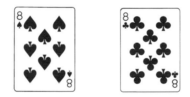

raise to three big blinds, and get called by a loose-passive opponent creating a $120 pot. The flop is:

and you both check.

In this hand, you may indeed have convinced your loose-passive opponent that you do not hold a set. So what? If you bet, he can still call with his pair of treys, ace-high, queen-seven, etc. So deception in this spot only nets you a smaller average pot when you rake in the chips at the river.

The one time where slowplaying is clearly correct is when you have the board so monopolized that your best chance of winning a sizeable pot is for your opponent to connect with the turn card or decide to bluff. The classic example is flopping quads.

Blinds: $10-$20
Note: Your opponent is tight-aggressive.

Your hand: 7♣4♠

Action: You limp in the small blind and your opponent checks. The pot is $40.

Flop: 4♣4♦4♥

Action: You both check.

Analysis: Clearly your opponent does not have a piece of this flop. The only possible hand of value he could have is a pocket pair, which is uncommon in heads-up, plus your aggressive opponent probably would have raised your preflop limp if he held a pair. So check this flop. If your opponent makes a full house on the turn, he might be willing to play a large pot. If he misses the turn he may bluff, figuring that it is unlikely you have connected.

In the following hands, you have a very strong hand. You must decide whether it is correct to slowplay.

Effective stacks: $14,000

Blinds: $100-$200

Your hand: 6♥6♣

Action: You raise to $500 on the button and Villain calls. The pot is $1,000.

Flop: Q♠T♥6♣

Action: Villain checks.

Question: *Should you check?*

> **Answer:** Your hand is strong enough that you will rarely be outdrawn on the turn, but you should still bet. You want to extract maximum value from your better hands, and doing so will require as many medium-large bets as possible going into the pot by the showdown. Declining a flop betting round limits the final pot size.
>
> Also, if Villain checks a queen or a ten intending to call or raise your bet, he may be much less willing to play a large pot if an ace or king hits on the turn. In addition, Villain will probably be expecting you to make a standard C-bet if you have been playing an aggressive style, and failing to do so may only make him suspicious. So you should go ahead and bet around $500-$800.

Effective stacks: $1,400

Blinds: $10-$20

Your hand: K♣K♠

Action: Villain min-raises to $40 on the button.

Question: *Should you just call?*
    Answer: No. You have a premium hand and should stick in a sizeable raise to around $150-$200. If you just call, not only are you offering any ace the free chance to outdraw you, but you are limiting the size of the final pot. If you raise and Villain calls, he will probably not be able to get away from a lower top pair. This is no longer true when you only call his raise and the pot is much smaller. So reraise for value rather than slowplay when you hold a premium hand preflop.

Action: You raise to $175 and Villain calls. The pot is $350.

Flop: K♦6♥5♥

Question: *Bet for value, or check as a slowplay?*
    Answer: Bet. Your check might look suspicious. Your failure to bet may make you forfeit a betting round. Also, if Villain has two hearts or a straight draw, he will often call a bet, but shut down if the turn or river doesn't improve his hand.
    Another reason not to slowplay is that draws that would call now cannot put more money into the pot after they have missed. So betting earlier in the hand may be the only time a drawing hand will call a bet.

Effective stacks: $1,000

Blinds: $20-$40
Note: Your opponent is aggressive.

Your hand: 8♠7♠

Action: Your opponent raises to $120 on the button and you call. The pot is $240.

Flop: 8♣8♦2♥

Question: *Should you check to slowplay?*
    Answer: Yes. Checking here is good strategy because your hand is best, and if you check you can expect to win at least your opponent's C-bet. There are no possible draws or turn scare cards, so you can check the flop, and then bet or check-raise the turn or river.

Effective stacks: $1,500

Blinds: $10-$20

Your hand: A♠4♠

Action: You raise to $60 on the button and your opponent calls. The pot is $120.

Flop: A♥9♦2♣

Action: Your opponent bets $80.

Question: *Call or raise?*
    Answer: Calling is good, but it is not a slowplay. With top pair you generally want three post-flop bets to enter the pot. Your opponent has made the first one, raising will usually win the pot outright when you are ahead, and put extra bets in when your opponent has a higher ace. A weak top pair hand figures to be best in heads-up, but it is not strong enough that "slowplaying" is an applicable word to describe your play.

Getting
Value from Quads

Chris Ferguson has a 3-to-2 chip lead in his match against TJ Cloutier.

Blinds: $4,000-$8,000

Cloutier's hand: A♠T♥
Ferguson's hand: A♣6♠

Action: Cloutier raises to $24,000 from the button and Ferguson calls. The pot is $83,000.

Flop: 6♣6♦6♥

Action: Ferguson checks. Cloutier bets $35,000 and Ferguson calls. The pot is $118,000.

Analysis: Ferguson is correct to slowplay since he has the board monopolized. Cloutier cannot improve to win so there is no danger in allowing a free card. Furthermore, if Cloutier has no piece of the hand now, then Ferguson's only hope of extracting more value is if Cloutier decides to execute a follow-up bluff, or the turn or river pair Cloutier, in which case he will probably assume that his full house is best and be willing to play a large pot. (Cloutier could also have a pair in his hand.)

Turn: 9♠

Action: Ferguson checks. Cloutier bets $80,000. Ferguson raises all-in to $317,700 and Cloutier folds.

Analysis: If Cloutier started with a low-mid pocket pair, or has just paired his nine, then he will very likely call an all-in reraise now, but he could get away from this hand if the river brings an overcard. So Ferguson's fast turn play is a much better time to apply pressure in this hand than the monopolized flop.

While Cloutier's bet prevents Ferguson from drawing to a free full house if behind, ace-high has strong showdown value on this board, so checking to ensure a cheap showdown would have been a good alternative to betting.

Handling a Full House

This next hand features Los Angeles Laker's owner Jerry Buss and Daniel Negreanu.

Blinds: $400-$800

Buss's hand: 6♣5♣
Negreanu's hand: Q♥5♠

Action: Negreanu limps on the button and Buss checks. The pot is $1,600.

Flop: Q♦Q♣5♦

Action: Buss bets $3,000 and Negreanu calls. The pot is $7,600.

Analysis: On the flop, Buss makes a solid lead bet, although betting more than the pot size is unnecessary. He has a hand likely to be best, yet many overcards devalue his holding and he is out of position.

Negreanu, meanwhile, is correct to slowplay by calling this bet. He has the board monopolized, and Buss's overbet is quite sufficient to build the pot. If Buss is on a bluff, Negreanu's only chance of winning more chips is if Buss improves on the turn, or decides to bluff again.

Turn: K♥

Action: Buss checks. Negreanu bets $3,000 and Buss folds.

Analysis: Buss correctly gives up when he has not improved after being called on the flop. Negreanu tries to eek out more value by making a callable turn bet, and there is nothing else he can do when Buss folds his marginal hand.

Playing a
Premium Hand Aggressively

In our next hand, Daniel Negreanu finds himself facing a monster hand, but his opponent, Antonio Esfandiari, elects not to slowplay. The problem? Negreanu has a premium hand as well.

Esfandiari: $34,600
Negreanu: $45,400

Blinds: $400-$800

Esfandiari's hand: T♠T♦
Negreanu's hand: A♥K♥

Action: Negreanu raises to $2,000 on the button and Esfandiari calls. The pot is $4,000.

Flop: T♥7♦5♥

Action: Esfandiari bets $2,500. Negreanu raises to $7,500. Esfandiari reraises to $17,500. Negreanu reraises again all-in and Esfandiari calls.

Analysis: First, note that it would have been reasonable for Esfandiari to reraise preflop. Given that he doesn't, Esfandiari's decision to bet with his top set is both unconventional and effective. Unconventional because he has the nuts, and most would be inclined to slowplay, particularly since Negreanu is likely to C-bet most flops after having raised preflop. The main reason Esfandiari's leadout is effective is that if Negreanu has caught any piece of this flop or has an overpair, he will often end up playing for all his chips because he knows most players would check a strong hand into him. Betting not only works toward Esfandiari's goal of pot growth, but it will probably appear weaker to Negreanu than would a check-raise or check-call.

From Negreanu's perspective, his flush draw and double-overcards make for fifteen outs. So unless Esfandiari has two-pair or better, Negreanu is 54 percent to improve to a likely best hand even if he is behind now. So Negreanu makes a semi-bluff raise, happy to build the pot immediately.

Esfandiari can either call or reraise immediately. How does he decide? Esfandiari knows Negreanu can call his unexpected leadout widely given the favorable odds and Negreanu's preflop show of strength. But Negreanu chooses to raise instead, indicating that he wants to build a big pot with a flop of T♥7♦5♥. Let's look at several holdings consistent with Negreanu's play, and consider the effects of calling versus reraising now.

1. **Negreanu holds a ten:** Even with three tens accounted for, there are still remaining hands that contain a ten, and Negreanu's actions so far are consistent with a top pair hand. Say Negreanu holds J♦T♣. Then he will be less likely to go all-in if the turn comes any card queen or higher, as well as a seven, five, or another mid heart. Negreanu might fold top

pair on the flop, but with the many possible draws, he is more likely to commit on the flop than he will be if many turn cards hit. So in this case, Esfandiari is indeed better-off three-betting immediately.

2. **Negreanu holds a strong draw, such as a straight draw or the two high hearts he actually holds:** If Negreanu improves to a straight or flush which does not pair the board, this is obviously the worst possible case for Esfandiari since he is behind. If Negreanu doesn't improve, he may be unwilling to go all-in with only one card left to come instead of two.

   With A♥K♥, for example, if the turn comes one of the eight hearts that do not pair the board, this is disastrous for Esfandiari. If the turn comes a blank (e.g. the 2♠), then Negreanu's perceived winning chances drop to under 3-to-1 if he is behind, and so he may no longer be willing to go all-in. Only if the turn comes one of the six remaining aces or kings will Negreanu be more likely to commit all his chips while still an underdog.

   Let us prove that Esfandiari should reraise if he knew that Negreanu held a strong draw such as A♥K♥. We will assume that if Esfandiari reraises the flop, Negreanu will commit all his chips since his draw gives him over 50 percent showdown equity against most hands. If Esfandiari calls instead, then the $19,000 pot will be nearly as big as the $25,100 left to be wagered. Thus we will assume that any remaining wagering is all-in, which is reasonable since a standard wager in proportion to the pot leaves stacks that are small relative to the pot.

   As for the turn card, if it is:

- A blank and Esfandiari bets again, then Negreanu could either call or fold because he will be getting pot odds of 2.3-to-1 which requires showdown equity of greater than

30 percent for a profitable call. Normally a 15-out draw would gives approximately 32 percent showdown equity, but Negreanu might correctly discount his 6 one-pair outs in the face of such strength. So let's assume that he is equally likely to call or fold facing the turn bet when a blank hits.

- A non-heart that pairs the board, let's assume that Negreanu will always fold since he must now discount all his outs.

- A jack or a queen, then Negreanu will always call since he now has three more outs to a nut hand.

- An ace or a king, then Negreanu will certainly commit the rest of his chips. And,

- A heart, then Esfandiari will check and fold since his 23 percent showdown equity is not sufficient to call.

These assumptions are clearly conservative since in practice Esfandiari would not actually know his opponent's hand with certainty and would therefore be more likely to pay off.

The turn will come a blank 40 percent of the time since 18 of the remaining 45 cards are non-broadway, non-hearts that do not pair the board. When a blank does fall, 50 percent of the time Negreanu folds and Esfandiari's stack increases to $44,100. The remaining times, Esfandiari will double his stack 84.1 percent of the time for an expected final stack of $58,200.

Here are the remaining turn possibilities

Esfandiari's Expected Stack
After the Hand as a Function of the Turn Card

Turn	Example	Number of Possible Cards	Probability	Esfandiari's Expected Stack
Blank	2♠	18 out of 45	40%	$51,150
Heart that pairs the board	7♥	1 out of 45	2.2%	$69,200
Heart that doesn't pair the board	J♥	8 out of 45	17.8%	$25,100
Non-heart that pairs the board	5♠	5 out of 45	13.3%	$44,100
Ace or king	A♠	6 out of 45	13.3%	$56,600
Non-heart jack or queen	Q♠	6 out of 45	13.3%	$53,470

Esfandiari's expected stack at the end of the hand when calling the flop bet is therefore $47,000.

$$\$47,000 = (.40)\big[(.50)(\$44,100) + (.50)(\$58,200)\big]$$
$$+ (.022)(\$69,200) + (.178)(\$25,100)$$
$$+ (.133)(\$44,100 + \$56,600 + \$53,470)$$

However if Esfandiari goes all-in at the flop, his expected stack size at the end of the hand is $51,500.

$$\$51,500 = (.744)(\$69,200)$$

Therefore Esfandiari does indeed have a higher expectation by reraising the flop rather than calling when Negreanu has a strong draw such as A♥K♥. This holds even if Esfandiari knew Negreanu's exact hand and never paid him off when he completed his draw on the turn.

3. **Negreanu holds two pair, most likely seven-five (since three tens are already accounted for):** Even in this case, there is no turn card that could come (besides one of the four remaining sevens or fives) that would make Negreanu more inclined to get his chips all-in than he would be on the flop.

So Esfandiari's flop three-bet is a good play for most hands that Negreanu is likely to have after raising the flop. Negreanu cannot be faulted for committing all his chips at this flop. Even though he knows Esfandiari must have connected after betting and raising, the strength of his hand combined with the already-sizeable pot compel Negreanu to continue with his mega-draw.

Playing Two-Pair Fast

This next hand features Paul Phillips and Phil Hellmuth.

Blinds: $400-$800

Hellmuth's hand: K♠9♠
Phillips' hand: 9♣6♣

Action: Phillips limps on the button and Hellmuth checks. The pot is $1,600.

Flop: J♣9♦6♥

Action: Hellmuth checks. Phillips bets $1,600 and Hellmuth calls. The pot is $4,800.

Analysis: Phillips makes a solid bet here. He has a strong hand, but bottom two-pair is also vulnerable to many turn cards, so making a full pot-sized bet is much better than checking or min-betting. Hellmuth could have bet out himself, and now he must at least call getting 2-to-1 odds with mid-pair and an overcard kicker.

Turn: K♥

Action: Hellmuth checks. Phillips bets $3,000 and Hellmuth calls. The pot is $10,800.

Analysis: Both players have two-pair. Paul Phillips has every reason to believe his two-pair is best, and he could even make a larger value bet. Any ten or queen puts four to a straight on board, and any jack or king counterfeits his second pair. So Phillips' hand, while strong, may not look nearly as good at the river.

Gabe Kaplan comments that Phil Hellmuth should raise Paul Phillips' turn bet. Hellmuth could have led out the betting this round, but having checked, it's also my opinion that he should check-raise. Hellmuth wants to get all his chips in the center with only one betting round to come, and there are many possible scare cards that could hit on the river, so raising immediately is better strategy.

River: A♥

Action: Hellmuth bets $3,500 and Phillips calls.

Analysis: Hellmuth has a tricky decision here. There is a slight chance his opponent has outdrawn him with a better two-pair, straight, or backdoor flush. Meanwhile, most hands Phillips liked on the flop such as queen-nine or jack-ten, will appear weaker now. Hellmuth must bet because if he checks, Phillips is likely to check behind with many weaker hands that would call a bet, and Phillips' call with bottom two-pair is a good decision.

Slowplaying the Slowplayer

This next hand features both Phil Hellmuth and Huck Seed making big hands.

Blinds: $1,500-$3,000

Hellmuth's hand: 2♦2♠
Seed's hand: J♦3♣

Action: Hellmuth calls on the button and Seed checks. The pot is $6,000.

Flop: J♠3♠2♣

Action: Seed checks. Hellmuth bets $3,000. Seed raises to $14,000 and Hellmuth calls. The pot is $34,000.

Analysis: Both players flop monster hands. Hellmuth makes a mandatory bet to build the pot, and Seed pulls the trigger on an overbet check-raise. With top two-pair on a rather coordinated flop out of position, a large raise-size is a solid play.

Gabe Kaplan points out that the match could easily end here, and that most players in Hellmuth's shoes would simply reraise all-in and Hellmuth should do just that. If Seed has an unlikely bluff, he will probably not keep on betting after Hellmuth calls this huge bet. If Seed is semi-bluffing a draw, Hellmuth should charge him now. If Seed has a made hand, such as a pair of jacks, many turn cards will kill the action — any overcard, in particular. So Hellmuth should reraise.

Turn: K♠

Action: Both players check.

Analysis: Both players should bet their strong hands for value rather than allow a free river which could allow their opponent to outdraw them, or possibly kill the action otherwise. And indeed, this is precisely what happens when the river comes a fourth spade.

River: 7♠

Action: Both players check.

Analysis: These checks are both correct with four spades on board. Either player is behind if his opponent has a spade (since Hellmuth's spade is the lowest in the deck), and so both want to show down their now-devalued hands as cheaply as possible.

But all good players switch gears, and in a hand during his match with Lyle Berman, Hellmuth plays a full house quickly on the flop.

Blinds: $800-$1,600

Berman's hand: A♦3♦
Hellmuth's hand: T♦8♦

Action: Hellmuth limps on the button. Berman raises to $7,600 and Hellmuth calls. The pot is $15,200.

Flop: T♥T♣8♠

Action: Berman checks. Hellmuth bets $4,000. Berman raises to $16,000. Hellmuth reraises to $37,000 and Berman folds.

Analysis: Hellmuth correctly decides to value bet this flop. He makes routine small bets with a wide variety of hands, and this is a paired board. So by betting, Hellmuth is building the pot in a way that looks like a cheap steal attempt. Meanwhile, Berman is getting nearly 5-to-1 on this call, and coupled with his considerable show of strength preflop, Hellmuth is confident that Berman will call with many hands. And even if Berman only calls this bet, the extra $8,000 in this pot will be significant in Hellmuth's quest to get Berman's entire stack by the river.

Berman's check-raise is reasonable given how few hands connect with this flop — ace-high will indeed often be best here. At this point, Hellmuth could put on the brakes rather than three-bet. The problem with three-betting is that Berman will probably require at least an eight to continue. Since Hellmuth has one ten and one eight, there are now a total of two eights and one ten left that Berman could hold. Unless Berman has one of these three remaining cards, or a higher pocket pair, he will probably fold.

But if Berman is on a bluff or semi-bluff, then he could put more chips in the pot at the turn or river if he pairs, makes a straight, or decides to bluff again. And by just calling, the pot will be nearly $50,000 after just a single round of betting. So Hellmuth should call Berman's raise rather than make a three-bet.

The biggest difference between this hand and the last one is the monopolization of the flop. In the hand against Seed, Hellmuth has bottom set on a board with two overcards and two low cards to a straight flush. So there are many hands Seed could go all-in with. But in this hand against Berman, Hellmuth has the nut full house on a paired board. Since there are fewer hands that connect with this flop, you should usually play it slower than the more coordinated flop with overcards and draws.

Bluffing Multiple Streets

While you must aggressively take stabs at many pots in heads-up, it is less often correct to bluff multiple streets, since by calling your first bluff (or two) in the hand, your opponent is saying he either likes his hand, or is willing to call bets lightly. You need a compelling reason to fire multiple bluffs. What are some of these reasons?

If you have bluffed the flop or turn with position, your opponent checks to you on the river, and your hand has no showdown value, then you should often bluff against most players because your opponent has shown a lack of interest in putting more money in the pot and your hand will lose a showdown.

Another situation is when the turn brings an overcard scare card. A common example is when you have position on an opponent, C-bet a missed a flop, and the fourth card to a straight or flush hits on the turn.

Blinds: $10-$20

Your hand: 5♠4♠

Action: You raise to $60 on the button and your opponent calls. The pot is $120.

Flop: Q♦9♣8♥

Action: Your opponent checks. You bet $80 and he calls. The pot is $280.

Turn: T♠

Action: Your opponent checks and you bet $175.

Analysis: The turn ten presents a good bluffing opportunity. Your opponent's flop call will often indicate a pair, and with four cards to a straight on board, as well as two possibly higher pairs to a flopped middle-bottom pair, this will be a tough bet to call. As always, be much less inclined to bluff against a loose opponent, but against a tight-passive or even unknown opponent, this scare card presents an excellent opportunity to steal.

So bluffing a turn overcard, or other scare card, can be another good reason to bluff multiple streets. A final reason is when you bluff the flop and pick up a draw on the turn, so betting is not a pure bluff since the draw component makes this a semi-bluff. Nevertheless, it is a situation where you are following up a bluff with another bet, still without a made hand.

Effective stacks: $2,200

Blinds: $25-$50
Note: Your opponent is tight-passive.

Your hand: 5♥4♠

Action: Your opponent limps on the button and you check. The pot is $100.

Flop: J♦8♥2♠

Action: You bet $75 and your opponent calls. The pot is $250.

Analysis: Your hand has no showdown value, so you attempt a steal. When your opponent calls, you resolve to shut down unless you improve.

Turn: 3♦

Action: You bet $175 and your opponent folds.

Analysis: With a draw to the nut straight, you would have to call a small bet were one made. Instead, you bet, hoping to win immediately, and if called you have the potential to hit a strong and disguised hand.

This play is best against a timid player capable of discarding second pair hands when faced with multiple post-flop bets. It is also a good play against an observant opponent if you have been routinely shutting down when you do not have a made hand and your flop bet has been called. Since you need to bluff occasionally on the later streets, partly so your opponents can not be sure that a second bet always means a strong hand, a good time to do this is when your hand improves to a potential semi-bluff such as the straight draw given here. Not only will this maximize expectation on these plays, but it will introduce a randomizing element into your strategy since you don't control the cards that come on board.

In this hand, Antonio Esfandiari attempts a multiple-street bluff in his match against Phil Hellmuth.

Blinds: $3,000-$6,000

Esfandiari's hand: T♦4♦
Hellmuth's hand: K♠Q♣

Action: Hellmuth limps on the button and Esfandiari checks. The pot is $12,000.

Analysis: Hellmuth limps with a strong hand. This would normally be a mistake, but Esfandiari has been aggressively attacking his button limps.

Flop: K♣6♠2♥

Action: Esfandiari bets $8,500 and Hellmuth calls. The pot is $29,000.

Turn: Q♦

Action: Esfandiari checks. Hellmuth bets $15,000. Esfandiari raises to $45,000. Hellmuth raises all-in to $417,000 and Esfandiari folds.

Analysis: Esfandiari's flop bluff is good strategy since his hand has no showdown value, and this two-thirds of the pot bet will often win immediately. The turn check-raise bluff is ill-advised. When you make a large bet which relies entirely on your opponent folding to show its profit, you want a reason to believe your opponent, who has already called one bet, will fold to a second. Hellmuth could decide to give up on a hand such as second pair against this show of strength assuming he would bet it in this spot, but these plays are much better when something new, such as two subsequent checks, a turn overcard, or a scare card, has happened.

When Hellmuth calls Esfandiari's bet at the raggedy flop, and then makes a solid turn bet, we can narrow his hand range. In particular, unless Hellmuth is on a stone bluff (which is possible), he is likely to have at least a pair of queens because he would probably not value bet third pair or a weaker hand.

So Esfandiari's bluff check-raise will work only if Hellmuth is bluffing or Hellmuth is willing to lay down a probable pair of queens or better when getting 2-to-1 odds in position. Since Esfandiari is risking $45,000 to win $44,000, he will show a profit if Hellmuth folds at least fifty percent of the time. But based on the strength Hellmuth has shown thus far, this assumption is unlikely to hold.

Meanwhile, if Hellmuth knew Esfandiari was bluffing, he would maximize his expectation by calling to induce a possible river bluff. But Esfandiari's show of strength indicates a real hand, so reraising immediately will often get all the chips in the center.

"Finishing Off" an Opponent

Suppose you are playing a standard online heads-up poker match with starting stacks of $1,500. You play well and get your opponent down to $500. It is often debated which is a better strategy: Should you go for the kill quickly so your opponent does not have an easy chance at reclaiming his chips? Or should you play a tight game so your opponent does not get an easy chance to double up?

The answer is that this question misses the point. We are only concerned with effective stacks, and so your strategy should not change whether you are the player with $500 or $2,500. Either way the most that can be wagered in a given hand is $500 since the player with the chip lead cannot bet anything beyond that. The leader's advantage is not that he can bet more in a given hand, but instead that if he does lose an all-in or fraction of his stack, he automatically reloads.

For instance, consider the following hand progression.

- **Hand No. 1:** Player A wins a $2,000 pot.

- **Hand No. 2:** Player A has $2,500 and Player B has $500.

Then both players can bet up to $500, but whereas Player B will be out of the match if he loses, Player A automatically reloads another $1,000 from the extra $2,000 he has behind him. Suppose Player B wins the hand.

- **Hand No. 3:** Player A has $2,000 and Player B has $1,000. Now both players can bet up to $1,000, with Player A automatically reloading from his additional $1,000 stack if he loses the hand.

So it is effective stacks that are important rather than which player is the chip leader and which player lags.

The second reason that our initial question on "finishing off" is difficult to answer is that optimal strategy depends heavily on the blinds. Let us return to the example of one player with only $500 chips.

With blinds of $200-$400, the blind alone is pot-committing and optimal strategy is simple: The player with the button puts in an extra $300, and the big blind calls for an extra $100.

However, with blinds of $10-$20, it would generally be a significant mistake to resort to shove-fold preflop poker with twenty-five big blinds in chips. With effective stacks this large, there is room to maneuver before and after the flop. So you would play whatever strategy you would normally pursue against this opponent with stacks twenty-five times the big blind.

In summary, the idea behind "finishing an opponent off" versus "preventing him from doubling up" is misguided in the context of heads-up tournament play. Instead, you should focus on the relevant parameters of effective stacks, stack-to-blind ratio, and exploiting your opponent's style. And whether you are the short stack or your opponent is, the same strategy applies.

Playing
the Very Short Stack

Suppose the effective stacks are small — say ten big blinds or fewer. Your emphasis will be on preflop play since there will be little room for post-flop maneuvering. This period of a heads-up is of crucial importance since many hands will involve putting your whole stack at risk. So let's look at the most important guidelines for short-stacked play.

First, if your opponent limps his button, raise all-in very widely because there is necessarily at least 20 percent of the effective stack size sitting on the table, and your opponent has not shown strength by calling.

For instance, the blinds are $50-$100 and you have a stack of $800. If your opponent limps, then the $200 on the table is a full quarter of your stack. In addition, if you check you'll be playing the remainder of the pot out of position. So by raising all-in you are seizing significant fold equity while nullifying your opponent's post-flop advantage.

Second, unless your opponent is a passive player, you should usually raise or fold before the flop. This is especially true if this person is a knowledgeable player since he will be significantly more likely to attack your button limp, or small button raise, than he would during lower-blind play. So when raising preflop, you should tend to raise all-in.

Suppose the blinds are $500-$1,000 with effective stacks of $10,000. You raise your button to $3,000, and your opponent reraises all-in. Then the pot is $13,000 and it costs you $7,000 to call. Getting pot odds of nearly 2-to-1, you are correct to call with almost any hand because the standard worst-case scenario is your opponent holding two overcards versus your undercards. In this case, you only are about a 2-to-1 underdog. (The classic example illustrating this last fact is that trey-deuce offsuit will beat ace-king 34 percent of the time.)

So rather than be forced into making a borderline call after raising, you should simply raise all-in. Then you might get an immediate fold.

Note that when you are raising preflop from the big blind, always raise your entire stack[9] because not only will your raise pot-commit you if you are reraised, but you will be out of position for the remainder of the hand if called.

Since the majority of short-stacked play consists of shove-call versus fold decisions, the best thing you can do to improve your play is learn when to make these decisions. For example, when considering an all-in move, how do you know whether it's more profitable to fold or shove?

The branch of math called Game Theory is often used to answer this question. While we do discuss unexploitable short-stack play below, for now, we'll stray from Game Theory and stick with decisions designed to exploit your individual opponent.

Hands to shove preflop depend entirely on what hands your opponent will call with. Suppose he is calling only with aces or kings. Then you could push all-in with any two cards since he will fold over ninety-nine percent of the time.

On the other hand, suppose he is calling with any two cards. Then you know you are getting called if you shove, so excluding the effect of the already-posted blinds, you should shove your above-average hands and fold the rest.

Of course, most opponents will not be quite so extreme. In the general case, you can have software analyze how many hands you can profitably shove when your opponent is calling with a

---

[9] "Always" is perhaps too strong a word. Possible exceptions occur when you have a premium hand and strongly want value, or you are "raising all-in without all your chips." See p. 164 of *Sit 'n Go Strategy* by Collin Moshman for more information.

given hand range. Here is a table summarizing the results for a loose caller.

Open Shoving Hands with Blinds of $50-$100 Against a Loose Caller

Effective Stacks	Calling Percentage	+EV Pushing Hands
$300	All Hands	Any pocket pair, ace, king, queen, jack, ten, 95+, 92s+, 86+, 84s+, 76+, 75s+
$500	Top 85%	Any pocket pair, ace, king, queen, J5+, J2s+, T7+, T5s+, 98+, 96s+, 87s+
$700	Top 55%	Any pocket pair, ace, king, Q5+, Q2s+, J8+, J6s+, T9+, T7s+, 97s+, 76s+
$1,000	Top 40%	Any pocket pair, ace, K8+, K6s+, QJ+, QTs+

(The software used for these calculations was *SitNGo Wizard*. Top N percent of hands in 5 percent increments are given in "Appendix C: Top N Percent Starting Hands" on page 381.)

How does the software decide on profitable shoving hands with five big blind stacks against an opponent who calls with 85 percent of the hands? It does an expected value calculation. 15 percent of the time you win 1.5 big blinds without a fight, and the remaining 85 percent of the time, you will be gambling for 5 big blinds with a hand winning X percent of the time against those hands (in the top 85 percent). If X is high enough such that your shoving EV is positive, then you should shove. Otherwise you fold.

From the loose opponent chart, we see that pushing any ace or pocket pair will almost always have a positive expectation with effective stacks of 10 big blinds or fewer. The larger the stacks, the higher the pushing standards you need. And as a general guide, push almost any two cards with effective stacks of 4 big blinds or less; with stacks of 5-7 big blinds, shove hands with either a high card or suited connecters; and stick with more recognizably solid hands with 8-10 big blinds.

The optimal shoving pattern facing a tight caller is much simpler:

Open Shoving Hands with Blinds of $50-$100 Against a Tight Caller

Effective Stacks	Calling Percentage	+EV Pushing Hands
$300	Top 65%	All hands
$500	Top 35%	All hands
$700	Top 25%	All hands
$1,000	Top 15%	All hands

The tight caller is easy to exploit. You win chips pushing on him with effective stacks of 10 big blinds or fewer, almost regardless of your holding, because he folds often enough that the immediate profit you make by stealing compensates for those times he calls with a better hand.

You will certainly encounter players against whom you can profitably open-shove any hand with short effective stacks. For instance, suppose you shove 3 big blinds into an opponent who

holds the

a hand just outside the 65 percent cutoff point. Despite getting 2-to-1 odds with ten-high, a hand that will win more than one time in three even when the raiser is discarding the entire bottom 50 percent of his starting hands, some players will fold because they do not want to gamble with a weak hand. Such opponents are very exploitable through wide shoving.

However, just because you can seize a slight chip profit shoving a junk hand into a tight opponent, you should not always make this play. This is particularly true against a passive player. An aggressive opponent is liable to attack your button limps, come over top of small steal-raises, and otherwise make life difficult if you play a non-shove-fold game. But passive players can often be outplayed with a smaller-pot strategy similar to how you would outplay him in deeper-stacked play. With very short stacks of 5 big blinds or fewer, it's usually not worth getting fancy with limps or smaller raises. But with stacks of 9 or 10 big blinds, you are often better continuing to chip away at a tight-passive player's stack rather than make a slightly +EV shove.

Note also that your opponent will tend to adjust his perception of your pushing range. Even a weak-tight player will usually widen his calling range if you push every hand. So realize that while the tight player may be unlikely to make a +EV odds-based call after you shove preflop once or twice, he will most likely loosen up if you make many pushes. This is another reason why you should sometimes limp, fold, or make a smaller raise even when you could earn a slight immediate profit with a preflop all-in.

In our section on the Metagame, we will address the question of adjustments and readjustments, and how they apply to pushing and calling ranges. Normally, however, the game lasts a limited number of hands once the effective stacks get to 10 big blinds or fewer because the first hand where the shorter stack goes all-in and loses will end the match. So you should concentrate primarily on what standards you think your opponent has to call an all-in raise, or make one himself ... and what hands are profitable to shove or call given these ranges.

Speaking of hands to call with, we reverse the focus of the above tables to see what type of hands merit a call for the tight and looser shovers. Recall that "Appendix C: Top N Percent Starting Hands" on p. 381 lists the starting hand percentiles.

All-In Calling Hands with Blinds of $50-$100 Against a Tight Shover

Effective Stacks	Shoving Percentage	+EV Calling Hands
$300	Top 60%	Top 86%
$500	Top 35%	31.5%
$700	Top 25%	16.7%
$1,000	Top 12%	5.9%

All-In Calling Hands With Blinds
of $50-$100 Against a Loose Shover

Effective Stacks	Shoving Percentage	+EV Calling Hands
$300	Top 100%	All hands
$500	Top 100%	81%
$700	Top 70%	70%
$1,000	Top 50%	26.8%

You are less inclined to play all-in pots facing a tight player's shove because they will have stronger hands when making this play. The loose-shover calling chart is particularly subjective since many hyper-aggressive players will shove nearly any two cards with effective stacks under 10 big blinds. And while such extreme aggression is usually not the best strategy, it is certainly preferable to the other extreme — folding until you get a good hand.

Let us summarize a calling strategy. Against a tight raiser, wait to raise yourself or until you pick up a sufficiently strong hand to call. Against a loose raiser, you will often have to make calls with many hands. If you are unsure, a good guideline is to follow the aggression principle — shove liberally since you may win immediately, and be more selective in your calls. Let's now put these ideas into action with short-stacked hand examples.

Effective stacks: $600
Blinds: $50-$100
Note: In this match, you have not raised all-in against a button limp.

Action: Your opponent limps on the button.

Question: *What is your play?*

    Answer: Raise all-in with any two cards. There is $200 on the table, a full third of your stack. Your opponent has shown no strength by limping, and you should attack no matter how weak your cards.

    The "no previous attack" clause is important. You should not play frightened poker, of course — but you must stay aware. An aggressive player will not usually limp with such short stacks, and even the most passive player will begin to feel foolish if you routinely take away his limps with shoves from the big blind. So whether you are facing a strong player setting a trap based on his perception of your aggression, or a weak player who makes an ego call ("He's pushed the last three hands on me, — that's it, I'm calling him!"), avoid pushing with junk when you have already established a reputation for attacking button limps.

Effective stacks: $1,500
Blinds: $75-$150
Note: Your opponent is loose-aggressive.

Your hand: A♠2♣

Question: *Call, raise, or fold?*

    Answer: Raise all-in. This shove is +EV regardless of your opponent's calling criteria. Meanwhile, low offsuit aces play poorly after the flop. Your hand is strong enough that you must at least call, and a limp or smaller raise will put you in a difficult position if your opponent raises all-in. So seize a guaranteed edge and shove preflop.

Effective stacks: $1,400
Blinds: $75-$150

Note: You have been routinely shoving your button against your tight-passive opponent.

Your hand: 6♠4♣

Question: *What is your play?*
    Answer: Call. From the chart above, we conclude that shoving would normally be +EV. And indeed, shoving is far from an unreasonable play regardless of your hand when facing a tight-passive opponent with short stacks. But calling is better for two reasons:

1.   Your opponent's calling range is likely to have loosened up since he has seen you pushing with such frequency, and with a wider calling range, these low suited semi-connectors will not do nearly as well.

2.   Even if shoving is slightly +EV, with effective stacks near 10 big blinds and a weak opponent, your expectation for the match will tend to be higher playing a smaller-pot strategy and continuing to chip away at his stack with plays like this limp, followed by a $150-$200 bet at any flop he checks. Be much more inclined to shove this hand against a player with a similarly tight calling range, yet with an aggressive style when he does play. Such a player in this situation is much more likely to attack a limp or small raise if you do not shove.

Effective stacks: $900
Blinds: $50-$100
Note: Your maniac opponent has shoved the past six hands any time you have not open-shoved yourself.

Your hand: K♠7♣

Action: Your opponent raises all in.

Question: *Call or fold?*
>   **Answer:** Call. If your opponent is shoving at least the top 50 percent of the starting hands, you have an edge calling with your mid-king. Based on our read and his recent play, your opponent is actually shoving much wider, perhaps any two cards.
>
>   Some will be hesitant to make this call, reasoning that even if your opponent is blindly shoving any two cards, a mid king is only an 11-to-9 favorite over the random distribution. And it's true, the pot is laying you slim odds, and you figure to be only a slight favorite on average.
>
>   What this illustrates is the strength of the hyper-aggressive playing style during short-stacked play. Your opponent may indeed be playing recklessly, but he is still forcing you to gamble as a marginal favorite or get blinded out. It is unlikely this match will last many more hands, and you cannot wait for a substantial edge which may never come. So seize any edge you can find, and calling your maniac opponent with this mid-king qualifies.

Effective stacks: $150
Blinds: $25-$50
Note: Your opponent is tight-aggressive.

Your hand: 9♠4♣

Action: Your opponent min-raises from the button.

Question: *What is your play?*
>   **Answer:** Commit the rest of your chips. Your opponent will not fold for another $50, so you are effectively considering whether to call your remaining $100 with $200 already on the

table. Getting 2-to-1 with a 9-high, you should call. Often you will be exactly a 2-to-1 underdog against two overcards. Occasionally you will be worse, such as when your opponent has you dominated. But many times you will only be a 3-to-2 underdog or better, facing hands like A♣2♣ or K♦8♥. So gamble now and hope for the best.

Now let us evaluate a series of all-in call-fold decisions in Huck Seed's match against Phil Hellmuth.

Effective stacks: $73,600
Blinds: $6,000- $12,000

Hellmuth's hand: A♣T♠
Seed's hand: Q♦8♠

Action: Seed raises all-in on the button and Hellmuth calls.

Analysis: With a stack of 6 big blinds, Seed is correct to shove wide even if Hellmuth is calling wide. A mid offsuit queen certainly merits a raise here, and with these high blinds, raising all-in is the best play. Hellmuth's call is clear with a high ace.

On Seed's next button, he shoves a slightly weaker hand with shallower stacks.

Effective stacks: $32,800
Blinds: $6,000-$12,000

Hellmuth's hand: K♣T♠
Seed's hand: J♣8♠

Action: Seed shoves $32,800 on the button and Hellmuth calls.

Analysis: Both men still play correctly. The noteworthy aspect of this hand is that either player could use this strategy without even looking at their cards. With a stack under 3 big blinds, Seed should push any two rather than get blinded out. And since the pot is laying Hellmuth better than 2-to-1, and he knows Seed will push any two, Hellmuth can also call no matter what his holding.

Seed survives, and makes a push that results in a seemingly loose call.

Effective stacks: $53,600
Blinds: $6,000-$12,000

Hellmuth's hand: K♦6♣
Seed's hand: J♣J♠

Action: Seed shoves $53,600 and Hellmuth calls.

Analysis: Hellmuth's call for another $40,000+ looks weak on TV when we see Seed's pocket jacks, but from Hellmuth's perspective, this is a reasonable call. He is getting better than 3-to-2, and he could even have the better hand. Indeed, Seed has shoved his last two buttons with weaker hands. Against many of Seed's better hands, such as A♠4♣, Hellmuth will still win about the 40 percent of the time he needs in order to show a profit.

Stop 'n Go

Whenever you are facing a button raise with a hand strong enough to commit all your chips, your one alternative to reraising all-in preflop is the Stop 'n Go. If you think your opponent will realize his bet has pot-committed him into calling a resteal, then you still might induce a fold if you only call his preflop raise and then bet all-in on the flop regardless of what hits.

If your opponent has missed, he might well fold rather than call a post-flop shove with a weak hand. A good time to execute this play is when holding a low-mid pocket pair. For example, you hold the

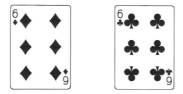

and your aggressive opponent makes a pot-committing steal-raise to $300. Your hand is too strong to fold, but if you call now and shove on the flop, he may fold if his hand does not improve. This betting sequence will win you a pot you would otherwise have lost when your opponent would have paired on a later street, or when the board double-pairs to counterfeit your small pair.

In summary, the stop 'n go is a technique used to increase pot-winning frequency when playing with short effective stacks out of position facing a pot-committing raise. You call the raise, then shove all-in on the flop regardless of what hits.

Effective stacks: $600
Blinds: $50-$100

Your hand: 4♠4♣

Action: Your opponent raises to $300.

Question: *What is your play?*

> **Answer:** Call, and then push all-in regardless of the flop. If you raise preflop your opponent will not fold another $300 having already committed $300 himself.
>
> But suppose the flop comes T♣6♠6♥. The pot contains $600 and you are betting $300. Your opponent holds Q♦7♦. He might fold his high card, figuring that you have a better hand. And when he does, you gain substantially despite being ahead because you are offering him 3-to-1 on the call and he is correct to call if he will win at least 25 percent of the time. Since any queen, ten, seven, or a running pair higher than four will give him the best hand, he is actually 38 percent to win. So you lose nothing by attempting this "stop 'n go," and when it works, you gain quite nicely.

Effective stacks: $800
Blinds: $50-$100

Your hand: K♠Q♣
Villian's hand: 4♣4♠

Action: Villain raises to $300 from the button and you call. The pot is $600.

Flop: 9♥8♥7♥

Action: You bet all-in and Villain folds two black fours.

This is an excellent result. Winning you $600 as opposed to being a 3-to-1 underdog with all your chips in the middle, as would likely have been the case if you had raised the extra $500 before the flop.

Going All-In
with a Raise Versus a Call

This next hand features Johnny Chan and James Woods.

Chan: $15,000
Woods: $25,000

Chan's hand: K♠T♥
Woods' hand: Q♠T♠

Action: Chan raises to $5,000 on the button and Woods calls. The pot is $10,000.

Flop: K♥J♥3♥

Action: Woods checks. Chan shoves $9,950 and Woods calls.

Analysis: Woods's chip commitment would be reasonable here if he had been the one to shove as a stop 'n go. Not only will he have the many partial outs to a straight or mid-high pair, but Chan might well fold a better hand if he does not hold a heart.

Check-calling this flop bet is the worst of Woods's options. He is a favorite to almost no hand Chan would push here. (He is even an underdog to two random cards.) And if he is willing to call this bet, he should go all-in himself. So due to the fold equity from the stop 'n go, hands that show positive expectation when you are the one initiating the all-in, become negative expectation plays when you call an all-in.

Action: The turn comes the A♣, but a river Q♥ gives Chan the hand-winning flush.

All-In
Calling: The 2-to-1 Rule

As we have stated, you should tend to call a preflop all-in bet when getting pot odds better than 2-to-1, almost regardless of your holding because pocket pairs are dealt with less frequency than unpaired cards — namely 16 no-pair hands for each pocket pair. And no no-pair hand is much more than a 2-to-1 favorite over another no-pair hand. This rule explains some unusual-seeming calls in many forms of tournament no-limit hold 'em.

Calling a Shove
with a Marginal Hand

This hand returns us to the second round of the 2005 National Heads-Up Poker Championship match between Phil Hellmuth and Paul Phillips.

Effective stacks: $13,100
Blinds: $2,000-$4,000

Hellmuth's hand: J♣5♠
Phillips' hand: A♣8♣

Action: Phillips shoves $13,100 on the button.

Question: Hellmuth, in the big blind, must put in $9,100 to call. *What should he do?*

Answer: The decision of whether to call or fold against this preflop all-in is strictly a matter of the pot odds Hellmuth is getting as well as his showdown equity against the range of hands Phillips will shove here.

Pot odds are easily calculated. The pot is $13,100 + $4,000 = $17,100, and it costs $9,100 to call. Therefore the pot odds are 1.88-to-1. In live play, it would be quite sufficient to estimate: "The pot's around $17k and it costs me about $9k to call, so I'm getting just under 2-to-1." We have said that you need a compelling reason *not* to call a preflop all-in when getting 2-to-1 or better. Here, Hellmuth is getting a bit worse than 2-to-1, but he does hold a face card. Since Phillips will (correctly) be pushing a wide range with his stack of barely over 3 big blinds, and Hellmuth's jack-high is a roughly average hand, he should call.

Another way of seeing this is that the J♣5♠ is a 53-to-47 underdog versus a random hand. Hellmuth's 1.9-to-1 odds mean that he needs to win 35 percent of the time to show a profit, and even against a hand as strong as Phillips's ace-eight, he exceeds this threshold at 36 percent. And Phillips could even be shoving a hand that Hellmuth is ahead of, such as the 7♦6♦.

Action: Hellmuth calls.

Final board: K♥J♦9♥8♠6♠ and Hellmuth wins the hand and the match.

Another pot odds call occurs in a match between Antonio Esfandiari and Ted Forrest.

Effective stacks: $34,000
Blinds: $2,000-$4,000

Esfandiari's hand: Q♠9♥
Forrest's hand: T♠T♣

Action: Forrest raises all-in on the button.

Question: Efandiari must pay $30,000 to call. *What should he do?*
Answer: Esfandiari could play for all his chips if he were the one shoving queen-nine offsuit. As the caller, the pot is laying him only slight odds of 5-to-4. So for the most part, Esfandiari should call this bet if he believes he is ahead of Forrest's range. The program *SNG Wizard* confirms that if Esfandiari thinks Forrest is pushing anything beyond the top 50 percent of starting hands, then this is a profitable call and so Esfandiari calls probably with this thought in mind.

Effective stacks: $300
Blinds: $50-$100
Note: Your opponent is tight-passive.

Your hand: 3♣2♠

Action: Your opponent shoves all-in from the button for $300.

Question: *Call or fold?*
Answer: You should fold. The pot is $400 and it costs you $200 to call. Getting exactly 2-to-1, you won't lose on average many chips by calling with your junk hand, but folding is better because you will almost never be better than 2-to-1, but anytime your opponent has a higher deuce or trey, or a less common pocket pair, you will be worse than 2-to-1. So you actually need a little better than 2-to-1 odds to show a profit.

Playing
Against Professionals

While you should not actively seek tough competition for a profitable match, if you do find yourself facing a much more skilled opponent, the nature of heads-up matches is such that you can partially neutralize this advantage by playing a hyper-aggressive style. One key skill that solid heads-up no-limit players all possess is an excellent ability to manipulate the pot size. Your mission, as the less skilled player, is to strip away your opponent's ability to accomplish this task.

First, make your default button raise larger than normal, say 4 to 5 big blinds instead of the more standard 2 to 3. This will force your opponent to play large pots out of position if he does not fold immediately.

Second, make large three-bets more often. When your opponent comes in for standard button raises, you should almost never call. A player who is both more skilled than you and has the button, will be able to outplay you postflop. This is fine, so long as you acknowledge the fact and avoid calling from the big blind. Instead, fold or force him to play a larger pot than he probably wishes to play.

Next, play aggressive post-flop. Make pot-sized C-bets almost any time you raise before the flop, and come over top of his bets widely when you have a piece of the board and your opponent might fold.

Lastly, lower your standards for calling an all-in bet. If you are getting good odds and think your hand may be best, then consider calling. Remember, skill is on your opponent's side. If you can turn the match into a gamble instead, you should seize the opportunity if the chip decision is close. By forcing your opponent to gamble, you are maximizing the importance of short-term luck in the outcome of the match.

A rich philanthropist buys you into the $25,000 *NBC National Heads-up Poker Championship*. In your first round match, you are pitted against a top-level professional with considerably more experience than you.

Effective stacks: $20,000
Blinds: $100-$200

Your hand: 7♥6♥

Question: *What is your play?*
    Answer: Raise to about $1,000. Remember, you want to maximize chip swings and big pots, and coming in with large preflop raises is an excellent way to achieve this goal.

Action: You raise to $1,000 and your opponent calls. The pot is $2,000.

Flop: T♦5♣4♥

Action: Your opponent bets $1,200.

Question: *What is your play?*
    Answer: Make a substantial raise to about $5,000. You have an open-ended straight draw, six outs to second pair which may be good, and a backdoor flush draw. Play this hand aggressively.

    A more standard play would be a raise to $3,000 or a flat-call, but you want to minimize late-street betting and aggressively force your opponent to fold or play large pots early, so make a large raise now.

You increase your stack size to $23,200.

Blinds: $100-$200

Your hand: K♥6♥

Action: Your opponent raises to $500 from the button.

Question: *What is your play?*
　　Answer: Fold or make a substantial reraise. Normally, you would not three-bet a low suited king, particularly not a large three-bet. But here we actively seek large chip swings, so when not folding you should make a large reraise.

Action: You reraise to $2,200 and your opponent calls. The pot is $4,400.

Flop: Q♣7♥2♠

Question: *Check or bet?*
　　Answer: Make a pot-sized bet. Anytime you raise or reraise before the flop, you will be making a large C-bet to exploit the fact that most flops miss most players. Furthermore, a professional player might call a smaller bet widely with position and his skill edge, but he will be less likely to play this strategy when faced with large bets.

Action: You bet $4,500 and your opponent raises to $11,000.

Question: *What is your play?*
　　Answer: Fold. Your opponent is effectively putting you all-in, and a lone high card is not strong enough to call.

You win several small pots in the following hands with large preflop raises. When the blinds hit $200-$400, you are back to even with $20,000 each.

Blinds: $200-$400

Your hand: 5♣4♥

Action: Your opponent calls from the button.

Question: *What is your play?*
>**Answer:** Consider making a big raise. You should attack his limps relentlessly. There is $800 sitting on the table, and your goal is to win this sum immediately. If he calls your large raise, then you will C-bet any flop.

Four hands later...

Blinds: $200-$400

Your hand: K♠7♣

Action: Your opponent limps on the button. You raise to $2,600 and he reraises all-in.

Question: *Call or fold?*
>**Answer:** Fold. If you call this bet, it is likely you will find yourself up against a mid-high pocket pair or ace-king. Even though you want to gamble, too often you will be a 70-to-30 dog. Since the pot is laying you slim odds, you should fold.

Analysis: One good thing is definitely happening. You have gotten the professional to play your game by forcing him to play preflop all-in poker, which was certainly not his strategy going into the match. Even though you lose over $2,000 this hand, his switch to "longball" suggests that your hyper-aggressive style is frustrating him.

Two hands later...

Blinds: $200-$400

Your hand: 6♥3♠

Action: Your opponent raises to $1,200 on the button.

Question: *What is your play?*
    Answer: Fold. You are playing a reraise-fold strategy from the big blind, and with this trash hand, fold and move on.

Several hands later.

Blinds: $200-$400

Your hand: T♠7♠

Action: Your opponent min-raises from the button to $800.

Question: *What is your play?*
    Answer: Throw in a sizeable reraise. Your hand is strong enough to attack.

Action: You reraise to $3,600 and your opponent calls. The pot is $7,200.

Flop: K♣8♠7♥

Question: *Check or bet?*
Answer: Make a pot-sized bet.

Action: You bet $7,000 and your opponent goes all-in.

Question: It costs you $9,100 to call. *Fold or call?*
Answer*:* Your first instinct is probably to fold bottom pair facing this all-in. But remember, you are looking to play big all-in pots against this person, so you should consider the situation carefully before mucking your hand. When considering whether to fold or call a preflop all-in, recall that you should always estimate the pot odds, and then assess how your hand compares to the range of hands your opponent might move all-in with.

The pot odds are straightforward. It is a live event and you will not have a calculator, so keep the math simple. The pot is roughly $7,000 (preflop) plus $7,000 (your post-flop bet) plus $16,000 (his reraise), or about $30,000. It costs you $9,000 to call so you are getting just over 3-to-1. Therefore you need to win 1 time in 4 (25 percent) to show a profit. How often should you actually expect to win?

With five outs to hit two-pair or trips, plus backdoor straight and flush draws, you have over six outs. So you will improve to beat a hand as strong as A♦K♦ 25 percent of the time. While you could be almost drawing dead against a made two-pair or set, you should still call.

One reason is that there is a remote chance your opponent is bluffing. Anyone who says your opponent is never bluffing is wrong. It may be unlikely, but as Dan Harrington observes, anytime an opponent puts a lot of chips into the pot, you can never fully write off a bluff. Any player can go on tilt and make an ill-advised play, or perhaps semi-bluff a hand such as ten-nine.

But more importantly, you do not need an edge to call here. Quite the contrary. If you could decide this match in the beginning with a coin-flip, you would gladly do so because it would take away the skill. Against this much better player, you must seize gambles that are chip-neutral, or close to it, because they negate his skill edge.

Action: After three minutes of thinking, your opponent calls the clock. Despite feeling embarrassed showing down with bottom pair, you call. Your opponent shows K♥Q♥.

Turn: 9♦

River: 6♥

You win the pot with a ten-high straight. Your opponent looks away in disgust as the dealer returns him $2,100 and the blinds rise to $300-$600.

Next hand, the Pro quickly goes all-in.

Blinds: $300-$600

Your hand: 8♦2♠

Action: Your opponent goes all in for $2,100.

Question: *With what hands should you call?*
Answer: All of them. The pot is $2,700 and it costs you $1,500 to call. Remember, if you are getting 2-to-1 or better, you should almost always call a preflop all-in. In this case, since you are looking to gamble, your odds of nearly 2-to-1 are good enough, even with a junk hand.

Action: You call. The Pro flips Q♣T♥, and you spike trip deuces on the flop to win the pot and the match.

Clearly you had some very good luck, but your strategy was what it needed to be. You played large pots and gambled as much as possible. You succeeded in minimizing the effects of his skill, and ultimately, this is what won you the match.

I do not mean for this fairy-tale ending to suggest that inexperienced players can immediately challenge a heads-up expert. It is just that in heads-up no-limit, particularly with shorter stacks, the amateur can play a fairly basic strategy of hyper-aggressive longball to counter the expert's strengths.

Playing with a Significant Skill Difference

You should also modify your style if you feel that you are significantly better than your opponent. Now you have the opposite approach: You want to play many small pots, avoid big all-in semi-bluffs, and stay away from calling all-in bets with only a small edge.

Let's suppose we have a heads-up match between a seasoned heads-up pro, The Professional, and The Amateur. What general strategy modifications should each player make?

As we have seen, The Amateur should be looking to play large pots, and generally force The Professional to call for all his chips or surrender the pot. But The Professional will want to stick with small pots, and only get all his chips in with a significant advantage. Also, The Professional will want to take advantage of his superior ability to interpret information by making bets on the late streets. So let us look at several scenarios, and see how they should be optimally handled by each player.

Effective stacks: $1,500
Blinds: $10-$20

Your hand: K♠2♠

Action: Villain limps on the button.

Question: *What is your move?*
    Answer: If you are The Amateur, you should make a large raise with your above-average hand — say to $100, to force The Professional to give up immediately or commit a lot of chips earlier in the hand than he would desire. But as The

Professional, you should be much more inclined to check and see a free flop. You would only attack if you knew that Villain was tight and likely to fold.

Blinds: $10-$20

Your hand: K♠2♣

Action: You limp on the button and Villain checks. The pot is $40.

Flop: K♥9♦3♠

Action: Villain bets $40.

Question: *What is your move?*

> **Answer:** The Amateur should put in a big raise with top pair. There is no reason to play a guessing game on the late streets. But as The Professional, you should just call. You are getting 2-to-1 with top pair and position, so at least calling is mandatory. However, since it is unlikely you will be outdrawn with a turn card, wait until the hand develops before deciding how much you want to commit.

Blinds: $10-$20

Your hand: 7♠7♦

Action: Villain limps on the button. You raise to $80 and he calls. The pot is $160.

Flop: Q♥J♥7♥

Question: *What is your move?*

    Answer: You should make a sizeable bet regardless of skill level. You need to get value from a premium hand and give incorrect odds to a possible drawout. As The Amateur, however, you should make a large overbet, as you are happy to win immediately. If another heart falls, you'll be in a difficult position. Even going all-in would be fine.

    The Professional should still bet, but he does not have to worry as much about winning immediately because he will be much better equipped to handle late-street decisions, such as a fourth heart on the turn or river.

Two hands later.

Blinds: $10-$20

Your hand: (A) J♥T♥; (B) K♠3♦

Action: Villain raises to $60 from the button.

Analysis: Both players should play the J♥T♥. While The Amateur should make a large three-bet, as discussed above, The Professional should flat-call. He has a strong hand and would rather see a flop than build a big pot preflop not knowing where he stands.

    Both players should be inclined to fold the K♠3♦. This hand is too weak for The Amateur to make his preferred three-bet, and The Professional's post-flop advantage is not enough to overcome being out of position and having a questionable hand.

    One such amateur-pro confrontation took place in the match between Jerry Buss and Daniel Negreanu.

Buss: $5,900
Negreanu: $14,100

Blinds: $400-$800

Buss' hand: 6♦6♣
Negreanu's hand: A♥8♦

Action: Buss limps on the button and Negreanu checks. The pot is $1,600.

Analysis: Buss should raise a pocket pair in position, and with effective stacks under 10 big blinds, raising all-in is his best play. It is an unexploitable shove. His hand is strong enough to win chips on average moving all-in regardless of Negreanu's calling range.

Similarly with a full $1,600 on the table, Negreanu could shove his decent ace to win a sizeable pot out of position. However, he prefers to play a smallball strategy against his amateur opponent. But with $1,600 to win immediately, a moderately strong hand, and lacking position, shoving tends to be the best play regardless of post-flop skill level.

Flop: Q♠6♥5♣

Action: Both players check.

Analysis: With deeper stacks, Buss would be making a significant mistake not betting for value and to build a large pot with a monster hand. As is, however, two pot-sized bets will still get all the chips in the center by the showdown, so slowplaying is okay strategy.

Turn: 8♠

Action: Negreanu bets $1,200 and Buss raises all-in to $5,100. Negreanu calls.

Analysis: Negreanu must figure his second pair, top kicker is the best hand, and so he is betting for value. Buss's play is also good strategy. With many turn cards, he might want to call and make a move at the river. But with three mid cards to a straight and two spades, raising all-in builds the pot, and it prevents Negreanu from getting a free chance to outdraw him or possibly giving up a worse hand if a scare card hits.

After Buss's raise, Negreanu's hand is too strong to lay down in heads-up getting better than 2-to-1. While deliberating, Negreanu muses about Buss being on a draw. That's another advantage to Buss's immediate raise. Negreanu would have to expect him to bet a queen on the flop, so his all-in with multiple possible draws camouflages the strength of his hand. That is, were the turn a blank, say the 2♦, then Negreanu would realize Buss could only have a monster or a bluff. But with the draws, he can now put Buss on a semi-bluff; and indeed, it is likely the weight he assigns to this possibility that cements the call. Negreanu is drawing dead, and Buss doubles up.

One final note. The short-stacked shove-fold material we have covered applies mainly to tournament formats. In "Part Five: Cash and Tournament Formats" coming up, we turn to a systematic treatment of cash versus tournament formats.

Part Five

Cash and
Tournament Formats

Cash and Tournament Formats

Introduction

Heads-up refers broadly to one-on-one playing situations, but the specific format of a heads-up confrontation often has bearing on your optimal strategy. In this section, we will examine:

- Converting Chip Stacks into Cash Piles
- Blind Versus Blind Play in Fuller Games
- Multi-Table Heads-up Tournaments
- Freeze-outs
- Playing with an Ante
- Folding your Button in Cash Poker
- Playing with a Straddle
- The Split Pot Rule

We will show a procedure for converting tournament blinds into their equivalent cash blinds based on the buy-in, and look at similarities and differences between tournament and cash situations. We will then discuss "accidental heads-up" situations occurring in fuller games when it is folded around to the blinds.

Many variations on tournament and cash matches are discussed, such as playing with an ante, playing with a straddle, the freeze-out match, and multi-table heads-up tournaments. The optimal strategy for these heads-up variations often varies considerably, and we will discuss the necessary strategy adjustments. The concluding section focuses on the particular case of calling to split a pot, applicable to all heads-up formats. We begin with more discussion on cash and tournament formats.

Cash Versus Tournaments

Cash heads-up play and tournament heads-up play are different in many ways. For one thing, the effective stack size will usually be much deeper in cash relative to tournaments, particularly the late stages of a tournament.

But cash play can be shallow as well, so this is only one difference. Tournament play often involves an ante, whereas cash usually does not. We address ante adjustments below, but this difference is also not universal. Cash could involve an ante (while not standard), and early heads-up tournament play rarely does.

So we ask, what are the universal differences between heads-up cash and heads-up tournaments?

1. **The blinds are constant in cash play:** Rising blinds benefit the player who can most readily adapt his style to suit the generally diminishing effective stack sizes resulting from increasing tournament blinds. Suppose that a talented heads-up cash player faces off against a less skilled tournament specialist. If they clash in a tournament format, the tournament specialist will have an edge by playing few large pots early, and doing his best to ensure the match plays out in the higher-blind segment of the tournament. And vice versa with a tournament pro in a cash situation. So the changing blinds, along with the generally shallower stacks at all phases of a tournament, constitute the biggest difference between cash and tournament play.

2. **You may stand up and leave during cash play:** If you are playing heads-up cash against a player you realize is outplaying you, simply quit playing. If you find his style more difficult to play against than your usual opposition, begin tilting, dislike the effective stack sizes, or dislike the situation

for any other reason, you should not prolong the match. You always want to have a definite edge in any variation of poker, and heads-up is no exception. But in a tournament, you have no choice but to complete the match.

3. **The shorter-stacked player can (usually) modify the effective stack sizes in cash play:** Suppose you are playing $2-$4 cash no-limit with $400 effective stacks and lose $200 the first hand. You could continue playing with $200 (50 big blind) effective stacks, or you can rebuy to $400, or possibly your opponent's full $600 depending on buy-in rules. Obviously you cannot reach into your pockets and add chips to the table a during heads-up tournament.

4. **There is no per-hand rake in tournament play:** This is generally an insignificant difference, but we will consider one potentially important ramification below.

In summary, the solid heads-up cash player will tend to be very comfortable playing with deep effective stacks, and he should also be able to quickly assess his edge against his opponent. The tournament player will be very comfortable playing with constantly- changing effective stack sizes, and he does not require the same deep-stack skills (100+ big blinds) relative to the cash player.

Here is a hand that exemplifies the difference between cash and tournament heads-up games. We consider it first in the tournament context, and then consider how a similar hand might play out in a cash game. Note: tX means "X in tournament chips" rather than dollars.

Stacks: t1,500
Blinds: t50-t100
Note: Your opponent is tricky and loose-aggressive.

Your hand: A♥2♥

Action: Your opponent raises to t300 from the button. You call. The pot is t600.

Flop: A♣7♠5♦

Action: You bet t400. Your opponent raises all-in and you call.

Resolution: Your opponent shows the 4♦3♦ and your pair of aces holds up to win the hand.

A reasonable tournament hand, right? But in cash, several aspects would be different. First, very rarely would the effective stacks only be 15 big blinds deep. It is possible if one player goes nearly broke and does not rebuy, but these shorter-stacked situations are much rarer in cash play relative to tournament play.

Post-flop, whereas your only consideration in the tournament hand is how to get it all-in with top pair, in cash games, you would have to decide how big a pot you want to play, and how to achieve this. (For instance, with 100 big blind stacks, you would not be willing to commit all or most of your chips.)

Lastly, in a cash game, you should tend not to voluntarily play a long match against a tricky, loose-aggressive player. Find easier opposition. If it's a tournament, you have no choice.

So how might this hand have played out in a cash context?

Effective stacks: $10,000
Blinds: $50-$100
Note: Your opponent is tricky and loose-aggressive.

Your hand: A♥2♥

Action: Your opponent raises to $300 on the button. You call. The pot is $600.

Flop: A♣7♠5♦

Action: You check. Your opponent bets $450 and you call. The pot is $1,500.

Analysis: You decide to check-call each street, only betting if he checks a prior street since your hand is probably not strong enough to play for four bets in case he raises. Your opponent might also bluff multiple streets if you keep on checking.

Turn: T♥

Action: You check. Your Opponent bets $1,200 and you call. The pot is $3,900.

River: T♦

Action: You both check. Your opponent shows 4♦3♦ and your aces win.

So the cash hand involved deeper stacks, a different post-flop strategy, and a decision to quit playing against a tough opponent. It also involved using the "$" sign as opposed to the "t" symbol.

Converting Chip Stacks into Cash Piles

In any heads-up match, you can convert a chip stack into a cash pile through simple math because you are playing winner-take-all and know how many chips you have and how much money you are playing for. For example, suppose you are playing an online heads-up sit 'n go with a $100 buy-in, $5 rake, and T1,500 in starting chips. Then the worth of each chip is $0.0667

$$\$0.0667 = \frac{\$100}{1,500 \text{ chips}}$$

From a cash perspective, the tournament progresses like a cash game with escalating blinds. Introducing a common blind structure, this tournament may have the following cash-equivalent progression:

Structure in Chips Versus Dollars for an Online $100 Tournament

Blinds (Chips)	Blinds ($ Equivalent)	Stack Depth
T10-T20	$0.65-$1.30	75 BB
T15-T30	$1.00-$2.00	50 BB
T25-T50	$1.65-$3.30	30 BB
T50-T100	$3.30-$6.60	15 BB
T75-T150	$5.00-$10.00	10 BB

So this tournament is like playing a cash game with one set of blinds, then another cash game with higher blinds, and so forth.

Here is another example of this chip-to-dollar conversion process. Suppose you are playing a major live tournament and get down to the final two. First place pays $1,000,000 and second pays $400,000. Since both players can finish with no less than $400,000, this situation is no different from one where both have already been awarded $400,000 and are now playing a heads-up winner-take-all battle for the remaining $600,000.

The blinds are t50,000-t100,000 with a t15,000 ante. The chips stacks are:

Player A: t3.5 Million
Player B: t1.5 Million

Then the cash value of each t1 chip is $0.12.

$$\$0.12 = \frac{\$600,000}{5,000,000 \text{ chips}}$$

So at this particular blind level, the two are effectively playing a cash game with the following parameters.

Player A's Stack: $420,000
Player B's Stack: $180,000

Blinds: $6,000-$12,000 ($1,800 Ante)

Usually a heads-up cash game between these two players would feature smaller blinds given these stack sizes, and not have an ante. Nonetheless, the players can think of the chips they are using as chips with direct monetary value which cannot be cashed out until one player remains.

And finally, because tournament chips can be so readily converted to cash, from here out we'll use the more standard $ sign rather than clarifying tournament chips with a "t." This notation should make the rest of this section easier to understand.

Small Blind Versus Big Blind Heads-Up Play

In this chapter, we discuss heads-up play that occurs in the context of a three-handed or larger game — cash or tournament — when everyone folds to the blinds. (From now on, we will abbreviate such "accidental" heads-up situations as AHU.) There is one fundamental difference between this form of heads-up play and conventional heads-up gameplay.

> The small blind now acts first on every subsequent betting round in addition to acting first preflop.

What are the implications of this difference? Being the small blind is now very undesirable. You have a positional disadvantage on every single betting round, and this is difficult to overcome. Getting 3-to-1 on your chips with a post-flop positional advantage, you should be inclined to play most hands as the small blind in normal heads-up play.

But this situation changes dramatically when AHU. If in doubt, it's usually best to fold. Specifically, fold your weaker hands or those that play poorly post-flop, such as low offsuit queens or jacks. When you do raise, you are generally doing so for value. Also, the stronger and more aggressive the big blind player is, the less inclined you should be to enter the pot since good players will be able to exploit their positional edge.

Conversely, when you are the big blind, the opposite holds — you are much more likely to call (or reraise) the small blind. This reraise can be for value, or to build a pot with position since you will have such strong stealing value even when you miss.

Let's consider several AHU hands and compare the optimal play to that in conventional heads-up. The following hand occurs in a nine-handed no-limit cash game.

Effective stacks: $400
Blinds: $2-$4
Note: The big blind is a shrewd, tight-aggressive player.

Your hand: T♠7♣

Action: Everyone folds to you in the small blind.

Question: *What is your play?*
   Answer: Tend to fold. You hand is not strong, and you should not be inclined to challenge a good player who will have position on every betting round. This is quite different from conventional heads-up where you should absolutely play a ten-seven from the small blind on the button.
   The times to consider playing this hand in AHU are against passive opponents in the big blind. For instance, you could complete against a calling station, and raise against a very timid player. But against an unknown or aggressive player this holding should hit the muck.

This hand occurs in a multi-table tournament.

Effective stacks: $300,000

Blinds: $4,000-$8,000 ($1,000 ante)

Your hand: K♥J♥

Action: Everyone folds to you in the small blind. You raise to $36,000 and your opponent calls. The pot is $79,000.

Flop: Q♦7♥2♠

Action: You bet $50,000 and your opponent raises all-in. You fold.

Analysis: Preflop, your two high suited cards are strong enough to play even as the AHU small blind. But after your opponent calls your preflop raise, you lack the extra information of post-flop action before you make your move. You elect to fire again, not willing to give up on the pot. Now he raises. Does this indicate a strong queen, or is your opponent on a stone bluff figuring that the pot is large and you are unlikely to have connected with this flop? You cannot afford to find out with king high, so you should fold. But regardless of his holding, your opponent was the one with the positional advantage since he got to see your action on both betting rounds before choosing his action.

Early in a multi-table tournament.

Effective stacks: $5,000

Blinds: $25-$50

Your hand: 5♦4♦

Action: Everyone folds to the small blind who completes. You are in the big blind.

Question: *What is your play?*
   Answer: Raise. If your opponent folds, then you have won immediately with five-high. And if he calls, then you are playing a potentially large pot with position.

Action: You raise to $200 and your opponent calls. The pot is $400.

Flop: A♥J♥9♠

Action: Your opponent checks.

Question: *Check or bet?*
  Answer: Bet. Your opponent has shown weakness, and you are not going to win by checking.

Action: You bet $250 and your opponent folds.

To summarize this chapter, small blind versus big blind heads-up play is a very good situation for the big blind, and a very poor one for the small blind. When in doubt, call or raise as the big blind, and fold as the small blind.

Multi-Table Heads-Up Tournaments

Multi-table heads-up tournaments are one example of the "shootout" format where a table does not break until one player has all the chips. Besides the *NBC Championship,* these heads-up MTTs are also widely spread online and are growing in popularity.

Should you have a different strategy for these matches? No. Every heads-up match you play is still winner-take-all. For instance, suppose you are playing a thirty-two man heads-up tournament with prizes of:

First: $10,000
Second: $5,000
Third and Fourth: $2,500

You make it to the final four. In your semi-final match, the loser receives a guaranteed $2,500 and the winner receives $7,500 in equity.

$$\$7,500 = (.50)(\$10,000) + (.50)(\$5,000)$$

Similarly to the final two in a regular multi-table tournament, this situation is equivalent to one where both players have already received $2,500 and are playing a winner-take-all battle for the remaining $5,000 in equity.

Thus at any stage of a multi-table heads-up tournament, you are still playing winner-take-all. Therefore, play as you normally would, seizing any chip advantage just as if it was a stand alone heads-up match.

Are Effective
Stacks Really Enough?

During a seminar I gave on heads-up, one participant strongly objected to effective stacks given in lieu of actual stacks. His argument was that he would often make a borderline laydown if his was the shorter stack because that way he could preserve his tournament life. Before I could reply, another gentleman argued that he would be more willing to make the marginal laydown with a chip lead so as not to risk doubling his opponent up.

From a math perspective, these men were both incorrect. As we have stated, in a winner-take-all heads-up match, chips and cash are effectively the same. Suppose you play a $100 buy-in heads-up match with t1,000 chip starting stacks. Then each chip is worth identically 10¢.

$$10¢ \text{ per chip} = \frac{\$100 \text{ buy - in}}{\text{t1,000 chips}}$$

The loser cashes $0, so each chip stays worth exactly 10¢. So chips in strictly heads-up tournaments are no different than cash.

And in cash poker, it is taken for granted that you should maximize your chips, regardless of stack size. The only time tournament play should affect this is if, as already discussed, you believe there is a noticeable skill difference between you and your opponent. For instance, if your opponent is playing a tight-passive style (the weakest in heads-up), and you have a slightly +cEV call for a substantial amount of chips, you would be correct to fold. This may also occur if you thought higher blinds, and therefore shallower stack sizes, conferred a greater edge upon you. And, as we mentioned in the last section, these types of strategy adjustments are to increase win rate percentage and not necessarily hourly rate.

Or perhaps you have significant experience playing turbo nine-man sit 'n go's, where the blinds quickly become large relative to the starting stacks. Then you would want a greater edge to gamble early in a heads-up tournament since your edge will increase with the rapidly-increasing blinds. And should you happen to find yourself out-matched, you might call a large gamble as a slight chip underdog for similar reasons.

But these plays and strategy apply regardless of whether you are the shorter stack or the bigger stack. If you are the better player, for instance, you should be less willing to take a marginal gamble regardless of whether it is for his entire stack or yours.

So while actual stacks often make for a more compelling heads-up story, the effective stack is the only stack-related criterion necessary for making strategy decisions. The reason for the confusion is that in multi-table tournaments where many places are paid, or in sit 'n go's that pay three places, many strategy adjustments based on stack sizes do come into play. But once it's down to two players, or it was a heads-up match to begin with, then it's winner take all and actual stack sizes have no impact.

Freeze-Outs

The freeze-out is a heads-up match with blinds that stay constant, that is played until one player has all the chips. In this sense, the freeze-out has a combination of cash and tournament elements. It is like cash in that you do not have to adjust for rising blinds. And if you are a cash player, you can convert the chips into dollar terms and think of all decisions like cash.

For example, in a $100 buy-in freeze-out with t50-t100 blinds and starting stacks of t5,000, this is equivalent to $100 starting stacks with fixed blinds of $1-$2.

However, like tournament play, neither opponent can leave until the match is finished. Also, neither player can rebuy, which benefits those who adjust well to different effective stack sizes.

The freeze-out can, in theory, proceed indefinitely. Normally it is the rising blinds that ensure any tournament will come to an end, so with static blinds, the match could last quite a long time. Of course the shorter stack will eventually lose an all-in, but a longer-lasting match benefits the better player.

Freeze-outs generally occur as challenges between two players who want to test their skills, and feel that playing with short stacks is less skillful. For example, suppose two heads-up masters face off in a traditional tournament match-up. After a sufficient number of hands, the blinds will have risen such that the effective stacks are 10 big blinds or shallower. While there is certainly a significant skill component involved in short-stacked heads-up poker, this largely preflop shove-fold game arguably has less complexity than deeper-stacked poker. So a freeze-out benefits the player who does not have to decide it all on a potential coinflip those times the blinds get high.

When should you play a freeze-out? Assuming your motive in playing is purely profit, you should agree to a freeze-out only when you believe you have a substantial edge over your opponent in deep-stacked play. You need to be confident that you have this large edge for two reasons:

1. You cannot stand up and leave if you are mistaken, like you could in cash. And,

2. The match can potentially last a long time, so you can play fewer of these in a given time frame. All else equal, this will tend to lower your hourly profits.

From a recreational standpoint, the freeze-out is often a convenient format for two friends to play live. This type of heads-up match does not require different chips for coloring up, a clock, an agreed-upon structure, and so forth. Thus it can be more fun and help add a social element to the game.

Playing with an Ante

Playing with the ante in heads-up is most common when playing the final two of a multi-table tournament. With an ante, you should almost always follow Dan Harrington's advice on heads-up and never fold your button (in tournament play with antes).

There has been some debate about whether this statement is also applicable to cash poker and ante-less tournament poker. It's my opinion that even without the ante, it certainly cannot be a big mistake to at least limp any hand from the small blind because you are getting good odds in position. (Of course, you will have to sometimes switch up which hands you limp and raise with if you want to play every hand; we discuss this in "Part Six: The Metagame" on Page 315.)

But in late-stage tournament play, not folding your button is a must since you are getting over 3-to-1 pot odds with position. In this situation, any two cards should show a profit.

Suppose we are playing without the ante. Theoretically, you should be able to play every hand when you are the button since you are getting good odds in position. But possible reasons to fold some hands are:

- The blinds are high, you have a weak hand, and your opponent is aggressive. Here you might consider limping a strong hand, but in general you should stick to a raise-fold game.

- You want your opponent to see that you sometimes choose not to play your button. And,

- Your opponent is a very strong player. This might make some of your worse hands unprofitable, so they should now be folded. In other words, against a weak opponent you would play everything, but against a tough opponent, this may not be the best strategy.

But again, in heads-up MTT play, the better than 3-to-1 odds you are getting are too good to pass up.[10]

You are heads-up in the WSOP main event.

Effective Stacks: $19,000,000

Blinds: $400,000-$800,000
Ante: $100,000

Your hand: 5♣2♠

Question: *What is your play?*
    Answer: At least call. Normally you should call because you have a weak hand, so you would rather play for a small pot … when all else is equal. But if your opponent is catching on to this tendency and raising your button limps, you should switch around and begin raising weak hands and limping strong ones.
    Regardless of your exact play, the pot is $1,400,000 with the antes, it costs you another $400,000 to play, and you will be in position during the hand. These three facts make any cards playable, even your weak 5♣2♠. (Again, with the exception noted in the footnote previously.)

---

[10] Unless your opponent will almost always raise if you limp and often reraise if you raise.

Folding Your Button in Cash Poker

There are two more practical reasons why you might fold your button when playing cash. Suppose you have a marginal hand that you believe could be played for a slight profit. You estimate your expectation at roughly +0.02 big blinds in a comparable tournament situation. This would equate to a winrate of 2 big blinds per each 100 hands — winning, for instance, an average of $20 each 100 hands in a $5-$10 game.

The first reason to consider folding is the effect of the rake. In a tournament, the rake is a flat fee for entering, independent of how many hands you play once you have bought in. So playing our marginal hand will still show a profit in tournament play.

But in cash play, if your expected rake contribution is greater than or equal to 0.02 big blinds, you will show a loss. Why? Suppose playing this hand, you win a pot of 10 big blinds or greater at least 10 percent of the time, and the rake is 2 percent. Then your expected rake payment for playing the hand is, at a minimum, 0.02 BB.

$$0.02 \text{ BB} = (.10)(.02)(10 \text{ BB})$$

Since we hypothesized your pre-rake winrate to be precisely this number, after the rake, you will no longer show a profit.

Furthermore, if you do fold, you can instantly begin another hand. By passing on these very marginal hands you can choose to only play those hands that figure to show a higher profit. Thus your overall winrate should be higher.

In summary, the button is still your bread-and-butter position in cash poker. However, even though you are getting good odds to play a pot in position, there is sometimes extra rationale for folding your weaker button hands.

Playing with a Straddle

A straddle is normally a third live blind in a cash game put out voluntarily by the player who would otherwise act first before the flop. Generally, the straddle occurs when players in a live game want to increase the action. Here is an example of preflop action from a full ring game with a straddle.

Blinds: $10-$20
Straddle: $40

Before the deal, the player to the left of the dealer posts a $10 blind, the player to his left posts a $20 blind, and the player one more to the left posts a $40 straddle. It is live. He can raise if everyone else just limps.

Action: Everyone folds to the cutoff who calls the $40. The button raises to $100. Both blinds fold. The straddle calls for another $60 and the cutoff calls $60.

We give this preliminary description for full ring because the straddle in the context of heads-up has a very specific meaning. The player first-to-act in heads-up is always the button. So using the above $10-$20-($40) structure, here are the differences between straddle and straddle-less gameplay.

Without the Straddle

Starting pot	$30
First-to-act preflop	Button
Possible actions	Fold, call $10, raise to $40 or higher
First-to-act post-flop	Big blind

With the Straddle

Starting pot	$60
First-to-act preflop	Big blind
Possible actions	Fold, call $20, raise to $60 or higher
First-to-act post-flop	Big blind

Therefore heads-up play with a straddle is fundamentally the same as accidental heads-up cash play. Recall that accidental heads-up is when a table of three or more all fold to the blinds. The reason the straddle makes the situation the same as AHU is because in either case, one player acts first preflop and in all subsequent betting rounds, and this player posts exactly half the amount of his opponent before the deal. The only difference is that this unlucky player is the small blind in AHU and the big blind in cash straddle matches. So you should now be willing to fold your weaker hands preflop when you are the big blind since you will have a positional disadvantage on all betting rounds.

Effective Stacks: $30,000
Blinds: $100-$200
Straddle: $400

Your hand: K♣K♠

Question: *You are the big blind. What is your play?*
Answer: Usually make a substantial raise to at least $1,600. Remember that not only are you acting first before the flop, but you are also acting first after the flop. Therefore you are much more willing to settle for an early win rather than be forced into playing the late streets acting before your opponent. (Of course, you should sometimes just call, especially against aggressive opponents.)

Action: You raise to $1,800 and Villain calls. The pot is $3,600.

Flop: A♦J♠J♣

Action: You both check.

Analysis: Your check is a smart move. You figure to be way ahead unless Villain holds an ace or a jack.

Turn: Q♥

Action: You bet $2,400 and Villain calls. The pot is $8,400.

River: Q♣

Question: *Should you check or bet?*
    Answer: Check. You cannot bet for value since:

1. No worse hand will call. Any lower pair has been counterfeited, so the only worse hands are high card hands. And,

2. It is unlikely a better hand will fold. A full house will certainly call here, and a straight or pair of aces will probably toss in a second postflop bet to look you up. However, your hand is strong enough to serve as a bluff-catcher, and a hand such as T♠9♠ or 7♣7♥ might bluff if you check.

Action: You check. Villain bets $17,000 and you fold.

Analysis: While this overbet will often be for value with a full house, your opponent could be bluffing. The problem is that you must be confident in your read to profitably call such a large bet. The moral: Playing even premium hands is a much more difficult task when your opponent gets to act second on all four betting rounds.

The Split Pot Rule

We now introduce a concept which will be quite familiar to those who have played high-low poker variations:

> Almost never call a large bet hoping for a split pot.

This concept is particularly crucial in deep-stacked cash poker, and relies on an expected value calculation with surprising results.

Effective stacks: $1,400

Blinds: $5-$10

Your hand: 7♣4♠

Action: Your opponent limps on the button and you check. The pot is $20.

Flop: 2♠2♦2♣

Action: You both check.

Turn: A♣

Action: You both check.

River: A♦

Action: You check and your opponent goes all-in for $1,400.

Question: *What is your move?*

    Answer: With a full house on board, this will be a split pot unless your opponent has quad deuces, or a third ace for a higher full house. You strongly believe your opponent would have bet earlier holding an ace, plus two of them are accounted for. Quads are not only improbable from a hand combination perspective, but you also think your opponent would have made a more reasonable value bet with this strong a hand.

Question: You therefore believe it very likely that calling will result in a split pot. *How often must you be correct to win chips from this call?*

    Answer: When you are right, you will win half the original $20 pot. Everything wagered on top is split. When you are wrong, you lose your entire $1,400 stack. Let p be the probability that you are correct. Then your EV for calling is

$$(p)(\$10) + (1 - p)(-\$1,390)$$

which we want to be positive. Simplifying, and setting greater than zero:

$$(\$10p) - (\$1,390) + (\$1.390p) > 0 \Rightarrow$$
$$p > 99.3$$

So you must be correct over 99 percent of the time to show a profit. Put another way, you are laying $1,400 to win $10, or 140-to-1, which is too optimistic. Indeed, your opponent could be aware that if you act on your read and call hoping for a split, then he has a massively chip-winning overbet opportunity with an ace or deuce. Do not oblige him.

    Similarly, if you hold an unexpected monster on a board that looks like it should "rightfully" be split, often overbet. If your opponent is not familiar with the frequency with which he must be correct to show a profit, you will come out way ahead with such bets in the long run.

While this split pot rule is important, you can certainly overdo it, as in this next hand between Ted Forrest and Antonio Esfandiari.

Antonio Esfandiari: $44,200
Ted Forrest: $115,800

Blinds: $600-$1,200

Esfandiari's hand: 9♠6♠
Forrest's hand: 6♥4♥

Action: Esfandiari calls and Forrest checks. The pot is $2,400.

Flop: 5♣4♠2♦

Action: Both players check.

Analysis: Forrest should bet here if he had a lone pair of fours, but with his accompanying straight draw, another card may help him. So checking is okay strategy, particularly with the intent to check-raise if the aggressive Esfandiari bets.

From Esfandiari's perspective, he wants a free card with his overcard, straight, and backdoor flush draws. So checking is reasonable for him as well.

Turn: K♠

Action: Forrest checks. Esfandiari bets $1,200 and Forrest calls. The pot is $4,800.

Analysis: After Forrest checks again, Esfandiari makes a reasonable bet. Forrest has shown weakness by checking twice, and it is unlikely that he would check a pair of kings with three low straight cards on board. If Esfandiari is called or raised, he has added a flush draw to his winning possibilities.

But the king only puts another overcard on board for Forrest. With his third pair and straight draw, he just wants to see a cheap showdown. If Forrest improves to a straight or trips, he will bet for value. If he misses, he can check and call most river bets.

River: 3♥

Action: Forrest bets $2,100. Efandiari raises to $6,100. Forrest reraises all-in and Esfandiari folds.

Analysis: Fireworks at the river, culminating with a huge fold. Forrest hits his straight and bets for value. This smallish value bet is a good size if Esfandiari has a pair, or other hand weaker than the ace-through-five straight (which would probably call a larger bet). But Esfandiari's failure to raise preflop makes it less likely that he holds an ace, and so Forrest could reasonably put him on a pair, possibly kings after the turn bet.

But Esfandiari has actually hit the same straight, and he raises for value. He knows that Forrest will assume the only hands Esfandiari would raise are the six-high straight or a stone bluff, but getting over 3-to-1 on the call against an aggressive player, Forrest may have to make a crying call with a weaker hand.

When Forrest three-bets all-in, he is basically saying, "Why not?" He is guaranteed to at least split the pot unless Esfandiari has precisely the seven-six, and if for any reason Esfandiari does decide to call this bet with an inferior hand — maybe because this overbet looks like a bluff, then Forrest gains tremendously.

Esfandiari actually lays down another six-high straight. He has already put $8,500 into this pot, so Forrest's reraise is effectively to $35,700. So it costs him $29,600 to call for a pot worth $58,800. He is therefore getting almost 2-to-1 when only a seven-six will beat him. Furthermore, he is holding one six, so there are only twelve remaining seven-six hand combinations — under 1 percent of the 1,326 possible starting hands. Note that Forrest would have to have checked an open-ended straight draw at both the flop and the turn, a very passive playing sequence.

It is true that Forrest likely has at least a six. The all-in overbet is indeed a strange one, and since Forrest knows Esfandiari won't call without at least a six, Esfandiari reasons that Forrest is likely to have the seven-six. And if not, the best he can do is split the pot. As we have seen, you want to be cautious calling in the hopes of splitting. How often must Forrest have the seven-six for this call no longer to be profitable?

Letting p be the probability of a split pot, then the EV on a call is

$$(p)(.5)(\$17,000) + (1 - p)(- \$29,600)$$

Note that $17,000 is the amount already on the table which Esfandiari gets to split if Forrest only has a six. Simplifying and setting greater than zero:

$$(\$8,500p) - (\$29,600) + (\$29,600p) > 0 \Rightarrow$$
$$p > 0.7769$$

So if Forrest has only a six at least 78 percent of the time, then even if he is never bluffing, Esfandiari will still profit from this call. This hand is an exception to the "don't call for half" rule, since the amount already on the table is large, and the one hand Esfandiari is afraid of is unlikely. Plus Forrest will indeed sometimes be bluffing, even if only rarely. On the other hand, if Esfandiari is able to reason out, perhaps because of the way the hand was played, that it is quite likely that Forrest indeed does have precisely the seven-six, then folding is the best play.

Part Six

The Metagame

The Metagame

Introduction

The Metagame refers to considerations affecting the entire match, rather than just the current hand. Specific topics include:

- Paying for Information
- The Metagame in Action
- Image
- When Your Opponent is Exploiting You
- Adjusting Midway Through the Match
- Exploitable Versus Unexploitable Play
- Counter-Adjustments and the Nash Equilibrium
- Unexploitable Short Stack Play
- Voluntarily Showing Cards.

While understanding your image is an important topic, we will see how some players place too much emphasis on it against unobservant opponents. We will also see that it becomes necessary to safeguard against strategies that perceptive opponents use to exploit your playing style. Thus we will also discuss unexploitable play, as well as situations when you should concentrate mostly on exploiting your opponent's weaknesses.

In the chapter "Counter-adjustments and the Nash Equilibrium," we will look at continually evolving style adjustments that players make to exploit each other and the equilibrium solutions that may result. One important application of these ideas is unexploitable short stack play, and we will return to short-stacked strategy discussion in the context of exploiting your opponent's tendencies versus playing in an unexploitable manner yourself. We then conclude with a section tying many of these ideas together in voluntary card-showing.

Paying for Information

Would you ever call a bet on the river with a hand certain to lose, such as 6-high on a board with four overcards? Usually not, but sometimes you might make a river call certain to lose, or other negative expectation play, to gain information.

For example, suppose it is early in an online heads-up match, and you are trying to get a read on your opponent. He makes a small river bet, and you want to find out what he's holding.

Effective stacks: $1,500

Blinds: $10-$20

Your hand: 8♠7♠

Action: Your opponent limps on the button. You raise to $80 and he calls. The pot is $160.

Flop: K♠Q♠2♥

Action: You bet $120 and your opponent calls. The pot is $400.

Turn: 3♥

Action: You both check.

River: 5♣

Action: You check and your opponent bets $20.

Analysis: Consider calling this bet. This call is not for the purpose of winning chips; your opponent will very rarely hold a hand you can beat.

But for only $20, you can find out what his holding is to make this unusual sequence of plays. For example, suppose he flips over:

- **Ace-king:** Your opponent is passive. He does not raise preflop with a quality hand, nor does he bet the flop or turn with top pair. This opponent figures to have a strong hand when he is the one betting or raising.

- **Six-four:** Your opponent is loose and passive based on his early calling with such a weak hand.

So for only a $20 investment, you buy a tentative read on your opponent. Meanwhile, he might assume for future hands that you cannot be bluffed when you call his bet with an eight-high.

Your willingness to purchase information should correlate with both stack depth and expected match length. If you are playing with short effective stacks, then even small bets represent too great a fraction of your stack. But if you are playing a tournament with deep stacks, then sacrificing a big blind or two is a small loss. The longer the match figures to be, the more valuable the information you gain on your opponent. Playing a single hand, you are simply throwing away chips making a losing call. But playing a best-of-ten series, any information is valuable.

While paying for information can be worthwhile, make sure that you do not let it be an excuse to make wild or significantly negative expectation plays. If you are altering your normal game plan to get info, make sure any expected loss is small and make sure that the information you are purchasing is worth the price. After making the play, you should be able to state what you have learned and how you intend to exploit this information as we did above. When in doubt about whether to buy information, make the play you normally would to maximize your chips.

The Metagame in Action

If you were to only play a single hand against your opponent you should play it in the best possible way. But if you are playing a series of hands, it can become correct to play one or more of these hands, especially when the blinds are small, in a less than optimal fashion. This is known as the metagame. Paying for information is one example of such a play. So to start, let's look at several examples of metagame concerns.

Slowplaying, normally a mistake, is sometimes correct for metagame reasons. Let's say you routinely play the same opponent. If you never slowplay, he will know that anytime you check, your hand is at best mediocre. Your opponent can exploit this fact by bluffing at a higher frequency. Even making an occasional exception will keep an astute player guessing.

Note that the "routinely play the same opponent" clause is key here. Metagame becomes more important when you are playing the same player often, especially if he is perceptive. For instance, if your opponent thought only on the "zeroth" level — only considering his cards to determine his action — then you would have no meta-concerns playing him even in repeated matches. By contrast, playing even a single match against a tough heads-up player might be cause for meta-concern.

When thinking about the metagame, ask yourself what notes a perceptive player could take on you if a particular action always had the same meaning. The longer or more complex the note, the less you should worry about giving away this information. For instance, you would not want your opponent to be able to note that you "Will not check-raise with a draw." But this knowledge would only do so much good for your opponent because it only allows him to rule out a drawing hand when you check-raise him, and he would still not know whether your hand was weak or strong.

Furthermore, your opponent would have to be analyzing your play over many hands to gain such a read.

By contrast, a more detrimental read for an opponent to have about your strategy is "Limps only with weak hands." This would be problematic for several reasons:

1. It does not take a player with advanced reading skills to deduce this. Even relatively early in a single tournament, a player with modest reading skills might notice that you are only showing down weak hands every time you limp your button.

2. You want to play most of your buttons, and a player who understood how you were accomplishing this goal (i.e., by calling with weak hands and raising with strong hands) would have a significant edge in the battle of reads.

3. This read is easy to exploit. For instance, the player who knows you will not check-raise semi-bluff has only limited room to exploit this information. All he can do is narrow your hand range to exclude a certain category of hands in those specific instances where you check-raise him.

    But the player who notices you limping only with trash hands can frequently raise out of position after you have limped, knowing you cannot call a substantial raise with a weak hand. So you should mix up your preflop play to deny him this knowledge, sometimes raising with a weak hand and limping with a strong hand.

Let's conclude this section with an example from a $1,500 heads-up match between two very successful online players which ends with this strange hand.

Player A: $1,440
Player B: $1,560

Effective stacks: $1,440

Blinds: $10-$20

Player A's hand: A♣5♠
Player B's hand: 4♦4♠

Action: A raises to $60 on the button. B reraises to $180 and is called. The pot is $360.

Flop: A♥8♦3♥

Action: B bets $200. A raises all-in to $1,260 and B calls.

Analysis: The early action is aggressive, but quite reasonable. A raises preflop holding an ace, B reraises with a low pocket pair, and A calls getting 2-to-1 with position. B then makes a standard bet to win immediately when the flop comes with two overcards.

But more conventional follow-up action would be for A to call or make a smaller raise, and B to then shut down his betting. One reason A likely raises all-in immediately is because he is a hyper-aggressive player, capable of making this raise with a draw or weaker pair. He knows that B is capable of picking up on such patterns, and therefore he needs to play his stronger hands fast as well.

And indeed, B calls over another $1,000 despite being ahead of only bottom pair, a flush draw, or a stone bluff. More specifically, getting 1.7-to-1 pot odds, he needs the best hand by the showdown at least 37 percent of the time for this call to be profitable.

- If A holds any pair above fours, B is only 8 percent to win the hand.

- If A holds two hearts higher than the 4♥, then B is approximately 45 percent to win.

- If A holds a pair of treys or two overcards with no flush draw, then B is 75 percent to win.

So B must place a high weight on A having a weak hand. For instance, even if he assumes A is just as likely to hold a flush draw or bluff as he is to have any pair above fours, then he is still only just getting the odds to call as a 58-to-42 dog. And most players, facing this substantial all-in bet, would weight a pair much higher.

So it is probable that B is factoring metagame into his decision. He has both seen A make plays like this with weaker hands, and he also wants his hyper-aggressive foe to think, "I can't get away with bluffing this guy because he'll call even large bets with a weak hand."

If this were their only match, then Player's B call would probably be ill-advised. Most random opponents you encounter will not shove this widely on a bluff, and furthermore, there could be no meta-benefits to calling in a single match. But because B anticipates future matchups, and is taking previous matchups into account, he elects to call. Similarly, a big reason Player A elects to simply shove his top pair is for these meta-concerns of balancing his (semi-)bluffing and value betting with all-in raises.

Image

Your image is how your opponent perceives you. Examples are tight-passive or wild-aggressive, although this definition presupposes that your opponent is actively observing you. It is possible that your opponent is not changing his perception of you, if he has one, based on your actions. Some players will only consider their own cards and strategy, and others will lack the knowledge to interpret what your betting patterns, tells, and so forth might indicate. (However, players this dense usually don't play heads-up matches.)

With these caveats in place, you should be aware of how your opponent perceives you, particularly if he appears to be observant. And if this is the case, you might modify your play to take advantage of your opponent's perception.

Effective stacks: $1,165
Blinds: $10-$20
Note: After 14 hands of play, you have been catching good cards and your normally loose-aggressive style would likely come across as a maniac to an observant opponent.

Your hand: K♠K♥

Action: You raise to $65 on the button and your opponent reraises to $195.

Analysis: You should strongly consider reraising all-in. While this line is not a mistake as a "default" play, it is not how you would normally play kings. You have position with a premium hand that figures to be at worst a 70-to-30 favorite, if not 88-to-12, over your opponent's hand. So in general you should either call, or make a smaller four-bet.

But there is a strong chance your opponent may have already concluded that you are recklessly aggressive, in which case his range for calling this all-in will widen substantially. Therefore, going all-in immediately is much better than it would normally be.

When you modify your normal play due to image, you want the new play to be reasonable as well. For instance, if you have what you believe to be a tight image, you might bluff more aggressively on the river; and with a loose image, you could value bet weaker hands. But in both cases, you would still be making reasonable plays with your cards. You just lean more toward one decision based on how your opponent is likely to perceive you.

In other words, you should have a good reason to deviate from your normal play for image reasons. Some players go to an extreme: "I start off just playing like a maniac, and once that image is established, I wait until a big hand comes my way and then get paid off." It isn't worth going this far out of your way for image. You should play a game you feel confident with, and only make decisions based on image when they are otherwise close, or your opponent begins exploiting your natural tendencies.

In the first hand of his match against John Juanda, Barry Greenstein makes an unusual preflop four-bet.

Effective stacks: $80,000

Blinds: $300-$600

Greenstein's hand: Q♣9♥
Juanda's hand: 9♦8♦

Action: Greenstein raises to $1,800 on the button. Juanda reraises to $5,800. Greenstein reraises to $21,800 and Juanda folds.

Analysis: Fireworks on the opening hand. Greenstein makes a reasonable three big blind raise with a solid queen, and Juanda makes an aggressive reraise with mid suited connectors. Juanda's disguised hand is a good one to take initiative with since most often when Greenstein calls, Juanda can steal the flop with a lead bet when Greenstein misses. And when Juanda does hit the flop, he will have a disguised holding.

However, Greenstein elects to throw in a heavy fourth bet preflop. He probably does not intend for this play to be particularly profitable in isolation. However, he wants Juanda to respect his button raises throughout the match, and Juanda will have a difficult time playing an aggressive style and continuing to three-bet marginal hands preflop when he sees Greenstein so willing to come over top of a reraise.

You do not want to make an image play that will lose you many chips, but Greenstein can win a substantial pot immediately, and his further decisions are simple. If Juanda reraises all-in he knows he is badly beaten and can make a clear fold. If Juanda calls this extra $16,000, he can leave the hand unless he connects well with the flop.

Image
Effects of a Big Fold

This next hand from the semi-final round features T.J. Cloutier and Chris Ferguson.

Blinds: $2,000-$4,000

Cloutier's hand: 7♦6♣
Ferguson's hand: 5♠2♥

Action: Cloutier calls on the button and Ferguson checks. The pot is $8,000.

Flop: 7♥3♣2♣

Action: Ferguson checks. Cloutier bets $4,000 and Ferguson calls. The pot is $16,000.

Turn: 5♥

Action: Ferguson checks. Cloutier bets $10,000. Ferguson raises to $32,000 and Cloutier calls. The pot is $80,000.

Analysis: Both players have strong, yet vulnerable hands, and both aggressively seek value. Cloutier's call of Ferguson's check-raise is better than raising since Ferguson will probably call a third bet only with hands that can beat top pair with a low kicker. But top pair is certainly strong enough to at least call, which Cloutier does.

River: 7♣

Action: Ferguson checks. Cloutier bets $20,000 and Ferguson folds.

Analysis: While Cloutier could not logically make a small bet on this dangerous board without at least trips, a straight, or a flush, Ferguson will show a profit by calling if his opponent is bluffing more than one time in six. But there is also another reason for him to call if this decision is close. If Cloutier knows that his opponent is capable of folding to small river bluffs, he can very profitably increase his frequency of such plays. For instance, if Cloutier could get Ferguson to make a similar laydown in a situation where he (Cloutier) held only a high card, he would profit enormously.

So even if you are confident that your opponent is almost never bluffing in a spot like this, be wary of folding. If you do fold, then be prepared to call future river bets much more liberally since a perceptive opponent is likely to attack this apparent tendency of folding to small river bets.

When Your
Opponent is Exploiting You

We have repeatedly stressed the importance of figuring out how your opponent plays, and then playing to exploit these tendencies. Examples include value betting relentlessly against loose-passive opponents, and playing loose-aggressively against tight opponents. But if your opponent is a good player, he will be doing the same to you.

There are several indications your opponent is paying attention to what you do. First, if you know he is a winning player, it is a fairly safe bet he is responding, in some manner, to how you play. You might know he is a winner, or at least knows enough to react to your style, based on how he's playing, reputation, or comments he has made.

Second, if his style appears to be changing as the match progresses, this is usually because he is purposely trying to mix up his play, often based on how he perceives your play. When this happens, you should decide which aspect of your playing style (or perceived playing style) he might be trying to exploit, and then how to take advantage of this.

Here's an example. You are playing a heads-up tournament against an opponent who appears to be loose-passive, and you are therefore limping many hands on the button, knowing that strong value bets can be made when your hand connects. So you limp your button with the bottom 25 percent of the hands, and raise the rest. After 10 or 15 hands, your opponent goes from raising none of your button limps to raising all of them.

Clearly your opponent has decided that your button limps indicate weakness and he begins to exploit this tendency. What do you do? Limp with some strong hands.

Now suppose the last four times your opponent has raised your button limp you have folded. The blinds have just risen to $50-$100, and you have a $2,200-to-$800 chip lead. You hold the

limp, and your opponent shoves. From his perspective, there is already $200 on the table, and you have yet to stand up to an out of position raise after limping your button, let alone an all-in. So you call. Your opponent flips over the

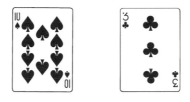

and despite getting outdrawn after a river ten, you got your money in as a significant favorite. Of course, not only should you stay aware of how your opponent might be adjusting to exploit you, you should also monitor adjustments in his style that occur due to tilt, a sense of urgency, or other factors.

Adjusting
Midway through the Match

Your opponent will often switch gears during a match, sometimes drastically. When he changes styles, you should adjust accordingly.

A classic example occurs during heads-up tournaments when you are facing a passive opponent. The passive style is a losing one. So you exploit it the straightforward way through aggressive play and value betting relentlessly. You pound away at his stack until the blinds reach Level III and you have a significant chip lead. Then you make a standard three big blind raise and he comes over top for all his chips.

Of course, anyone can pick up a hand. But the very next hand, your opponent raises his button to eight big blinds, and this is followed by an all-in resteal the following hand. While your opponent might have gotten several consecutive strong hands and decided to play them fast, more likely your weak opponent has become annoyed with you taking away pot after pot with aggressive play. He might also feel greater urgency to make a move since the blinds have gone up.

Such players actually have the right idea. They should be playing more aggressively. But shoving a wide range of cards has a poor risk-reward ratio. For instance, if the effective stacks are $1,500 with blinds of $25-$50, and your opponent is routinely reraising your $125 button steals with all-in resteals, he is risking $1,450 to win under $200.

So you must put yourself in position to exploit his new style — the maniac. For instance, if your opponent has shoved two or three straight hands preflop with effective stacks of 15 big blinds, call him more liberally than you normally would such a large push. Hands like a mid pocket pair, decent ace, and the better broadway hands such as king-queen or king-jack suited all qualify.

When should you begin adjusting your strategy from how you would normally play to exploit your opponent's new tendencies? If you adjust the first time, you could easily be adjusting to exploit a non-existent tendency. After all, any player can make an uncharacteristic play or catch an unexpected holding. But suppose you wait until witnessing this new play 10 times. Clearly such an extreme delay would be too much.

A guideline that works quite well is, "three times is enough."[11] That is, as a general guideline, you can safely adjust to your opponent's new strategy after observing three such occurrences.

For instance, suppose your opponent calls three straight C-bets when he has been folding a lot. The probability of him having a pair or better on an unpaired flop assuming you have none of these pair cards is around 35 percent.

So even if we increase this number to 0.4 to account for made straights and flushes, as well as decent draws, the probability of your opponent having any piece of the flop three straight times is approximately 6 percent.

$$(0.064) = (0.4)^3$$

Possible, but unlikely enough that you should go with the assumption that your opponent does not need to have hit the board to call your bets. (And of course, we can always modify this assumption as the match progresses.) So you can make a reasonably safe assumption that this opponent is now loose-passive, and revert accordingly to a value-betting game.

---

[11] A similar phrase is used by Tony Guerrera in *Killer Poker by the Numbers*.

We may draw a similar conclusion about our opponent's aggression based on consecutive button-raises. In particular, we ask: What is the probability our opponent now requires a good hand to raise his button given that he has raised his N most recent buttons?

The answer depends, of course, on which hands we label "good." Since this is heads-up, and he has position, let us label anything besides junk as good. This is roughly the top 65 percent of the hands, which includes all aces, kings, pocket pairs, suited jacks or tens, offsuit hands as weak as nine-seven, and suited hands as low as six-four.

Now let us examine the last question we posed.

Number of Consecutive Button Raises	Probability This Will Happen if Our Opponent Needs a Good Hand to Raise
1	65%
2	42%
3	27%
4	18%
5	12%
6	8%
7	5%

So we cannot draw a conclusion quite as quickly, but an opponent raising his button four straight times is unlikely to be doing so just for value, and an opponent with seven straight button raises is almost certainly doing so with trash hands such as ten-deuce or six-trey.

Exploitable
Versus Unexploitable Play

An unexploitable strategy is one where an opponent who knew your strategy would not be able to profit from it. An exploitable strategy is one where an opponent who knew your strategy could take advantage.

Playing exploitably leaves you vulnerable to an opponent profiting from his understanding of your actions, but it also allows you much more flexibility to make optimal plays against less observant opponents. If someone is only acting on the basis of his own cards, for instance, then playing an unexploitable strategy would offer no benefits. Also, if an opponent knows your strategy but cannot figure out how to take advantage of it, then it is fine to play exploitably. For instance, if you are playing like a maniac to attack a weak-tight opponent, and he realizes this but does not know how to adjust, then your exploitability is not hurting you.

What does it mean, in a practical sense, to play unexploitably? Suppose you are the button, have raised preflop, and your opponent checks on the flop. The pot is $1,000. If your C-bet decision is independent of hand strength, then this is an almost unexploitable strategy since your opponent, no matter how observant, can deduce nothing about your hand based on your flop play.[12]

Now let's suppose you bet smaller when you miss and want an immediate fold, say $500. And when you hit, you bet a full pot-sized $1,000. Clearly "hitting" is not such a black-and-white idea, but categorizing hands is not the point of this example. You think

---

[12] It's not totally unexploitable if you always bet because your opponent knows he can always check-raise. The unexploitable strategy would have you betting *all* hands *most* of the time.

your opponent will fold to either bet when he has missed, and call or raise either bet when he has a caught something.

But suppose your opponent is observant. He notices that you always fold to a check-raise or show down a weak hand when you bet the $500, and similarly your strong hands are correlated with $1,000 bets. He may exploit your strategy by check-reraising even his weakest hands when you bet $500, and folding hands normally strong enough to call or check-raise when you bet the pot. This is a bleak situation because you are losing your $500 every time you bluff, and not getting value for your strong hands.

In general, whether your exploitable play will actually be exploited depends mainly on three questions:

1. **How observant is your opponent?** The more experienced and skilled at opponent-reading your foe is, the more likely he is to determine and exploit your strategy.

2. **How often do you play against this person?** The more often you play against him, the more significant the metagame and the more data he will have at his disposal. And,

3. **With what frequency does the situation arise?** The relationship of bet-sizes to hand strength is easy to exploit because betting occurs almost every hand, but there are more subtle examples.

One common situation is your strategy when you are first and your C-bets get called. Let's suppose you adopt the C-bet strategy of two-thirds the pot regardless of your hand strength. When your opponent calls, one appealing strategy choice is check-folding with your weaker hands that do not improve, and continuing to bet your stronger hands. This strategy is difficult to exploit because you are only offering this information on those hands where you raise preflop, C-bet, and then get called.

But how might an observant player who knows you are employing this strategy exploit you? The first point your opponent gains information about your hand is after your turn action. If you bet again, you are strong. If you check, you are weak.

So this opponent may now increase his C-bet calling frequency as a "semi-bluff call." He knows he can win not only by having or improving to the best hand, but also by bluffing the river when he does not improve and you check the turn.

If you were playing long enough to observe your opponent river-bluffing often after your turn checks, you could then respond by either checking some strong hands on the turn, or bluffing a few weak ones.

Counter-Adjustments
and the Nash Equilibrium

When playing against a new opponent, do not assume he will take advantage of exploitable elements of your strategy. Many players are too concerned with their own cards, not sufficiently observant to pick up patterns, or simply unable to exploit your strategy even if they have some understanding of how you play. Wait until your opponents show you they are capable of correctly adjusting before you make any changes in your strategy.

When you know your opponent has begun exploiting you, that's when you begin to switch gears. Make a play with a weak hand that you would normally only do with a strong holding. Your opponent can make new adjustments in turn, and this process will continue, given enough hands and sufficiently observant opponents, until no player can make a profit exploiting his opponent through further adjustments. When both players become unexploitable, such that neither one can gain an edge through further adjustments, this is called a Nash Equilibrium.

The most important aspect of Game Theory for heads-up play is to be aware of the underlying concepts of exploitability, strategy adjustments, and so forth. Playing an equilibrium strategy is generally detrimental to profits because an exploitative strategy attacking your opponent's particular weaknesses will win you more in the long run. If your opponent is indeed playing unexploitably, and such foes are certainly the exception rather than the rule, you won't do as well. So let us determine a Nash Equilibrium for our previous example of button-limping.

Player A wants to play 100 percent of his buttons. His starting strategy is: Raise all strong hands, limp all his weak hands. (For the purposes of this example, we assume that "strong" versus "weak" is a black-and-white distinction.) When Player B raises his limp to 4 big blinds or greater, A folds. B's starting strategy as big blind is to usually check when A limps, raising only when he has a premium hand. Now suppose after some number of hands, B discovers A's starting strategy.

Question: *Since Player B knows Player A's button strategy from the button, could he adjust his own strategy to exploit it and increase his expectation?*

Answer: Yes. In particular, he can now begin raising Player A's button limps more liberally since this will force A to either fold or play with a weak hand. So Player B's adjusted strategy is to raise to 4 big blinds when Player A limps regardless of his (B's) holding. But after more hands pass, A notices that whenever he limps, B is raising to 4 big blinds. So A counter-adjusts. For instance, he could limp some or all of his stronger hands, and then call or reraise B's raises from the big blind. A could even limp only strong hands and raise or fold his weak ones.

After a while, suppose Player A's decision is to continue to play all his buttons now deciding at random whether to raise or limp, rather than based on the strength of his cards. Player B then also makes the raise/fold decision randomly himself, rather than based on A's action, since A's limp/raise decision reveals no information. Perhaps they eventually reach a point where B can no longer profitably attack limps based on his opponent's action since A can now have a hand of any strength. And A cannot profitably limp any more hands due to the frequency that B is attacking his limps. This is a Nash Equilibrium with respect to A's button-limping.

Unexploitable Short Stack Play

Our earlier section on playing the very short stack gave the important strategic guidelines for exploitative play with effective stacks of 10 big blinds or fewer, but we would be remiss not to say more about this topic in the context of unexploitability. So whereas previously we considered this approach as one of attacking opponent weaknesses, now we determine how to avoid having exploitatable tendencies which our opponent could attack.

There has been some controversy about the best approach for optimal heads-up shove-or-fold gameplay. By "shove-or-fold," we mean that the button will only raise all-in or fold, and therefore the big blind must call or fold. It is not rare for high blind heads-up battles to indeed play out in this manner.

The pioneering Sklansky-Chubanov Numbers (S-C Numbers), appearing in *No Limit Hold 'Em: Theory and Practice* by David Sklansky and Ed Miller, approach this question from an interesting standpoint. Suppose the big blind will call your shove precisely with those hands that are positive. The S-C Number for a hand is the highest effective stack size (in big blinds) where you can go all-in and still show a profit (compared to folding) even if your opponent somehow knew your hand. So anytime you shove with effective stacks "permitted" by its S-C Number, your play is unexploitable.

In addition, the jam-or-fold tables in *Mathematics of Poker* each give Nash Equilibrium solutions. That is, if you and your opponent are both following the strategies given in these tables, then neither of you can profit more by changing strategies. So you are playing an optimal (profit-maximizing) strategy so long as your opponent is in the same Nash Equilibrium. Otherwise, you can modify your strategy and win more through exploitative play.

Earlier, we gave guidelines based on whether our opponent was "tight" versus "loose." Now let us look again at the shove decision. Suppose you knew your opponent was calling with the hand range, for any stack size, that made your optimal shoving range as narrow as possible. If conditions were most unfavorable, what hands would you still be correct to shove?

Narrowest Range of Profitable Shoving Hands at $50-$100 Blinds

Effective Stacks	"Worst" Calling Range	Shoving Range
$1,500	15%	55+, AT+, A9s (10%)
$1,200	24%	All the above and 22-44, A5+, A2s+, KQ+, KJs+ (19%)
$1,000	30%	KT+, K9s+, QTs+, JTs (25%)
$800	42%	K6+, K3s+, QT+, Q9s+ (33%)
$600	58%	K2+, Q7+, Q4s+, J9+, J8s+, T9s (43%)
$400	70%	Q2+, J6+, J2s+, T7+, T6s+, 98+, 87s+ (58%)
$300	92%	J3+, T6+, T3s+, 97+, 95s+, 87+, 86s+ (66%)
$200	100%	T2+, 94+, 92s+, 85+, 83s+, 76+, 54s+ (80%)

The leftmost column of this table gives the effective stack size assuming, for simplicity, blinds of $50-$100. This is the stack size of the shorter-stacked player before posting blinds. The

Calling Range is the collection of hands that our opponent can call with that minimizes the number of starting hands that we can profitably shove. At first glance it may appear that this number should be 100 percent, that is, we can profitably shove fewer hands whenever our opponent is calling more often. But we actually want our opponent to call with most hands weaker than our own.

Profitability of Shoving Jack-Deuce Offsuit with an 8 Big Blind Effective Stack

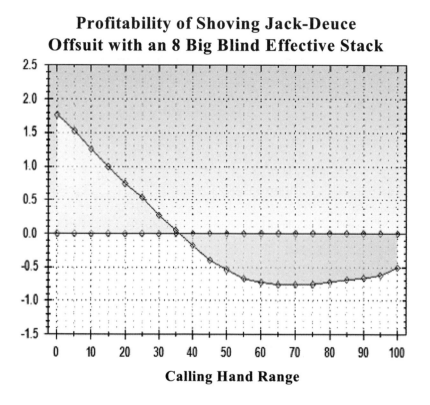

Calling Hand Range

Note: Y-Axis is: **Profitability of Shoving Jack-Deuce Offsuit**

In this graph, we look at the profitability of shoving jack-deuce offsuit with $800 effective stacks at $50-$100 blinds. We used the commercial software *SitNGo Wizard* to generate the tables and this graph. The range percents are therefore based on

S-C Numbers, and the Y-Axis in the graph gives profitability (as a function of a sit 'n go prizepool). But we are only concerned with the trend in this graph, which is that shoving becomes less and less profitable as our opponent adds on more and more calling hands … until around 72 percent. At that point, our profitability increases because as long as our opponent is calling with hands such as queen-deuce, we would rather he keep lowering his calling standards to ten-deuce and nine-deuce hands that we are ahead of.

So for any effective stack there is a "worst calling range" which minimizes the number of profitable shoves. Thus the hands in the Shoving Range are unexploitable shoves since they assume the worst calling ranges for the effective stack size. *Note that each entry includes all hands in the row above, in addition to what is listed.* For example, you should clearly still shove pocket pairs 55+ with a $1,200 effective stack. Lastly, while it is not until around $125 or fewer that you can show a profit shoving any two cards, it is a close approximation for any stacks shallower than $200.

The problem of unexploitable calling is tougher. Suppose, for instance, that your opponent shoves with effective stacks of $1,000. You have

This is not a strictly unexploitable call for all shoving strategies. If, for instance, your opponent's shoving range is aces down through queens, then you do not show a profit by calling. (In this case, your profit would come from your opponent getting blinded out due to tightness.)

So instead, we pose a question. Suppose our opponent is shoving with only the unexploitable hands in the above table, but no wider. What hands can we now call with?

Narrowest Range of Profitable Calling Hands at $50-$100 Blinds

Effective Stacks	Shoving Range	Calling Hands
$1,500	10%	88+, AQ+ (5%)
$1,200	19%	55+, AT+, A9s+ (9%)
$1,000	25%	33+, A8+, A7s+, KQs (13%)
$800	33%	22+, A3+, A2s+, KT+, K9s+, QJs (23%)
$600	43%	22+, A2+, K7+, K4s+, QT+, Q9s+, JTs (31%)
$400	58%	K2+, Q2+, J7+, J3s+, T8+, T6s+, 98+, 96s+, 54s+ (58%)
$300	66%	All hands besides two low, offsuit cards (85%)
$200	80%	100%

To reiterate, you should be calling with more hands than those in this table against most opponents who will be shoving a much wider range of hands than this table assumes.

Now we end this section with a disclaimer. It will benefit you to understand the concept of a Nash Equilibrium solution to short-stacked jam-or-fold gameplay. Knowing unexploitable shoving hands for different stack sizes is indeed quite valuable, as is knowing profitable calling hands assuming a narrow shoving range.

However, against most opponents, you will do best to exploit their weaknesses. If your opponent is hyper-tight, shove any two cards with 5 big blind effective stacks. Doing so is not unexploitable, but it will take advantage of your opponent's weakness of calling too tight. If your opponent is loose and passive, limp a marginal hand with 10 big blind stacks on the button. Could he now make an unexploitable shove with any two cards based on your limping range? Possibly, but if your opponent does not know this or will not act in this respect, then it does not matter.

> In most short-stacked battles, you will do better playing a strategy to exploit your opponent's weaknesses even if such a strategy is not strictly unexploitable.

Let's conclude by comparing unexploitable versus exploitable plays in two short-stacked situations.

Effective stacks: $800
Blinds: $50-$100
Note: Your opponent is tight-passive.

Your hand: 8♣6♠

Action: You are on the button.

Question: *What is your optimal preflop action?*
    Answer: You cannot make an unexploitable shove here, but you should not fold either. This is because you can actively exploit your tight opponent by shoving or possibly limping or min-raising. We saw in the earlier section on short-stacked play that you can shove any two cards facing a tight caller

with 8 big blind stacks. If your opponent will fold immediately at least 50 percent of the time facing a min-raise, then this play is more profitable than folding even ignoring the chance of winning the pot post-flop.

Focusing on unexploitability when facing a tight-passive opponent misses the point. You have a great opportunity to exploit this player through loose-aggressive play, and you should do so. Perhaps David Sklansky or Bill Chen could exploit your "inoptimally" loose-aggressive play, but your tight-passive opponent in this particular match can't.

Effective stacks: $700
Blinds: $50-$100
Note: Your opponent is tight-aggressive. So far during this heads-up battle he has shoved any time you have limped your button, and he has folded each time you have raised all-in.

Your hand: A♠A♣

Question: *Should you shove this hand preflop?*
    Answer: You should limp. Shoving is unexploitable and will obviously show a profit, but here you should exploit your opponent's tendency to shove widely facing a button limp. In fact, it is probably better to limp if you *know* he would not shove. Two aces has little interest in taking the blinds, and with stacks this short, they do not need to build a pot early.

Voluntarily Showing Cards

In most poker variations, a good basic rule would be to never show your cards since any of the other players in the game could get valuable insight into your playing style.

Suppose you win a large pot at the turn holding a set. You are a loose-aggressive player who would have made similar bets with many weaker holdings, so you decide to show your hand to get more respect for future bets in similar situations where you will often have a worse hand. But if you show, your opponents will know how you played your hand preflop and on the flop as well.

For instance, perhaps you held

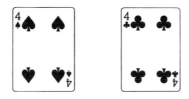

under-the-gun and limped. An astute player could now assume you will be limping small pocket pairs from early position. This is far from devastating information for an opponent to have, but you have offered him a free look at your playing style. And certain shows are particularly ill-advised, such as when you are the big blind and reraise a button raise with a premium hand — you are suggesting that you require a strong hand to defend your blind. So in most poker variations, you need a very compelling reason to show your cards.

The same rule holds in heads-up, but there is an exception. When you show in heads-up, there are no other players besides your lone opponent to take advantage of this information. Thus, if the following two statements hold, you now have a reason to increase your frequency of voluntary shows:

1. Your opponent tends to show his hands in rough proportion to the rate you show your hands. And,

2. You can draw more information from your opponents' shows than he can from yours.

If your opponent begins showing, recpicrocate if you can exploit this information better than he is likely to be able to exploit your shows. Otherwise pass. This process is more feasible live than online. Assessing whether Criterion No. 2 holds will be much easier by talking to your opponent. Furthermore, many online players have options set to muck cards they are not forced to show.

Assuming that card-showing is an option, you should not dismiss it in heads-up play. If you believe Criterion No. 2 would hold but your opponent is not showing, begin showing yourself. Make it clear, in a friendly manner, that you expect your opponent to reciprocate. For instance, if he wins the pot with a substantial turn bet at a board of the

you might smile, say "Nice bet. You have it?" and look toward his cards. If he shows, praise him regardless of his holding to encourage future shows. If he refuses, then end your own shows.

Suppose your opponent shows the

and the action had him calling a preflop raise, and then leading on both the flop and the turn. Then you know he is a loose caller preflop, and furthermore, his unexpected leadout bets seem to correlate with strong hands.

But if you make a similar show in a future situation, your opponent's thoughts might be more vague, such as, "He just comes right out and bets when he has it," or even, "Wow, he had three kings."

In summary, showing your cards should still be the exception rather than the rule in heads-up, but if you can establish a reciprocal showing arrangement, this may be beneficial.

Showing at the Wrong Time

Here's a short but important hand between Johnny Chan and James Woods.

Effective stacks: Under $20,000
Blinds: $1,000-$2,000
Note: Woods has a slight chip edge

Chan's hand: T♠3♠
Woods' hand: A♥9♠

Action: Chan raises to $4,500 on the button and Woods folds throwing in his hand face-up.

Analysis: Woods commits a serious blunder. With a top 10 percent hand, significantly more skilled opponent, and effective stacks of under 10 big blinds, he should happily commit all his chips regardless of Chan's opening move. Even if Chan is shoving narrowly and moves all-in, Woods will show a profit calling. And since his opponent is not pot-committed and he might pick up the $6,500 on the table without a fight, he should reraise all-in.

An almost as large mistake is that Woods shows his strong ace. He is effectively saying, "Despite the short stacks, I will need a premium hand to defend my blind." It is also probable that the professional Chan will be better equipped to exploit the information given in a show, so the amateur Woods should in general keep his hands concealed, and showing this hand was particularly bad.

You should also be more inclined to show hands that give the wrong impression as to how you actually play. For instance, suppose you normally use a "straightforward" style of value betting strong hands and rarely bluffing. Then you raise your opponent's river bet on a board of A♣6♠6♣4♦4♠.

If your opponent folds, be much more inclined to show a hand like T♣8♣ than a legitimate raising hand such as A♠A♥ because showing the nut full house confirms your opponent's impression of your playing style, namely that you require a strong hand to make this type of play. So showing the strong hand will not only provide free information, it will also increase your opponent's confidence in his ability to read you.

However, when you show a ten-high, your opponent may lose confidence in his ability to decipher your actions. Now when you make future raises with legitimate holdings, he may pay you off with a wider range of hands. On the other hand, if you plan to look for bluffing opportunities in the future, it might be worthwhile to show the A♠A♥ if you believe this will strengthen his belief that you always bet with only strong hands.

With deep stacks, you could even misplay a hand to give the wrong impression. Of course, this idea should not be taken too far since it's usually best to make what you believe to be the best possible play, and only deviate as necessary to remain unpredictable. But when you do take an uncharacteristic line or misplay a hand for any reason, or perhaps plan to do this in the future, then you should be much more inclined to voluntarily show.

Part Seven
Career Play

Career Play

Introduction

With the growing popularity of heads-up no-limit hold 'em, an increasing number of professional online players are switching to fulltime heads-up poker. In this section, we will discuss the key topics necessary for career heads-up play. These crucial topics on heads-up no-limit career play include:

- Bankroll
- Rake
- Table Selection
- The Buy-in Decision
- Seizing Online Edges
- Pace-Setting the Match
- Tilt Control
- Heads-up Versus Other Games
- Timing Tells and Reverse Tells
- Continually Improving your Game

Topics such as bankroll and rake may not be glamorous, but they are vitally important in maintaining a professional heads-up poker business. The process of table selection, furthermore, is what can distinguish solidly winning players from equally-skilled losing or breakeven players. And while many of the career concepts here are universal to many poker variations, the process of pace-setting is unique to heads-up gameplay and can be incorporated by players of all skill levels. Lastly, we tackle the important topic of how to keep on improving. Top players never let their skill level plateau, and we discuss the process of continually improving your game in the final chapter.

Rake

The rake is an often-overlooked aspect of most poker variations, but its long-term effects can be substantial. Unless you are playing home poker ... the casino, online site, or other venue will charge a vigorish for allowing you to play this match. Rake is a part of life in any poker game where non-participants provide services such as dealing, resolving disputes, and so forth. The rake is fundamentally no different than charges for any other goods or services. And just as you should closely monitor these fees, so must you familiarize yourself with the rake market as slight differences accumulate quickly.

Let us consider a player who wins 55 percent of his matches at the $100 level. How do his profits fare with an escalating rake?

Long-Term Profit as a Function of Rake*			
Rake	Win Rate	ROI	1,000 Games
0%	55%	10%	$10,000
2.5%	55%	7.5%	$7,500
5%	55%	5%	$5,000
10%	55%	0%	$0
20%	55%	-10%	-$10,000

* per match, not per hand

With a standard 5 percent rake, Hero's $10,000 profits halve; double the rake, and the profits disappear. It is easy to overlook rake since its effect will not seem consequential in any given match because you will either lose slightly more, or win slightly less. Realize, as this table illustrates, that the rake adds up significantly long-term.

Table Selection

In any poker variation, table selection is a critical aspect for maximizing your profit. There is a common saying, which modified for heads-up is: "If you're the second best heads-up player in the world, but your opponent is the best, then you're the underdog."

And indeed, we can even switch around the focus: "If you are the second worst heads-up player in the world, and you are playing against the absolute worst, then you're the favorite." Hopefully, this latter saying will not apply to you, but the point is irrefutable: Skill level in heads-up is not an absolute; you should instead be concerned with your skill relative to your opponent's.

Suppose you are considering staking one of two players, Sam and Todd. Assume that while both are winning players, Sam is more skilled than Todd, and if the two were to play each other over a large number of matches, Sam would win the majority of the time. Both will also be completely honest in honoring the staking arrangement. Would you necessarily be correct to choose Sam for your staking agreement?

No. If this were all we knew, then certainly Sam would be the better choice. But we can add an additional hypothesis that would make Todd the superior choice. Can you spot it?

Let us suppose that Sam believes he is one of the best players in the world, and he routinely plays against fellow top players. Meanwhile, Todd exercises strict table selection, and he will only play against opponents whom he knows are long-term losers. Perhaps he determines this through online research, searches out rich recreational players live, or otherwise ensures his competition is always weak, even if this means he must sometimes change limits or avoid playing.

Even though Sam is the superior player skill-wise, you would still want to stake Todd because he will enjoy a much greater edge in his matches unless he limits the number of matches so much that he can't make any real money.

In *The Psychology of Poker*, Dr. Alan Schoonmaker instructs his readers to fill out a chart quantifying their motives for playing poker. Besides making money, other possible options include having fun, the thrill of competition, and taking pleasure in a tough challenge. Just as with the bankroll decision, these other motives might give legitimate cause to otherwise questionable decision-making.

But if you are playing heads-up poker to win as much money as possible, or at least this is your primary motive, then table selection can be huge as long as you are playing at large enough stakes where many skilled players exist. Indeed, it could be the single biggest factor in your success as a professional heads-up player. Whether you are the best player in the world or simply above-average, you will win more money the weaker your opposition is (as long as you have ample games to play).

So in a cash game, stand up and leave if you find yourself against a shark. In a sit 'n go tournament, do not be the second to sit down if you know the first player to be strong. By declining these matches, you are not admitting that you are worse than these players or that you are frightened. Indeed, you may still be a favorite. You are merely refusing to play against a good player whom you will expect to win less from in the long run, than you would from the plenty of bad players out there.

Two objections are sometimes made to this line of argument. The first concerns hourly win rate. If you feel you are up against a good player against whom you still have an edge, then continuing to play is reasonable (unless your bankroll is in jeopardy) if you cannot quickly find a softer opponent. But be sure that you have an edge, even if it is less than ideal. Situations where there is no one else to play are uncommon, particularly online. Unless you are playing extremely high stakes or at unusual times, there should be plenty of potential opponents.

The other exception to the "weaker is better" rule is only an illusion. Suppose you have the opportunity to play someone who is overall worse than you, but against whom your style does not play well. Would you not be correct to decline this match-up in favor of playing a better opponent against whom you do match up well?

The reason this question is misguided is that if you cannot adjust to play well against your opponent's style, then you are not actually a better player than he is. Heads-up is a dynamic game requiring strategy modifications based on observation of your opponent's tendencies. Being a good heads-up player requires adjusting well to the many different styles you will come across. So if you have a naturally loose-aggressive style, for instance, and feel that you play poorly against calling stations, then you are not actually better than these weak players unless you can adjust your strategy to exploit them.

In summary, try to develop an awareness of who the good players are, and practice careful table selection. This may not be the most glamorous aspect of professional heads-up play, but from a profit maximization standpoint, it's frequently well worth it.

The Buy-in Decision

Related to table selection is buy-in differences. What separates the $2 micro-stakes players from the $5,000 nose-bleed players? The answer is that the $5,000 player wants to play for much more money than the $2 player. If this reply seems tautological, that's because it is. Many players assume that there are a fixed set of differences between players of different stakes, but the reality is that while the player willing to put up $5,000 is often a much more skilled heads-up player, he could also be severely tilting, rich and playing for fun, heavily intoxicated, or simply a "decent" player with poor bankroll management.

It is true that generally speaking, the higher the buy-in the stiffer the competition. But this pattern is not set in stone. You should be willing to play at least two different buy-in levels to take advantage of where the weak players are. This will also allow you to play a higher buy-in only when your opponent is particularly soft, and stick with your normal level otherwise.

Another reason why you will find some strong players at low buy-ins and vice versa relates to the priorities between professional and recreational players. The professional must ensure he does not go broke, and doing so entails risking only small fractions of his capital in any given match. He wants to grind out a large number of solid investments, and have a small risk of ruin.

However, the recreational player may not be concerned as much about bankroll. This decreased level of risk aversion isn't simply irrational (although bankroll ignorance may play a role); those playing heads-up matches for fun, rather than business, can afford to take much bigger risks with their poker capital. For these players, losing their playing bankroll is not nearly the catastrophe it is for a solid grinder using heads-up poker to pay his rent.

Seizing Online Edges

The online climate is perpetually evolving, but there will always be tools available to the shrewd to gain an edge. The software and tools discussed in this section may change, but the concept of seeking them out will remain sound.

One simple step is to determine whether your opponent is multi-tabling. Online players routinely play more than one table at once, and for some players, this trend continues into the realm of heads-up. If the site allows you to search for your opponent, see if he is playing other games concurrently.

Whether he is four-tabling heads-up matches or simply playing one full ring game in addition to his match against you, he is concentrating on more than just your match. Such players are more likely to have a default style that they like to play, often one that is tight-aggressive. In this case, you should play in a particularly loose-aggressive manner. Their attention is more divided, so there is relatively less need to mix up your play for the sake of deception.

Next, use tracking software. Programs such as *PokerTracker* and *Holdem Manager* can overlay opponent statistics directly on the table. The most common set of statistics to employ is:

- **Number of hands:** The sample size you are considering.

- **VPIP:** Percentage of hands your opponent voluntarily pays chips to see a flop.

- **PFR:** Percentage of hands your opponent raises with before the flop.

- **AF (PF):** Measure of post-flop aggression.

These statistics have less value than they do in full ring games or when you are multi-tabling yourself — contexts where you may not be directly monitoring each hand your opponent plays, but they are still useful in heads-up for two reasons. First, you may confirm the manual reads you are getting with these statistics. For instance, if your opponent always seems to be raising and reraising, your initial read might be loose-aggressive. But if his stats are, 50/45/5 (VPIP/PFR/AF) after 20 hands, then you might decide that while he is indeed hyper-aggressive those hands that he plays, he does have starting hand standards for playing a hand.

Another benefit to stats is that you might replay this same opponent in a subsequent match. Then you can see his statistics from prior matches and have a solid idea of his style before the match begins even if you otherwise did not remember your prior match.

So take advantage of datamining when possible. This is the process of recording game data as an observer which you can do at many sites with your own software by having open tables with tracking software running. You can also find a commercial datamining program that tells you how your opponent has done. Avoid playing the winners, and actively seek out the losers.

Pace-Setting the Match

Heads-up poker has a quick pace. Unlike other variations, you have no rest time between hands. If you suffer a bad beat or get bluffed out of a large pot, there is no time to regroup as you would in fuller games.

While you may not have hand breaks, there is time to make decisions. So don't let the fast pace of the game prevent you from taking time to make your decisions. There are two ways to gain maximum advantage from time. The first is clear: don't rush. If a player puts you all-in, do not react based on instinct. Consider the pot odds, his likely hand range, and so forth — even if doing so "interrupts" the natural fast rhythm of the match.

The second way to use the time resource is to regroup. While sitting out a hand may not be possible, you can slow the match down simply by elongating the decision process. Do not stall without reason to slow down the game, but if taking extra time will help you regain your bearings, by all means do so. Verbalizing can also help in this process.

For instance, suppose you get involved in a large pot with second pair against a hyper-aggressive all-in opponent, and he ends up holding a low set and doubles up. Your incorrect read, coupled with the chip loss, may cause your confidence and playing ability to temporarily plummet.

To combat this tendency, play the next few hands as follows.

Effective stacks: $750

Blinds: $15-$30

Your hand: K♠2♠

Analysis: Think "Okay, I have a weak king on the button. I think I'll make a small raise." Let five or ten seconds elapse, and then raise.

Action: You raise to $75, and your opponent reraises to $350. Think to yourself: "Now the pot is four twenty-five and it costs me two seventy-five to call. But doing so would commit me to the hand. Even though this guy is loose, I can't commit the rest of my stack here." After another five or ten seconds, you fold.

Playing several consecutive hands in this manner, with a verbal thought process and allowing plenty of time to elapse between decisions, will take the place of sitting out several hands. So when necessary, slow things down.

The contrary principle also holds. If your opponent has just taken a bad beat or been called out on a big bluff, you should speed up the pace of the match. Play the next few hands quickly and aggressively. Of course, you cannot force your opponent to act quickly, but you can take your own actions without delay and increase the pace as much as possible. Your opponent will often play passively the next several hands, lacking confidence, and you should exploit this tendency when you observe it.

In summary, the time resource is a valuable one — seize it to gain any extra edge. Set a slow pace when you want one, and do your best to force a fast pace when your opponent will tend to benefit from a slow down.

Tilt Control

A player is "on tilt" when his mindset is such that he cannot make decisions in his usual manner. Tilt can be caused by having an opponent show he has bluffed you off a hand, when an opponent outdraws you as a significant underdog, or for many other reasons depending on the individual.

As we discussed in the last chapter, heads-up is a much faster-paced game than short-handed play or full games. While you can stick to playing premium hands in fuller games, at least for a few orbits, you will get blinded out playing this way in heads-up. So we must consider a different strategy for combating tilt.

First, pace-set the match slower. When you are tilting is the primary time you want a slow match, and simply delaying each action for several orbits will go a long way. Remember to verbalize the thought process.

Second, realize that there is nothing fair or unfair about the cards that hit. It is easy to remember those times we are outdrawn and forget about the times we hit a miracle card ourselves. But your weak hands will crack your opponent's aces at the same frequency that this particular bad beat happens to you.

The toughest recovery process is arguably after making a significantly flawed read, such as when you get called on a bluff or believe your opponent is making a play and call him down lightly when he actually holds a strong hand.

Since heads-up is a game of constant reads, it can be tough to play well when you lose confidence in your ability to make them. Your best option is to temporarily switch to a more straightforward style. Still play aggressively, but play a tighter game based more heavily on hand selection. Only get involved in large pots if your cards warrant it.

Blinds: $10-$20
Note: In the hand before this one you mistakenly called an all-in bet facing the nut hand.

Your hand: 7♥4♣

Action: You raise to $60 on the button and your opponent calls. The pot is $120.

Flop: 9♣8♥2♣

Action: Your opponent checks. You bet $80 and he calls. The pot is $280.

Turn: K♥

Action: Your opponent checks and you bet $180. Your opponent folds.

While this is a very aggressive approach, it is reasonable. Preflop, unless you are playing against a calling station or a maniac, it is never a significant mistake to come in for a standard raise. C-betting the flop is not unreasonable. And when the turn comes an overcard not completing any of the draws, you have a solid follow-up bluff opportunity. Loose-aggressive? Absolutely. Reckless? Not unless your opponent never folds.

If you lacked confidence in your reads going into this hand, you should tend to play it in a more straightforward manner. In particular, you should tend to either fold or limp preflop.

Blinds: $10-$20

Your hand: 7♥4♣

Action: You limp and your opponent checks. The pot is $40.

Flop: 9♣8♥2♣

Action: Your opponent checks. You bet $30 and he calls. The pot is $100.

Turn: K♥

Action: You both check.

River: T♠

Action: You both check.

Analysis: You take only one stab at this small pot after limping preflop. You give up on the turn and elect not to bet the river even though a bluff is probably your only chance of winning this pot outright.

Switching temporarily to a more literal strategy, while playing slower and more deliberately, is a good way to regain your bearings if you begin to tilt. It might not seem like the best way to play, but if you are having trouble making good strategy decisions, then it becomes a better approach.

Heads-Up
Versus Other Games

In this chapter, we review the similarities and differences between heads-up matches versus other forms of poker. Heads-up requires you to assimilate incomplete information and use logic to decide on an optimal decision, like all poker variations.

Heads-up requires you to play a skilled loose-aggressive style. You cannot sit back and wait for premium hands. While many winning players of fuller games, particularly no-limit, also play loose and aggressive, these games are often beatable by applying strict hand selection guidelines. For instance, in a ten-handed no-limit cash game, you could fold fifty consecutive hands and only be down 7.5 big blinds, well under 10 percent of the typical 100 big blind buy-in.

In heads-up, this type of rigid hand selection would get you blinded out. So to play heads-up well, you must become comfortable with a loose-aggressive style and handling marginal situations.

In heads-up, you are definitively in position or out of position each hand. So the power of position makes itself clear much quicker than in fuller games where multiple positions coupled with such ideas as relative position render the benefits of the button less obvious. To succeed in heads-up, you must be comfortable playing the button, and quickly learn the limitations of being out of position after the flop.

Heads-up also emphasizes opponent-reading much more than fuller games. Clearly, a player who is paying attention to his opponents will do better than his unobservant counterpart in a game of any type. But you could fail to pick up on many opponent tendencies and still do relatively well in some full games, again just through hand selection. This is probably not true in tough shorthanded games, and almost never true in heads-up. Even against weak competition, you must respond to how your opponent is playing to be a significant winner. Heads-up is a battle to gain information since you face only one opponent, and do so each hand.

To use the language of heads-up limit professional Bryce Paradis, heads-up is an "information saturated environment" compared to the "information sparse" full games. You have access to much more data facing a single opponent whose actions and cards you observe with high frequency, relative to many opponents — any combination of whom might be involved in any one hand.

And finally, playing heads-up can be a good way to improve your reading, positional, and aggressive skills in other forms of no-limit hold 'em, and even poker in general. So becoming skilled in this form of poker is certainly worthwhile.

Timing Tells
and Reverse Tells

The subject of tells for live poker is beyond the scope of this book. But we will address time-based tells since they are not only important in live poker, but are one of the only form of tells in online poker.

The four basic time-based tells are:

1.   Longer than normal to act indicates strength.

2.   Longer than normal to act indicates weakness.

3.   Quicker than normal to act indicates strength.

4.   Quicker than normal to act indicates weakness.

Note that you should witness such a correlation multiple times before acting on it. If, for instance, your opponent waits ten seconds before raising all-in after hitting a gutshot straight draw on the river, this might be because he always pauses before betting the nuts — possibly because he thinks most players will interpret such a delay as weakness, but it could also be for many other reasons. Perhaps your opponent was deciding whether to raise all-in, or to make a smaller value bet. Maybe he wants to make 100 percent sure he actually did hit his straight before betting. Or if playing online maybe he was distracted by another table or a ringing phone.

If your opponent is not trying to manipulate you through timing tells, then longer pauses before betting will generally indicate weakness over strength, and vice versa with quick actions because many players will generally have to think before deciding to execute a bluff (unless he is reckless, on tilt, etc.); and a player who knows he wants to bet generally feels this way due to hand strength. Therefore, when a player *is purposely* trying to deceive you, he will often reverse these defaults. Here is an example.

Effective stacks: $1,380
Blinds: $10-$20

Your hand: J♥J♦

Action: Your opponent raises to $60 on the button. You reraise to $200. He pauses for 15 seconds and reraises all-in.

Question: *What is your play?*
> **Answer:** This delay could be feigned hesitancy with aces or kings. More often, your opponent has a genuinely difficult choice with a hand like ace-jack or a medium pair. Unless you have a read on what his pauses tend to indicate, you should be inclined to select the action you would normally choose absent the tell. In this case, facing an unknown opponent, you should generally be willing to get all your chips in the center with jacks preflop — particularly at the lower buy-ins.

Similarly, if you want to asssure an astute opponent cannot get a read based on your own timing, try to let a similar amount of time pass before making any significant decision. This strategy has the added benefit that it incorporates time to think about the tough situations.

You should familiarize yourself with the tell literature before playing live. Tells can often have significant bearing on live hand decisions. This is especially true short-handed or in heads-up. However, if you otherwise play poorly but are good at tells, your results should still be disappointing.

This next hand features Jerry Buss and Daniel Negreanu.

Daniel Negreanu: ~ $30,000
Jerry Buss: ~ $10,000

Blinds: $250-$500

Buss' hand: Q♠T♦
Negreanu's hand: Q♣9♠

Action: Negreanu min-raises to $1,000 on the button and Buss calls. The pot is $2,000.

Flop: Q♦T♠4♠

Action: Buss checks. Negreanu bets $1,400 and Buss calls. The pot is $4,800.

Turn: A♥

Action: Both players check.

Analysis: Buss's flop slowplay was reasonable with top two-pair, particularly since he knows Negreanu will usually bet after he checks. But it is better to lead on this turn. Negreanu will now often check if Buss checks since Buss has called his flop bet, and the ace is unlikely to have helped Negreanu. And any ace, king, jack, or four could slow the action. Buss also needs to build the pot to have a chance of getting all-in.

Negreanu's check is fine. Buss has shown strength, and second pair is a good hand for two bets to enter the pot. He can then call a river bet if Buss bets, and bet for value if checked to. The downside to this strategy is when a king or jack hits, or possibly a spade, and Buss hits a free draw. (Or misses a draw he would have paid for.)

River: 9♦

Action: Buss shoves $8,750 and Negreanu folds.

Analysis: A great fold by Negreanu with a rivered second pair in heads-up, one that most would argue is incorrect had it not been for a tell Negreanu is able to induce from Buss. Negreanu shows his cards face-up and smilingly comments, "I have no idea what to do." Buss smiles, looks away, and says, "Tell him to call."

Gabe Kaplan comments, "I don't think Jerry should have said that, he looked too relaxed when he said that." And he is completely right — Negreanu would almost certainly not have folded his two-pair without this read. So be aware that a keen opponent may be studying you intently in a live environment, and you may also be able to improve your decision-making based on live tells.

Continually Improving Your Game

By virtue of reading this book, you should have a distinct advantage over most of your opposition, but reading alone is not enough for good players who continually strive to build upon their game.

Question: *What is the best way to continue to increase your knowledge and skill-level?*

Answer: The best way is to review hands and matches that you have played. While it is impossible to have every single possible scenario already thought through, there are enough commonalities between different hands that you should do a post-game analysis on hands that gave you trouble. Doing so will be of benefit any time you encounter a similar situation.

The most common method of achieving this is self-review. For instance, perhaps you are on the button with the

and do not know whether you should shove an 8 big blind stack. After the match, you would then review the tables in this book, or plug the hand into poker-analyzing software such as *SNG Wizard*.

Thinking away from the table will greatly benefit you. To really take advantage of this technique, try to modify one or multiple parameters and decide how such changes would affect your decision.

Consider the above question of shoving the J♣2♣. You can answer it by writing down the hand range you believe your opponent is likely to call an 8 big blind shove with, and then having software analyze whether you should shove or fold. Perhaps your opponent was tight, and you think he would only call with a mid-high ace, two suited broadway cards, king-queen offsuit, or any pocket pair fours or higher. You folded, and now you learn that shoving is a better play.

Then you might ask: How wide a range could my opponent call and I still be able to show a profit by shoving? This is again a question that software can answer: the top 45 percent of hands. You learn that unless your opponent is calling with many hands, you can profitably shove a marginal hand such as J♣2♣ with effective stacks of 8 big blinds.

Next you ask: How weak a hand could I shove into the initial hyper-tight opponent and still show a profit? You use software to determine that the answer is 100 percent. You learn that you can exploit a tight caller by shoving any hand with effective stacks of 8 big blinds or fewer. Another few clicks and you learn that this "any two are profitable" shove works against your tight opponent if the effective stacks are roughly 10 big blinds or less.

If you did this, you would more than make up for any money you lost by folding in the actual hand, with money you would make from applying your new knowledge in future hands. The chapter, "All-In Calling: The 2-to-1 Rule" in "Part Four: Crucial heads-Up Concepts and Situations" on page 271, gives more examples where software, mathematical analysis, and hand range estimation can give you a quantitative answer to your question.

Of course, not all hands can be solved so precisely. For hands in this latter category, if you cannot decide on a satisfactory solution, take advantage of the experience and expertise of others. In particular, you can discuss hands with a friend, post on an Internet message board (such as the excellent heads-up forum at www.twoplustwo.com), or even consult an expert through paid coaching.

Perhaps in the J♣2♣ hand, you realize that since your opponent is passive, perhaps pushing all-in is not your best move. Maybe you should make a small raise or even limp? If you cannot come up with a satisfactory numbers-based answer to this question, posting on an Internet message board is a solid next step. Often you will get good replies, but even when you don't, the process of actively writing down the hand and analyzing it will benefit you in and of itself. Doing so forces you to reason.

It is worth asking why it is that good players will take the time to compose quality answers for free in public forums. Actually, these players benefit from answering your question as well. Considering someone else's hand and writing an answer helps you because it is an exercise in the type of reasoning required to succeed at the tables. So being active on poker forums is a worthwhile use of your time as you will benefit from analyzing situations that others have found challenging.

In short, to continually improve your game, you should give a lot of thought to hands and analysis even when away from the table. Don't think this too time consuming. It is well worth the effort.

Appendix A
Preflop Hand Probabilities

Bad beats are often not actually so bad. In hold 'em, the most common worst-case scenario is finding yourself a 2-to-1 underdog heading into the flop. And many hands are actually much closer in value.

Preflop Match-Up	Examples	Favorite
Two Overcards versus Two Undercards	AK versus 72 AK versus 54s	68-to-32 59-to-41
One Overcard, Two Cards In-Between	A5 versus K8 A5 versus T9	60-to-40 55-to-45
One Overcard, One Card In-Between	A6 versus Q2 A6 versus Q2s	64-to-36 60-to-40
Pair versus Two Overcards	22 versus J5 22 versus T9s	53-to-47 46-to-54
Pair versus One Overcard	66 versus K6 66 versus K5	69-to-31 70-to-30
Pair versus Two Undercards	KK versus Q6 KK versus 54s	88-to-12 77-to-23
Overpair versus Underpair	KK versus 33 77 versus 44	81-to-19 81-to-19

Appendix B
Drawing Odds Chart

You should know the odds of your hand improving when you are deciding whether to continue playing after the flop, and your opponent has bet or raised. Here is a chart with this information which you should keep with you if playing online, or memorize if you are playing live.

Note that all cards that improve you are distinct "outs," even if they are of the same rank. For instance, if you have ace-high on a board of low cards, and you believe your opponent has a one-pair hand, then there are three cards that improve you rather than one since there are aces of all three remaining suits unaccounted for.

For example, you hold

on a board of

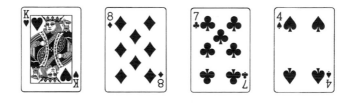

You believe your opponent has a one-pair hand (without an ace). Then you have three outs to make the best hand: A♥, A♦, and the A♣.

But this is not all you need to consider when deciding whether you should call, even if you appear to be getting the proper odds. First, you do not want to be drawing to a second-best hand. For instance, with your ace-high on a raggedy flop, improving against a player with a made set does not help; in fact, it will likely cause you to lose a large pot. In other words, tend to discount outs that may only be improving you to an inferior hand. For example, straight outs with three cards to a flush already on board. (Although on the opposing end of the spectrum, you should consider that your ace-high might currently be the best hand, in which case you do not need to improve at all.)

Second, realize that sometimes you should raise instead of call. Recall that a raise gives you the opportunity to win the pot immediately, or build a larger pot when you hit a premium hand. For instance, if you hold A♥K♥ on a flop of J♥T♥4♠, you should strongly consider raising since your twelve full outs for a straight or flush, and six additional outs to top pair actually make you a favorite over a hand as strong as top-pair.

Type of Draw[13]	No. of Outs	Chance of Hitting an Out with One Card to Come (%)	Odds Against Hitting an Out with One Card to Come	Chance of Hitting an Out with Two Cards to Come (%)	Odds Against Hitting an Out with Two Cards to Come
Trips — Quads	1	2.2	45.5-to-1	4.3	22.5-to-1
Pocket Pair — Set	2	4.3	22.3-to-1	8.4	10.9-to-1

---

[13] Please note that in most cases, the draws listed in this table represent only one example of a type of draw resulting in the specified number of outs. For example, a pocket pair with a four flush drawing to a set or flush represents an alternative example of an 11 out draw.

Type of Draw	No. of Outs	Chance of Hitting an Out with One Card to Come (%)	Odds Against Hitting an Out with One Card to Come	Chance of Hitting an Out with Two Cards to Come (%)	Odds Against Hitting an Out with Two Cards to Come
One Overcard — One Overpair	3	6.5	14.5-to-1	12.5	7.0-to-1
Gutshot Straight Draw — Straight	4	8.6	10.6-to-1	16.5	5.1-to-1
One Pair — Two-pair or Trips	5	10.8	8.3-to-1	20.4	3.9 to-1
Two Overcards — An Overpair	6	12.9	6.8-to-1	24.1	3.1-to-1
Gutshot Draw + One Overcard — Straight or Overpair	7	15.1	5.6-to-1	27.8	2.6-to-1
Open Ended Straight Draw — Straight	8	17.2	4.8-to-1	31.5	2.2-to-1
Four Cards to a Flush — Flush	9	19.4	4.2-to-1	35.0	1.9-to-1
Gutshot Draw + Two Overcards — Straight or Overpair	10	21.5	3.7-to-1	38.4	1.6-to-1
Open Ended Straight Draw + One Overcard — Straight or Overpair	11	23.7	3.2-to-1	41.7	1.4-to-1
Flush Draw + Gutshot Draw — Flush or Straight	12	25.8	2.9-to-1	45.0	1.2-to-1
Open-Ended Straight Draw + Pair — Straight, Two-pair, or Trips	13	28.0	2.6-to-1	48.1	1.1-to-1

Type of Draw	No. of Outs	Chance of Hitting an Out with One Card to Come (%)	Odds Against Hitting an Out with One Card to Come	Chance of Hitting an Out with Two Cards to Come (%)	Odds Against Hitting an Out with Two Cards to Come
Flush Draw + Pair — Flush, Two-Pair, or Trips	14	30.1	2.3-to-1	51.2	1.0-to-1
Flush Draw + Open Ended Straight Draw — Flush or Straight	15	32.3	2.1-to-1	54.1	0.8-to-1

Note that there is also a simple rule to give you a quick approximation if you are under stress and/or have otherwise forgotten your drawing odds. ("~" is used to indicate "approximately.")

• Probability of improving with one card to come ~ 2 x (# of outs)

• Probability of improving on the flop ~ 4 x (# of outs) (8 outs or fewer)

• Probability of improving on the flop ~ 4 x (# of outs) — (# of outs — 8); (9 outs or more)

For instance, suppose you hold 5♣4♣ on a board of: J♣3♦2♣. Then you have 15 outs: 9 clubs for a flush, and 6 non-club aces and sixes for a straight.

• Your probability of improving by the turn ~ 30 percent [(15)(2)]

• Your probability of improving by the river ~ 53 percent [(15)(4)] - [(15 - 8)]

Appendix C
Top N Percent Starting Hands

There are different ways to organize preflop starting hands; here, we use the popular *PokerStove* algorithm of evaluating hand performance. Note that hands listed in a higher percentile still qualify, of course. For instance, 88 is the weakest hand that qualifies as being top 7.5 percent, and clearly AA down through 99 are also in the top 7.5 percent.

- **5%:** 99 - AA, AK, AQs, AJs

- **7.5%:** 88, AQo, ATs, KTs, QJs

- **10%:** AJo, A9s, KQo, QTs

- **12.5%:** 77, ATo, KJo, JTs

- **15%:** A7s, KTo, K9s, QJo

- **20%:** 66, A9o, A4s, K8s, Q9s, JTo, T9s

- **25%:** A7o, A2s, K9o, K6s, Q8s, J8s, T8s

- **30%:** 55, A5o, K5s, Q9o, Q7s, J9o, T9o

- **35%:** A4o, K8o, K3s, Q6s, T7s, 87s

- **40%:** 44, A3o, K7o, K2s, Q8o, Q4s, J8o

- **50%:** 22, A2o, K5o, Q7o, Q2s, J7o, T7o, T6s, 98o, 86s

- **100%:** All hands

Glossary

Accidental Heads-Up (AHU): One-on-one play between the small blind and the big blind when all other players fold in a fuller-handed game.

Ante: Chips in addition to the blinds that each player must put into the pot before the start of the hand.

Backdoor: A draw on the flop requiring both turn and river cards to complete.

Big Blind: The player who posts the big blind acts last before the flop, and first on all future betting rounds.

Bluff-Catcher: A hand that can only beat a bluff.

Button: This is the player who posts the small blind. He acts first before the flop, and last on all subsequent betting rounds.

C-bet: Abbreviation for Continuation Bet — a bet made when the preflop raiser makes a follow-up bet on the flop.

Complete: See "Limp"

Deep: Effective stacks of many big blinds, usually at least 50 or more.

Effective stacks: The shorter of the two stacks.

Expected Value (EV): The number of chips a given play will win or lose on average. It is calculated by taking the sum of all possible rewards weighted by their likelihoods.

Exploitable: An action or playing style which your opponent could profit from if he knew your strategy.

Fold Equity: The gain when your opponent folds to a bet or a raise. It is calculated by multiplying the amount you win due to an immediate fold by the likelihood of such a fold.

Freeze-out: A heads-up tournament where the blinds do not rise.

Hero: The player whose actions we are considering

Implied Odds: The ratio of the expected pot size after future betting rounds relative to the current cost of calling.

Kicker: The other card in your hand when you have a pair with one of the board cards.

Limp: When the button calls the big blind before the flop. Also called complete.

Metagame: Considering how a given play will impact not only the present hand, but future interactions you expect to have with your opponent.

Nash Equilibrium: A situation when both players in the game are using strategies such that neither one can profit more by changing strategy.

The Nuts: The best possible hand.

OOP: Abbreviation for Out of Position — the big blind who must act first (and therefore lacks position) on all post-flop betting rounds.

Out: A card that will improve you to the best hand if you are currently behind.

Paired Flop: A flop that comes with two cards of the same rank, such as K♣K♦J♠ or T♥4♦4♠.

Pot Odds: The ratio of the pot size to the amount needed to call.

Push: To raise all-in. See "Shove."

Price-Setting: Betting the river out of position not for value or bluff purposes, rather to size the bet according to the pot size you want rather than let your opponent determine it.

Rainbow: A flop containing cards of three different suits.

Runner-runner: Hitting two consecutive cards to improve by the river.

Semi-Bluff: To make a bet or raise with a hand you believe is currently behind, but has the potential to improve if called or win immediately.

Set: Having three-of-a-kind with a pocket pair in your hand.

Shove: To raise all-in.

Sit 'n go: In heads-up, a tournament or freeze-out match that starts as soon as two players have sat down and posted the buy-in.

Slowplay: To check or call a bet, rather than bet or raise immediately, with a hand that figures to be considerably ahead of your opponent's.

Stacking: Winning a pot from your opponent where the full effective stacks have been wagered.

Straddle: A third blind posted by the player who would normally act first before the flop.

Three-bet: A reraise of a prior raise. Preflop this term is used when the button raises and the big blind reraises (thereby putting in the third bet). Post-flop a three-bet occurs when one player bets, his opponent raises, and he reraises.

tN: A chip stack of size N in a tournament, as opposed to $N in a cash game.

Trips: Having three-of-a-kind without holding a pocket pair.

Unexploitable: An action or playing style in which your opponent could know your exact strategy and still not be able to profit from this knowledge.

Villain: The player in a heads-up hand who is not Hero.

Index

NOTES

NOTES

NOTES

NOTES

NOTES

NOTES

Books from Two Plus Two